THE ANONYMOUS POET
OF POLAND

T0382396

CAMBRIDGE
UNIVERSITY PRESS

University Printing House, Cambridge CB2 8BS, United Kingdom

Cambridge University Press is part of the University of Cambridge.

It furthers the University's mission by disseminating knowledge in the pursuit of
education, learning and research at the highest international levels of excellence.

www.cambridge.org
Information on this title: www.cambridge.org/9781107461048

© Cambridge University Press 1919

First published 1919
First paperback edition 2014

A catalogue record for this publication is available from the British Library

ISBN 978-1-107-46104-8 Paperback

ZYGMUNT KRASINSKI

(after Ary Scheffer)

THE ANONYMOUS POET
OF POLAND
ZYGMUNT KRASINSKI

BY

MONICA M. GARDNER

AUTHOR OF

ADAM MICKIEWICZ: THE NATIONAL POET OF POLAND;
POLAND: A STUDY IN NATIONAL IDEALISM;
ETC.

"He who speaks truth to an unhappy nation is her
noblest son, for he brings her life."
Letters of Zygmunt Krasinski.

CAMBRIDGE
AT THE UNIVERSITY PRESS
1919

TO THE MEMORY OF
EDMUND S. NAGANOWSKI

"Serca podniosłe pękły. I myśl wszelka,
Byleby tylko wolna— silna— wielka—
Żegna się z nami."

ZYGMUNT KRASINSKI, *Fryburg.*

PREFACE

IN the following study on the Anonymous Poet of Poland I have attempted to give the English reader some idea of Zygmunt Krasinski as the poet, the patriot, the mystic, who endowed his nation with much of her greatest poetry and noblest thought, and finally as the man of tortured and complex character. I would ask my Polish readers to overlook the many omissions that of necessity I have been compelled to make in a subject too vast for one volume. I have restricted myself to those details that seemed to me calculated to further the object for which this book is written, that is, to draw English attention to a poetry and a line of thought that are, on one side, not only of a national but of a world-wide appeal, and, on the other, of high spiritual significance to the individual.

I have tried to let the poet speak mainly for himself both in his work and letters. For this purpose, and because the very name of Krasinski is unknown in this country, I have given extensive translations of his writings.

On certain aspects of Krasinski's life we are unable to speak with full certainty, as the voluminous correspondence with his father and Delphina Potocka remains at present unpublished in the family archives. To Dr Józef Kallenbach, who has had access to the letters between father and son, and who has freely used them in his monograph on Krasinski's youth, students of Krasinski owe their knowledge of much that would otherwise be obscure : but unfortunately Dr Kallenbach's work ends with the year 1838, and he has not as yet given us the completed biography. As it is, Krasinski's published correspondence comprises several volumes. Although I have drawn largely upon them, yet I have reluctantly been obliged, through want of space, to pass over much in these magnificent letters that can ill be spared either from the artistic or psychological point of view. It is however my intention to publish some of their most striking passages in a separate form.

My grateful thanks are due to Dr Kallenbach of the Lwów University for his gifts of his writings on Krasinski, and for the interest he showed in my work before the war put an end to my correspondence with Poles in Poland; to Prof. Zdziechowski; to Mr Ladislas Mickiewicz, who kindly lent me a volume of the Krasinski letters that in these difficult days I could obtain in no other way. But above all I wish to express here my indebtedness to my friend, the late Mr Edmund Naganowski. He was my first and constant guide in my Krasinski readings. From the hour that I began my Polish studies under his direction, twenty years ago, until the outbreak of the war cut off all possibility of communication between us, his help, his advice, his unfailing sympathy, were ceaseless. He died in Poland while the war was ravaging his country. It is to him that as a small tribute of affection and gratitude for a long and most precious friendship I dedicate this book.

M. M. G.

May, 1919.

CONTENTS

CHAPTER I

THE INITIATION
(1812–1829)

A biography of the great Polish poet, Zygmunt Krasinski, is one that offers to its writer no easy task. It can concern itself but little with outward events; for of such there are very few in Krasinski's life. The son of a soldier, with the blood in his veins of men who had helped to make the history of Poland, he was compelled by the tragedy of circumstance to stand aside from what is commonly, and perhaps erroneously, termed action. Nor can a study on Krasinski be merely a piece of literary criticism. With scarcely an exception Krasinski's work, for all its high literary beauty, is the organ of a great idea to which he regarded art as subservient. The history of the poet, who during his lifetime was known only as the Anonymous Poet, and after death had revealed his secret was, and is still, honoured under the same title, is that of an overmastering thought and of its development through a soul's travail. The poet who began his career by being unable to write verse ended it, by force of devotion to a cause, as one of the three supreme singers in the magnificent literature of Poland. The Pole who was driven to the brink of despair by grief for his country, who spoke in his early youth the language of pessimism, became the most sublime teacher of his nation, the herald of hope, the prophet of resurrection. The life of Krasinski, therefore, resolves itself into the record of a moral conflict and of the message that it wrung forth, which, primarily intended for the poet's own nation, yet appeals most powerfully to all humanity and to the spiritual necessity of every human soul.

It was in Paris on the nineteenth of February, 1812, that Zygmunt Krasinski was born to a noble and wealthy house; the greatly desired son of a marriage that, save for an infant daughter who did not survive her birth, had been childless for nine years. His family was related to the Royal House of Savoy. His mother was a Radziwiłł, one of the oldest names in Lithuania, written on nearly every page of Polish history. Behind him stretched a distinguished line of ancestors; soldiers who in the splendid, brilliantly coloured annals of Poland had led their armies of retainers into the battle-fields against Tartars, Turks, Russians; statesmen who had rendered conspicuous service to their country.

The father of the poet, Wincenty Krasinski, like so many Poles of his epoch, fought under Napoleon's flag. Among the Polish legions, devoted by a chivalrous and passionate attachment to Napoleon upon whom they looked as the future saviour of their nation, Wincenty Krasinski gained considerable distinction. He was above all things a soldier, with a soldier's physical courage and lightheartedness; vain, ambitious, and fond of show. With his character and temperament those of his only son were at life-long odds : and yet the confidence and affection, proof against the bitterest of tests, that united a wholly dissimilar father and son went so deep as to be exceptional. Zygmunt's mother gave him her plain face, her keen intelligence, her profound religious sense, and the fatal inheritance of melancholy and disordered nerves that tormented him all his life.

The conditions of Krasinski's infancy were strangely inconsistent with those of the shadowed life that followed. He entered the world amidst the clash of arms: he was the little son of a regiment, the plaything of the soldiers under Wincenty Krasinski's command. Moreover, he was born into that spring of high hope for the Polish nation, of which Adam Mickiewicz sang as the one year of gladness that he as a Pole had ever known. Those were the days of Napoleon's march upon Russia when all Poland enthusiastically hailed him as her deliverer. Wincenty Krasinski shared to its utmost the devotion to Napoleon that even the betrayal of their cause could never shake in the hearts of the Poles. Zygmunt was brought up in the Napoleonic tradition. Napoleon was the first of the five names which his parents gave him, among which the Zygmunt that remained by him came last; and in his childhood he was called by a pet Polish diminutive, equivalent to "Little Napoleon." The Napoleon cult played a very large part in the influences that shaped his views: and his final solution of his national and spiritual enigmas was in part based upon his theories of the Napoleonic conquests.

The downfall of Napoleon ended Wincenty Krasinski's career in the Polish legions. In 1814 he returned with his wife and child to the family palace in Warsaw; and, after the establishment of the autonomous Kingdom of Poland by the Congress of Vienna in 1815, he received a high command in the Polish army. The childhood of Zygmunt Krasinski synchronized therefore with the last days in which his nation possessed any vestiges of freedom. The Kingdom had been granted her own administration, her national army and constitution under the Russian Tsar, crowned king of Poland; but Krasinski was not out of his boyhood before the portents of tempest were fast gathering about his country. Her rights were attacked by Russia on every side, her liberties outraged. There could be but one end:—the Rising of 1830.

Although Krasinski was the idol of both his parents his childhood, even before his mother's death, was no happy one. He was brought up with as little relaxation and as few amusements suited to his age as any prince in a rigidly ceremonious court. The precocious brain of the frail and highly-strung child was forced at a pace that to our modern ideas seems frankly appalling. Between the father's ambition for his son and the pedagogic severity of the tutors, the delicate boy, despite his mother's entreaties, was kept at his lessons for the greater part of the day. Both head and heart were too soon developed. At four years old, the pretty, little ringleted boy, in the low-necked frock and high sash of the pre-Victorian era, such as we see him in a charming early portrait, recited to Alexander I at the latter's request verses of his own choosing : and with eyes fastened on the Tsar of all the Russias he spouted Brutus's defence of democracy from Voltaire. A child of seven, he made courtly repartees to the Dowager Empress. Clear signs of the acute sensitiveness and strong affections that were his characteristics through life already foretold the future. In his childish sicknesses his entreaty was that his invalid mother must not know what he was suffering.

Nor could Zygmunt Krasinski carry away from his

home the remembrance of a domestic hearth united by deep family attachment such as we find in the free, happy, boyish days of Adam Mickiewicz. He was the chief bond between his parents. Their marriage had not been a love-match. Although the high moral character of his mother was unimpeachable, her melancholy, her forebodings, her nervous petulance, her jealousies—for which her husband, gay, handsome, younger than herself, gave her good reason—made her no easy inmate of a household. Long before her death she retired from society, a mental and physical invalid, and occupied herself with the religious and moral training of her boy. She died in 1822, when Zygmunt was ten years old, of the lung disease that he inherited: her parting wish for her son, recorded in her will, being that he might grow up a good Christian and a good Pole.

It is said that the grief of the orphaned child was far more profound than that of his father for his dead wife. But what between the detestation with which Wincenty Krasinski has been regarded by many of his fellow-Poles and the white-washing process by which others have defended his memory, it is difficult to arrive at a correct judgment upon a character that was, moreover, in itself one of contradictions. All agree that to supply the loss of a mother's love he redoubled his fondness to the child. Father and son spent hours together in the General's private room. There Wincenty taught his son the national history. He spoke to him at length of the glorious deeds of his ancestors whose portraits, hanging round the walls of the palace such as the poet later described in a famous scene of his *Undivine Comedy*, impressed upon the boyish mind the realization of the patriotic inheritance and obligations of his house. Krasinski was, in fact, brought up in the spirit of devoted attachment to his country. This close intimacy between the soldier and his son deepened the latter's enthusiastic hero-worship for a father who had fought so gallantly himself for Poland[1]. It stands out with the most tragic significance when the trial of Zygmunt Krasinski's life swept down upon him. Beyond his father's love all the tenderness that Krasinski knew as a motherless boy was supplied by a French governess, to whom in his letters after he had reached manhood he always alludes with strong affection. His father's mother, it is true, lived in the palace; but her presence introduced no motherly or womanly influence into her young grandson's lonely life. Her rigid severity was the terror of her servants and all who approached her, and had early driven her son when a youth from home.

Such was the environment of Krasinski's childhood. His attainments were so far beyond his years that when he had reached the age of twelve his father invited the most learned men and best teachers in the country to put his son through an elaborate examination in his palace. It is consoling to learn that as a reward for his brilliant performance in an ordeal of which, badgered and overworked as he was, he entertained no agreeable remembrance, his father gave him a gun; and the one pleasingly childish picture that stands out from an unnatural childhood is that of a little boy going out with wild joy, in the short holiday that was allowed him, to shoot partridges and ducks in his country estate.

In the chapel of that country home—Opinogóra—Krasinski's mortal remains now lie. The happiest

[1] J. Kallenbach, *Zygmunt Krasinski* Lwów, 1904 (Polish).

moments of his boyhood were passed there. The long, plain house, built on one story, stood on a low hill, and was encircled by a flat, marshy landscape. Although the scenery was dreary and monotonous, it inspired Zygmunt with romantic fancies. In his time young people read and worshipped Walter Scott. Inevitably, therefore, the ruins of a castle near the mansion filled Krasinski's head with the dreams of bygone history, common to all poetic boys. But in his case they took a strong national colouring, tinged by the melancholy of the Pole looking back to the great past of his dismembered country, and seeing around him the life and death struggle of his nation to preserve even that shred of liberty that was still hers. He describes these surroundings of Opinogóra in a sketch that he wrote when he was sixteen. His manner of expression is the conventional one of a boy of his age; but the deep patriotic feeling behind it is significant.

I mused in this castle. I laid my gun upon the ground, and recalled the history of my country. The wind at times broke the silence. At times the raven with its ill-omened voice recalled the unhappiness of the present. The moon, rising behind the clouds, often found me leaning on an insensate stone, deep in old times. The rays of heaven's torch flowed on me and, suffusing with a mournful light the remnants of ancient glory, struck upon fallen stones, on wreathing plants, and when they chanced on fragments of a sword or armour, flowing in fiery streams, they seemed to rejoice that in a land of slavery they had met with the traces of our freedom of yore.

Oh, thou, freedom, exiled from this land, inspire my strains, and, if thou mayest not be in our native country, take refuge in our hearts, and beautify these feeble songs with thy divine accords. (*The Lord of the Three Hillocks.* 1828.)

When Krasinski had turned fourteen, he was sent to the Warsaw Lyceum to prepare for the University. Everything in his unwholesome training had been cal-

culated to encourage in an impressionable childish mind
an overweening self-estimation. Yet all his life Krasinski was singularly free from the slightest tendency
to vanity. Morbid and introspective as he undoubtedly
was, egotism was unknown to him. He idealized others,
himself never. His human sympathies that made him
the most generous, the tenderest of friends were far
from being stifled in the mental forcing-house of a
necessarily self-absorbed childhood. He gave his whole
heart to those he loved with an unreserved devotion.
He made friendships that endured for life with the boys
who were his school companions: notably, with Konstanty Gaszynski. The latter is known in Polish literature as a graceful and patriotic poet, albeit of no very
marked order. An exile after the Rising of 1830 in
which he fought, the victim like the majority of his
Polish contemporaries of bitter afflictions[1], he became
one of Krasinski's closest intimates and constant companion, at times the amanuensis during his blindness.
To Gaszynski, in the long series of letters that began
in early youth and ended only when the pen fell from
his dying hand, Krasinski poured out his sorrows,
his confidences, his passion for his country with a self-
abandonment expressive of the entire sympathy that
reigned between them.

There is little of note in Krasinski's year at school.
He worked well, and entered the University of Warsaw in the autumn of 1827.

The plunge of the fifteen-year-old boy into University life was not in reality so great a change from the

[1] The mother to whom he wrote a touching sonnet in their separation
was shot by Russian soldiers on the doorstep of her house. His last years—
after the death of Krasinski—were darkened by the national tragedies following the Rising of 1863.

school benches as it appears. At that time the students
at the University were hedged in by such strict regu-
lations that they were more like schoolboys than what
we should call undergraduates. Young Krasinski was a
lively, witty, turbulent boy, troublesome to his professors,
touchy and quarrelsome with his colleagues. In class
hours he was under strict discipline; but at home,
during the frequent absence of his father, he was completely left to his own devices. The atmosphere of the
palace when Wincenty Krasinski was there was one of
social brilliance and a festive coming and going. Loving
display and popularity, Wincenty Krasinski kept open
house, and gave weekly dinners at which the guests
were men of distinction in the world of politics and
letters. Zygmunt was too young to take part in these
reunions; but the accounts of the literary discussions
that went on there, reported to him by Gaszynski who,
several years his elder, was present at them, added
fresh fire to his burning ambition to write[1]. When the
master of the house was absent, the palace sank into
a petrified stillness and tedium. According to Krasinski's letters to his father, the only sounds that broke
the dragging silence of the long winter days and nights
were the howling of the wind and the storm shaking
the silver on the table[2]. He sat for hours in his grandmother's room, dull and bored, irritated by her ill humour,
trying, as he says, to please her by reading aloud to
her. His leisure time he spent in writing crude stories
after Walter Scott and falling in love.

It was no doubt inevitable that a poetically minded
and precocious boy, left so much alone, should have
worshipped at the shrine of a handsome young woman,

[1] J. Kallenbach, *op. cit.*   [2] *Ibid.*

a good many years older than himself, with whom he was thrown into close contact. His cousin, Amelia Załuska, a ward of Wincenty Krasinski, was staying under the protection of his roof while her husband was in prison with other Polish nationalists in the famous affair, to which we shall return. She looked upon Zygmunt as a young brother : but he, believing himself to be in love with her, lived in constant and feverish agitation. Watching her every mood, he worked himself up, mentally and physically, into a condition of unnatural excitement and exaltation, for which he afterwards, in letters to Henry Reeve, bitterly blamed himself. He ruined his already overstrung nerves by inordinate tea drinking, diluted with rum. He read to excess poetry and romance. With no one to control his proceedings, he sat up late into the night, writing stories. One of these, *The Grave of the Reichstals*, he saw when he was only sixteen printed in a Polish paper, probably through the complaisance of the editor who was a friend of his father. His father was not only the confidant of his first literary attempts ; he was also their somewhat unsparing critic. It speaks much for the unusually intimate relations between father and son that we find Zygmunt solemnly offering his *Lord of the Three Hillocks* to the General, sending him his manuscripts, and describing to him minutely his projected characters and plots. The father frankly thought the story presented to him poor stuff, and his son's absorption in his pen waste of time.

The great romantic revival in Polish literature was just then setting in, with Adam Mickiewicz as its chief and magnificent spokesman. While Krasinski was still a boy in his father's house, Mickiewicz, fourteen years his senior, had already entered into his exile in Russia. His words and movements were under the supervision of the Russian police ; his genius was held in shackles ; and yet he wrote his *Konrad Wallenrod*. Using the figure of the struggle of Lithuania against the Teutonic Knights he told a tale, understood by every Pole who read it, of the vengeance to which an oppressed nation may be forced [1]. The poem was given to young Krasinski by a cousin. He too was in his turn to write, on widely different lines, of the son of a conquered race preparing the destruction of the victor. But neither he nor those around him could have guessed that the boy of brilliant intellect, indeed, but with no capacity for writing poetry, who read with ecstasy Mickiewicz's splendid verse set against a great patriotic theme, was to stand with the author of *Konrad Wallenrod* as one of the trinity of Poland's most inspired poets. Knowing as we do that the basis of Krasinski's future teaching was the abjuration of revenge and hatred it is instructive to note how, when a youth, lurid Byronic avengers, albeit not Byron but Walter Scott was Krasinski's first love, always took his fancy. He chose them for the heroes of his own novels : and, speaking of *Konrad Wallenrod* to his father, he records the fascination exercised upon him by the patriot whose weapons are those of treachery and undying hatred. With the sadly ripe experience of the Polish boy living under a foreign yoke, he adds : " All the poem breathes grief and sadness, the grief that is so appropriate to us [2]."

In after years, when circumstances had not only driven him from his home, but robbed it of all joy for

---

[1] See my *Adam Mickiewicz*, Dent, 1911.
[2] J. Kallenbach, *op. cit.*

such short periods as he ever unwillingly returned to it, Krasinski looked back yearningly to those hours of his youth, the last before the catastrophe struck his life. Gaszynski was his frequent visitor. The two talked endlessly in Krasinski's room, or hunted, or roamed the countryside round Opinogóra. The "pipe era": so Krasinski in his later letters to Gaszynski fondly calls this part of his life from a joke they shared together. Forbidden by his father to smoke, Zygmunt enjoyed a pipe on the sly with Gaszynski till the General gave in; when Gaszynski, finding Krasinski celebrating the victory by smoking like a chimney, scrawled on the mantelpiece in high glee : " Hail, era of the pipe !"

The end of 1828 saw Krasinski in a University scrape, of a rather mild description, though it was taken very seriously by the authorities. Headed by Krasinski's friend, Leo Łubienski, a band of youths stamped down one of the professors to mark their disapproval of the public reprimand of a student. Krasinski was foremost among the ringleaders, and was sent to prison for two days. Thence he scrawled on his blotting-paper repentant letters to his father, promising that he would never do such a thing again. " Please forgive me," he writes in a very chastened frame of mind: "I solemnly swear that I will keep my given word[1]."

With this, our last, glimpse of a boyhood free from tragedy, we may close the account of Krasinski's early years. If we have dwelt somewhat at length upon their influences and circumstances, it is because these were of extraordinary significance to his subsequent history, and because, at the same time, the character that his life shows us is in strange—in noble—contradiction to

---

[1] J. Kallenbach, *op. cit.*

many of them. The paradox is part of the complex personality of Zygmunt Krasinski.

Those national events were now going forward which changed the whole tenor of Krasinski's life, and precipitated his country into the Rising and its long and mournful sequel. The promises given by Alexander I had fallen to the ground. The history of the Kingdom of Poland had resolved itself into one desperate struggle on the part of the Poles to preserve their guaranteed rights. In 1825 Alexander died. He had begun his career as a liberal ruler and the friend of Poland. He ended it as a weak reactionary who had violated the liberties that he had solemnly pledged himself to respect. On his death the famous Decembrist rising broke out in Petersburg. The Russian Liberals—those friends of Mickiewicz whose fate he has mourned in one of the most tragic of his poems—died on the gallows or were sent to the mines.

The Russian government then discovered that in touch with the Russian Liberals there existed a patriotic society in Poland, whose object was the restoration of Polish independence. The leaders were sent to join the numbers of their fellow-Poles who were already languishing in the prisons : and Nicholas I demanded their trial by the Senate of the Polish Diet. They were brought before this tribunal. Bielinski presided over it, and among its members sat Wincenty Krasinski.

The Polish court was between two most difficult alternatives. It must either obey the will of the Tsar and condemn to death men who had been guilty of no crime except the desire of their national restoration ; or it must declare the innocence of the accused, and thereby, by placing the nation in direct opposition to the Tsar, jeopardize the very existence of the Kingdom, where conditions were by now unworkable and strained to the last point.   It was manifestly impossible for a Polish tribunal to brand as criminals Poles whose only aim had been that of Polish independence.   After a long and intricate process, those who were convicted of actual knowledge of the Russian Decembrist plot were condemned to varying terms of imprisonment.   The remaining members of the patriotic association, amidst the acclamations of the whole nation, were liberated.

One, and only one, member of the court voted for the death sentence.   That man was the father of Zygmunt Krasinski.   Opinions differ as to his motives. Some say that he yielded to the dictates of his ambitious and time-serving nature, and was determined to stand well with the Tsar.   Again, his friends maintain that he saw the danger of Poland irrevocably losing that which was still hers to lose if she and the Tsar came to conflict on this matter.   But, whichever of these judgments be correct, the immediate result of his conduct was a storm of execration that gathered against him. Many of those who had been his best friends and the most habitual intimates of his house would never set foot again in the Krasinski palace.

The decision of the tribunal was given in the end of 1828.   In March, 1829, Bielinski, who had been its president, died.   All Warsaw determined to honour him by following his coffin to the grave.   The funeral in fact was to be a great national demonstration.   The University authorities, fearing a scene at this highly delicate and critical moment, gave orders that the students should not attend the obsequies, but should be present at the lectures as usual.   When the day came, every student—with one exception—followed the bier of the dead patriot, and, with wild enthusiasm, rushed upon the coffin and tore pieces from the pall as relics. The lecture halls were empty—still with the exception of one student.   That student was Zygmunt Krasinski. In obedience to his father's command, the unhappy boy, in dumb despair and rage, sat alone in the class-room, while all his compatriots mourned at the grave of the man who had defended Poland.   It seems difficult to conceive how a father, who was most fondly attached to his son, could have had the cruelty to expose an abnormally sensitive and intensely patriotic boy to such a position. It is said that his vanity, always his master-passion, was pricked by the knowledge of the unpopularity that he had brought upon himself, and that he was in consequence resolved to brave the opinions of his countrymen[1].

On the following day Zygmunt went to the lectures as usual.   There was never any lack of physical courage in his character, and he showed no outward sign of the mortal dread that must have filled his soul.   As he entered the class-room, crowded not only by students but also by a public audience, a murmur of disapprobation greeted him, only silenced by the entrance of the professor. It must be remembered that it was a time of great national tension when patriotic ardour, especially among the young men, ran at fever heat.   In the eyes of these boy companions of Krasinski, many of whom in less than two years were to fall fighting for Poland, who, moreover, naturally could not enter into

[1] Count Stanisław Tarnowski, *Zygmunt Krasinski*, Cracow, 1892 (Polish).

the extraordinarily difficult situation in which Krasinski was placed, both father and son were equally something like renegades to the Polish cause. When the lecture was concluded, Zygmunt was set upon by his fellow-students and mobbed. The ringleader who tore from Krasinski's uniform the badge of the University as one unworthy to bear it was his own friend, Łubienski. Konstanty Gaszynski, and in a further riot of the kind that occurred another Konstanty, Danielewicz, stood by Zygmunt's side and stoutly defended the delicate, undersized boy.

These scenes blasted the youth of Zygmunt Krasinski. They were his baptism of fire. Never, in all his after life, did he outlive their suffering and disgrace. Years later he told the story in accents of passionate pain in his *Unfinished Poem* : and obviously he could only bring himself to lift the veil for that once in order to render a tribute of gratitude and affection to Danielewicz, who had died in his arms. He repaid the intervention of Danielewicz by a life-long love. On the other hand when, two years afterwards, Łubienski approached Krasinski in Switzerland with some attempt at a renewal of friendship, Krasinski could neither forgive him or pronounce his name except with loathing[1]. Matters were patched up with the other youths who had taken part in the demonstration against him when, a few days after the original incident, Krasinski in the University hall called upon them to prove that he was a traitor to Bielinski's memory. But on the same

[1] I shall return to this meeting of the two in Switzerland, as it gave rise to a correspondence on the subject between Krasinski and Reeve that throws very important light on the psychology of Krasinski and of his *Iridion.*

occasion he publicly branded as a liar Łubienski, who had added to his original insult aspersions on Krasinski's patriotism, and he then and there challenged him to a duel. Brodzinski, the professor of Polish literature and the father of its romantic revival, was hurriedly summoned to the hall. By his temperate and kindly persuasions, he got the two to the point of shaking hands: but the reconciliation was only perfunctory, and the deadly offence remained unwiped out in Krasinski's mind. Duelling was against the rules of the University. For this cause, and also, as is clear from the correspondence between the Rector of the University and General Krasinski, because the authorities foresaw that the position of the excitable, hotheaded boy among his fellow-students would lead to endless difficulties, Wincenty Krasinski was requested to remove Zygmunt privately from the University for a year[1]. The father on his side realized that his son's life in his own city had become unlivable, and he decided to send him to complete his studies in Geneva. The boy spent the last months of his stay in his country—the last in which that country was to be his home—between Warsaw and Opinogóra, writing feverishly to distract thought. The tales and historical romances moulded on Scott that he then wrote were published the following year. One of them at least—*Władysław Herman*—is somewhat above the run of an ordinary boy's similar attempts; but as Krasinski, when past early youth, never followed up this line we need not linger on these first writings.

In the autumn of 1829 he left Poland. He was never to see his beloved country again except as a conquered province, given over to the fate of the

---

[1] The correspondence is given by Dr Kallenbach, *Zygmunt Krasinski*.

vanquished.   He was sent abroad with a sort of tutor, Jakubowski, whom in their letters Krasinski and Henry Reeve call Jacky.   Unable to tear himself away from his son until the last moment possible, Wincenty Krasinski went with the travellers for some part of the way.   Father and son then took farewell of each other, separating under painful circumstances, in deep affection. "The parting in 1829 was a sad one," writes Dr Kallenbach : "but the meeting in 1832 was to be still more bitter and tragic beyond all expression[1]."

[1] *Op. cit.*

CHAPTER II

THE FIRST EXILE
(1829–1830)

The homesick boy wrote sheaves of letters to his father and to the friends he had left in Poland, at every stage of his journey. His imagination was enthralled by his first sight of the Lake of Geneva: but, writes he to his father, "Poland with her sandy stretches stood out to me in far more alluring colours than the Swiss mountains, and I would not give up the memory of the pond at Opinogóra for the Lake of Geneva[1]." To Gaszynski he pours out the rapture of a poet at the spectacle of the autumn sunset over the lake; yet in his description of the waves curling like fiery serpents, of the deep blue lapis lazuli where the shadow of the mountains fell upon the water, he pauses to note a "lonely pine, reminding me of Poland." "My eyes are fastened on Leman," he ends his letter, "but my heart sighs for Poland[2]."

With his tutor, Zygmunt settled down in a pension, kept by a widow, the age and undecorative aspect of whose daughters displeased him greatly. His landlady, who was related to the principal families in Geneva, made haste to introduce him to Swiss society. It is amusing to read that he was considerably annoyed by

[1] Given by Dr Kallenbach, *Zygmunt Krasinski.*
[2] *Letters of Zygmunt Krasinski*, Vol. I, Lwów, 1882. To Konstanty Gaszynski. Geneva, 1829 (Polish).

the bombardment of ignorant questions put to him by
his new acquaintances as to whether, says Dr Kallenbach, "this or that were known in Poland": an ordeal
with which the Polish visitor in present-day England
has good reason to sympathize. Two days after his
arrival in Geneva Krasinski met at a party a tall, fair
English boy, with the face of a beautiful girl. "It is
difficult to judge of him at first sight," Zygmunt
cautiously tells his father[1]: for, curiously enough,
Krasinski, who passionately loved, never lost his heart
at the outset, but surveyed the objects of his future
adoration rather coldly and critically. The English boy
was Henry Reeve, the most beloved companion of
Krasinski's youth.

In these early days Krasinski sorely missed his
father, home and friends. He wrote to his father his
boyish resolves to keep straight; recounted to him the
details of his new life; told him of his sadness at being
parted from him. "Except Poland, except you, except
Warsaw, there is nothing for me in the world[2]." But
for all that there is, as Count Tarnowski observes,
already a reserve in the son's letters[3]. On one subject
he cannot speak: and Dr Kallenbach notices that his
effusions to his father are more those of a pupil to a
master, of whom he stands in some fear, than of a son
on terms of perfect ease and affection with a parent.
How extraordinarily sensitive he was to the approval
or disapproval of his father may be gathered from his
answer to the latter after Wincenty Krasinski, having
heard that his son had fought a duel, had written to
him in anger.

[1] Given by Dr Kallenbach, *op. cit.*   [2] *Ibid.*
[3] St. Tarnowski, *Zygmunt Krasinski.*

"Picturing to myself your uneasiness," replies Zygmunt, "I sought in vain for any relief to my sadness, and could not sit down in peace to my writing. I read a book, but did not understand either the words or the sense. Even your portrait hanging above my head looked changed to me. I reached such a point that I dared not look at it. Although I was entirely innocent, my father's anger tore my heart cruelly. The distance that divides us, your ill health, the uncertainty whether you would believe my words...and a thousand thoughts coursing uninterruptedly through my mind made a most painful impression upon my soul[1]."

Although Krasinski yearned with homesickness towards a country which draws those who are hers with a spell peculiar to herself, although he passed lonely hours cut off from his friends and relations in Poland by a silence increasing with the difficulties of the times, his first year at Geneva held many compensations. The memory of what had exiled him from his country was, it is true, burnt into his soul; his father had already taken the first steps on the road that severed him morally for ever from his son ; but they were only the first steps, and at present Zygmunt could not have foreseen what was close upon him. The boy worked hard at his studies. He did not take the regular University course, but chose his own subjects ; philosophy, political economy, jurisprudence, and Roman history. The Roman history lectures were given by Professor Rossi. Zygmunt followed them with close attention: and it was upon them that at a later period he built the splendid colouring of *Iridion*. He made a special study of French and devoted himself with ardour to that of English; took up mathematics with the idea of learning military tactics, and, in the amateur fashion of his epoch, dabbled with music. His capacities for work were, according to

[1] Given by Dr Kallenbach, *op. cit.*

Dr Kallenbach, quite unusual[1]. He read enormously, and now laid the stores of his profound after-knowledge. In the afternoons he went for rides in the beautiful neighbourhood of Geneva, or sailed on the lake with young Reeve and a Polish youth, August Zamojski. The evenings were often broken into by dinners, soirées, dances. The undiluted Geneva society appears from Krasinski's descriptions to have been decidedly dull. Everyone knew each other too well, and a stiff conventionality reigned in the salons. However, the strong cosmopolitan element brought in some variety. The foreign visitors were chiefly English: and, to an English biographer of the Anonymous Poet of Poland, it is gratifying to record that the favoured two to whom the heart of the sad and lonely boy went out in special manner, during the first year that he spent alone in a strange country, were an English boy and an English girl.

Henry Reeve, the future editor of *The Edinburgh Review*, the political leader writer during many years for *The Times*, was in 1829 living with his mother in Geneva, finishing his education. In those days he was romantic, poetical, enthusiastic even as Krasinski himself. The two became inseparable. To Henry Reeve not only the student of Krasinski, but the whole Polish nation, must ever owe a debt of gratitude. The discovery in 1892 of the correspondence between Krasinski and Reeve, consisting of a hundred and sixty-three letters, mainly Krasinski's, which range from the early summer of 1830 to the spring of 1838, has thrown invaluable light upon a period of the poet's life that is of the highest psychological importance, and of which much

[1] *Op. cit.*

hitherto had been left to conjecture. After the first
affectionate relations of their youth, Krasinski and
Reeve dropped entirely out of each other's lives[1]. But
more than forty years after Krasinski had left this earth
a Polish youth, a stranger—thus Dr Kallenbach describes the scene[2]—found his way to the country home
of Henry Reeve, then in extreme old age. Reeve saw
before him a young Pole whose face seemed vaguely
familiar. It was the grandson of the gifted boy, with
the strangely tragic history, whom Reeve had loved
when himself young. The old man handed over to
Count Adam Krasinski a bulky packet, containing not
only his and Krasinski's letters, but also some then unknown literary fragments of Krasinski's French prose
that the poet had sent him directly they were written[3].
All these were edited and published with an illuminating
introduction by Dr Kallenbach in 1902.

From these letters it is apparent that during the
years in Geneva Krasinski and Reeve were like
brothers. They boated and rode and walked together;
shared every confidence; discussed literature, philosophy, and politics; read and criticized each other's
literary productions; and sighed in company over the
respective ladies of their affections.

For Krasinski fell in love with an English girl, a
certain Henrietta Willan. Krasinski, the only son and

[1] But that Krasinski spoke often and with strong affection of Reeve we
know from a letter that the poet's wife wrote after his death to Reeve, in
reply to the words of condolence that the latter had addressed on his loss
to Count Ladislas Zamojski, one of Krasinski's greatest admirers. John
Knox Laughton, *Memoirs of the Life and Correspondence of Henry Reeve*,
London, 1898.

[2] See his Preface to *Correspondance de Sigismond Krasinski et de
Henry Reeve*, Paris, 1902.

[3] *Ibid.*

heir of a great Polish magnate, could never hope to obtain his father's consent to marriage with a young Englishwoman of no standing. Both he and Henrietta knew this well, but they promised each other endless attachment. Under the inspiration of his love Krasinski poured out French compositions, written for Henrietta, given to Reeve, and only known to Poland after they had lain seventy years in English keeping.

These semi-autobiographical pieces, a fragment of a journal, Krasinski calls them, or a fragment of a dream, are impregnated with the exaltation of a boy in love. They contain certain characteristics that strongly illustrate the psychology of Krasinski. It was but natural that the imagination of a highly-strung boy who had been born after a great political crime had been inflicted on his country, and who had been brought up with the results of that crime as a part of his daily life, should occupy itself with lurid scenes of cataclysm and bloodshed. These figure largely in the passages he wrote for Henrietta, and to this nightmare style he returns much later in his Polish prose poems: *The Dream of Cesara* and *A Legend*. In these early productions the vision of Henrietta is always there, but it is never far away from the thought of his country. So, in after life, is the image of the woman for whom Krasinski wrote his love poems, intimately, inseparably, united to a patriot's passion. Then, too, Krasinski's sentiment for the English girl was ethereal and unpractical, the germ of that idealization of human love that gave *Dawn* to the Polish nation.

"I did not love her lips but her smile," writes the young lover, "not her body but her immortal soul. I neither saw her body nor mine," he continues, speaking of their reunion after death, "but I felt that she was near me. We understood each other better than on earth. All our beautiful thoughts, all our sublime feelings, formed one chain that bound us together and kept us near each other. Our memories stood to us in the place of hope, for we were in a perfect beatitude. Her soul mingled with mine." (*Fragment d'un Journal.* March 24, 1830.)

The Willan family left for England in the spring of 1830. Krasinski remained behind in a youthful lover's despair. He relieved his feelings by the exchange of letters with Henrietta and by literary composition. "Two days after her departure": "Five days after her departure, at ten, eleven, twelve at night": so he heads the writings in which he deplores his solitude without her. He dreams of fighting for freedom in the Polish ranks, with her face before his eyes, or he chooses an eternity of woe rather than be divided from her beyond the grave. He sat in his room, overlooking the magnificent panorama of the Lake of Geneva, covering reams of paper by the light of two candles till far into the night[1]. He wrote chiefly in French—sketches, memories, reflections—but also short pieces in his native language which were printed in the Polish paper of which Gaszynski was sub-editor. It is a striking fact that prophecies of woe and struggle, strangely prescient of the Rising that the Polish nation was to see before the year was out, repeat themselves again and again in Krasinski's writings at this time. There is also the sense not only of impending disaster, but of personal frustration. No doubt we can find one reason in the ever rankling wound of the blow that had befallen Krasinski before he left his country. Furthermore, he must have lived, if scarcely consciously to himself, under a weight of oppression in those days when it was obvious that the tension between the Kingdom of Poland and

[1] J. Kallenbach, *Zygmunt Krasinski.*

Nicholas I was bound to end in some sort of explosion. But it must also be taken into account that now, like every youth of the epoch, Krasinski was becoming strongly affected by Byron.

It is a curious anomaly in Krasinski's history that he who was to be one of the greatest of his nation's poets, who read poetry with passion, was so far without the instinct for self-expression in verse native to every poetical boy or girl. While in Geneva he fell under the spell of the English romantic poets. He was fascinated by Southey, Campbell, Moore—whose name he invariably spells wrongly—and Keats. With enthusiasm he read Shakspeare under Reeve's auspices. "If it were not for poetry," he tells his father, "I don't know what a man would do in this world, and how he could live, surrounded only by cold reality[1]." Yet, for all the hours that, consumed by literary ambition, he spent composing, he seems hardly to have even attempted to write poetry, and when he did he failed. Romantic, too, as were the tendencies of Krasinski's mind, he possessed even when a boy—he kept it through life—a curiously clear vision and accurate power of observation.

His sarcastic descriptions of the Geneva salons are, as Dr Kallenbach notes, borne out in every detail by the accounts of other frequenters of the same society. For all his dreams, Krasinski never lived with his head in the clouds. If we may be permitted the expression, he was always "all there." His interest in politics, inevitable in a Pole ever awaiting the turn of events that would affect his country, was already strong. All manner of subjects attracted his attention: and among

---

[1] Given by Dr Kallenbach, *op. cit.*

his French essays written in his first summer at Geneva is an argument for and against the advisability of a state clergy.

In the summer of 1830 Reeve and his mother left Geneva for the vacation. Krasinski devoted his evenings to solitary rambles, ending in a garden near the house in which Henrietta Willan had lived. In this spot, gazing on the lake at his feet and at the snowy peaks reddening to the setting sun, he wrote down the poetic fancies with which his head was filled. His reflections were faithfully handed on to Reeve: and now began the eight years' correspondence between the two friends.

Had Krasinski left no line of poetry behind him, he would still have lived in the literature of Poland by the depth of thought, the beauty of expression, in the several hundred of his letters that have as yet been published. As regards literary power, his letters to Reeve naturally cannot be compared with those to Gaszynski, Sołtan and his other Polish correspondents. In the former Krasinski is writing in a foreign language, admirably as he manipulated it. The greater part of them were penned in early youth before he had reached either the maturity of his genius or the full development of his leading idea. But as an index to his character—that strangely complicated, contradictory and most appealing character—as the illustration of a poet and philosopher's mental evolution, the letters to Reeve are a priceless asset to the Krasinski student. They are written in French with, at times, an excursion into an English so peculiar that we can only describe it as the reverse of conversational. This interchange of ideas between two clever and enthusiastic boys is of course largely coloured with the romanticism of the early thirties when Byron, Shelley and Keats were the idols of the hour. It shows a certain amount of youthful exaggeration, here and there boyish folly, a distinct tinge of the posing that was then the fashion. But, as Dr Kallenbach bids us notice, side by side with the often callow sentiments of the earlier portion of the correspondence, may be found those deep reflections that were to make of Krasinski one of the most profound and truest thinkers of his nation[1]. The first letters were written before tragedy and shame had changed a boy's heart, while he still played with emotion and, to a certain extent, caressed a Byronic grief. After the Rising of 1830 had broken out, bringing upon the young Pole its double weight of national and private anguish, the tone of the letters changes. They are no longer those of a morbid and romantic boy who had been reading a good deal of Byron, but of one whose youth was immersed in an abyss of suffering where he found his manhood. Studying these self-revelations of an over sensitive and highly pitched nature, we see the young Krasinski penetrating at the outset of life with an almost startling acuteness into the mysteries of pain and the spiritual psychology of conflict. That insight is of itself a greater proof of the deep waters through which his soul passed than even those many passages in which he directly confides the details of his grief into the ears of those he loved.

The letters to Reeve open, as we should expect, with lamentations for Henrietta Willan's absence. Krasinski complains that the peaceful scenery of the Swiss lakes ill accords with the mood of two lovers:

[1] J. Kallenbach, *Préface. Correspondance de Sigismond Krasinski et de Henry Reeve.*

for Reeve was more or less enamoured of a Swiss girl, Constance Sautter.

"I must tell you that the day before yesterday I was in such a state of distress, of *disgust*"—Krasinski underlines his English words—"boredom, melancholy, that life weighed on me more than ever and, for the first time, the degrading idea came to me of finishing with this world which has brought me but few joys, taken from me as soon as I felt them. It was the first time in my life that I have had the idea of suicide, so I marked it down in my pocket-book. But I soon repulsed with disdain that thought which can sometimes rise in a delirious brain, but which can never be carried out except by a cowardly heart that lacks nobility.

"The night before last, being unable to close my eyes, I read the work of M. Boissier, 'Shall we find them in a better world?' and I found there consolation, life and hope, though the style is dry and dusty—and not one grain of poetry. When I have finished the romance that is occupying me at present, I shall write a work like it in Polish, but adding to it all the charms of imagination and poetry that my weak mind can put together—and I shall dedicate it to Her who inspired me with it. You can well understand that it will be *without name*. People can take it for a work of my imagination, and it will rather be that of my heart[1]."

Krasinski then gives Reeve a sketch of an essay he had just been showing to their French teacher, and asks for his opinion. It contains so strange a foreboding of what he suffered during the Rising that we cannot altogether pass it by. Beginning with the words: "I have known a really unhappy man," it goes on to describe a youth at heart a poet, but who cannot express himself. He loves, and his love, too, ends in failure, his beloved casting him off by reason of his seeming ineptitude. He becomes "dumb and stupefied" by his misfortune. "It was given to the voice of an oppressed country to wake him from this fearful lethargy. The love of his native soil gave him back his moral strength. Like the others, he was fain to march with a rapid step to glory." He goes to battle, but, worn out with grief, is physically too weak to fight.

He was forced to exchange the field of honour for a bed of suffering, while each of his brothers gave his blood for liberty. Thus could he never express himself either in action or in word. Despised, his heart torn by the cries of victory in which he could not share, he died, leaving no name, exciting no enthusiasm and moving no pity. (*Fragment*. June 24, 1830.)

Both Krasinski and Reeve were devoured with the passion of the pen. Krasinski carefully keeps Reeve informed upon everything that he writes and plans. These include a pleasing story of the Polish legions, animated with patriotic feeling and with the *verve* of a soldier's son who had been brought up on the traditions of the legions, which came out in a Swiss magazine, besides *The Confession of Napoleon* that stayed unknown in Reeve's possession for more than half a century. The last-named is very typical of the almost religious veneration for Bonaparte that was to stand for so much in the Anonymous Poet's philosophy.

On his side, Reeve sent Krasinski his verses for inspection. Krasinski's friendships were always of a markedly robust nature. He idealized every man and woman he loved : but he never hesitated, as we see from his correspondence with his friends, to remonstrate fearlessly when he disapproved in any way of their conduct or opinions. In his letters to Reeve, he candidly criticizes the latter's literary attempts; yet the generosity of a man who, in his own career as a writer never envied or detracted another's fame, is already patent. He thinks Reeve immeasurably superior to himself, and although he takes exception to some of his friend's expressions he is always eager to seize upon anything that he can praise. In this case it must be confessed that Krasinski's heart triumphed over his head, for it is obvious that he genuinely admired the shocking doggerel that Reeve turned out.

"I have received," writes he, italicizing as usual his English phrases, "your piece *about Polish Freedom*, '*Here a nation lies*' *is exceedingly good and beautiful.* But, my dear fellow, I will tell you my opinion frankly. The verses are written rather hastily and carelessly; but as for the rest it is a beautiful piece, the more beautiful for me because it reminds me both of a native country and of a friend who wrote it.

"You are, my dear Reeve," he goes on, reverting to their love affairs, "admirably cold blooded for a man in love. You write me these words: 'whom perhaps I shall never see again': without a fault in spelling, and without so far as I can see your pen having trembled in your hand. My dear fellow, I envy you that energy, that strength, that want of feeling, or rather that calm, that resignation. I could not be capable of them[1]."

"'Those whom the gods love die young,'" writes, on another occasion, the poet who was never to see old age. "It is the truest saying I have ever read or heard. And what shall we do, my dear Henry, when life will be only vegetation? The rose we once loved and adored as an emblem and a symbol, we shall be dissecting then to find out how many petals it has and how many lines lengthwise its calyx has. Where we saw soul and life we shall only see matter and weight. A pair of compasses and circle are what await us. Love and poetry are what we shall leave behind us. But perhaps God will not let us thus change; perhaps our grave is not far off, *and the flowers are about to grow above us*[2].

"If we might only be consumed away with great thoughts and a slow agony in the arms of those we adore! This is my wish as a poet, but as a man, as a Pole, can it be the same? No. I must think of other things; and while for you *the heart may be your world*, for me *love is only a song piped in the intervals of the acts of life*; and yet I would give all for love to be my life. My dear Henry, do not think that my affairs are going so badly. No. *She loves me still....* And even if that

---

[1] *Op. cit.* To Reeve. July 8, 1830.

[2] The italics in the text are always Krasinski's own which he employs when he writes in English.

were not the case She has loved me. That is enough. The thoughts that have turned towards me can no more be lost. Thought is immortal, and her love will be immortal as her thought is. In the same manner if C. has loved you each of her great and sublime thoughts has departed from her heart like a ray of the sun, and mounted to heaven. You have a great, an enormous advantage over me. Your kingdom can be not of this world, *if you will.* Mine is in part chained to the earth by my country. I am like Vulcan falling from heaven, and unable either to return to heaven or reach the earth. I am suspended in space by a chain of steel that penetrates my heart, that gnaws it and will perhaps break it[1]."

Here, with Reeve's return to Geneva, the correspondence ceased for some months. In August the friends took a trip into the mountains. Among the beautiful scenes through which they passed Krasinski dreamed constantly of Henrietta. He beguiled away a tedious journey on muleback by writing a poem to her : apparently a very bad one, for he and the Polish poet, Edward Odyniec, to whom he showed it, laughed over it together.

Odyniec, who had been a frequent guest at the Krasinski palace, was now in Switzerland, travelling with Mickiewicz. When he had last seen Krasinski in his father's house he had thought him nothing more than a lively and clever boy. He found now, he says himself, a youth full of fire and genius, "if not yet a thinker, at least a dreamer-poet ; though he does not know how to write poetry and only tries his powers in prose[2]."

In common with all Polish youths Krasinski worshipped Mickiewicz and had devoured his poems : but, brought face to face with him, the enthusiastic boy's first impressions were those of disappointment. The

---

[1] *Op. cit.* To Reeve. Geneva, July 14, 1830.
[2] J. Kallenbach, *Zygmunt Krasinski.*

three—Mickiewicz, Odyniec and Krasinski—started on a tour through Switzerland. They had not been together long before Krasinski was carried away with admiration for the great poet whose devotion to the moral welfare of the youth of Poland had sent him into prison and exile.

" I have learnt from him," wrote Krasinski to his father, " to look at the things of this world more coolly, in a finer way, more impartially. I have got rid of many prejudices and false ideas[1]."

The journey at close quarters with one of the greatest poets in Europe filled Krasinski with inspiration. Its first result was that in a French journal of the expedition which he wrote as he went along, nominally for Henrietta, he had already corrected some of the affectations in his style[2]. The descriptions of scenery given in this diary are so true to life that Dr Kallenbach speaks of its pages as "impregnated with the breath of Switzerland." But, poetical as are Krasinski's pictures of nature, they always lack the wonderful charm of Mickiewicz's magnificent word-paintings. Krasinski loved nature : but the moments where she plays any part in his poetry—exquisite and ethereal moments, it is true—are rare, and are invariably only there as the necessary accompaniment to a deeper passion behind.

In the dungeon of Chillon Mickiewicz, looking round at a scene that reminded him of the prison where he and his dearest friends had once languished, spoke to his companions of human tyranny and its incapacity to touch the soul. Zygmunt, hearing for the first time Mickiewicz discoursing in his own particular

[1] J. Kallenbach, *Zygmunt Krasinski.*   [2] *Op. cit.*

and enthralling manner, hung on his words so that, even in the spot immortalized by Byron, he forgot the English poet to whom his heart had hitherto gone out. This episode in the castle of Chillon was to give Polish literature one of Krasinski's most tragic poems: *The Last*.

It was after a conversation with Mickiewicz that Krasinski wrote the essay on the meeting of souls in the next world, of which he had spoken to Reeve. It was published the same year—1830—in Warsaw under the title: *Fragment from an old Slavonic manuscript*. Tender and poetical, philosophical rather than religious, it bases the certainty that there shall not be endless parting on the power of the will to compass its desire, on the innate love planted by the Creator in the soul for no transitory purpose, and on the fact of that love being stronger than death. It presents a decided spiritual link with the *Treatise of the Trinity*, written years later. The mystical bent of Krasinski's mind shows itself already in the tendency of his youthful writings to deal with semi-spiritual topics, which from an orthodox point of view he handles rather vaguely.

The French papers that streamed from Krasinski's pen, in the autumn months of 1830 before he left Geneva, range for the most part on melancholy themes. Death is the subject of many of them. *Écrit la Nuit*, "with emotion and fear," he adds in Polish, where his soul goes out with questioning and yearning to the spirits of the dead, is the anticipation of his *Three Thoughts*[1]. *Le Journal d'un Mourant, La Vie*, the latter a morbidly gloomy description of man's life,

----

[1] J. Kallenbach, *Préface. Correspondance de Sigismond Krasinski et de Henry Reeve*.

and other fragments of the kind, close Krasinski's first and singularly strenuous year in Switzerland.

In the October of 1830 it seemed probable that war between Russia and France would follow on the Revolution of July. Krasinski's father was anxious to remove his only son from the vicinity of a belligerent country, and sent him into Italy, deaf to Zygmunt's entreaty that the England of his Henrietta might be his destination. On the third of November Krasinski and Jakubowski set out over the Simplon. Reeve and the Pole, Zamojski, went with Krasinski as far as the first mile out of Geneva, and then the boys bade each other a regretful farewell. Krasinski, giving himself up to the pain of parting with those who had been his favourite companions for a year past, cared nothing for what he saw before his eyes during his journey, and his chief emotion on arriving at Florence was that he had reached a crisis with Henrietta Willan. He wrote to her from Florence in reply to some apparently rather hysterical letters that he found waiting for him there, telling her clearly that though he would love her for ever he could never marry her, and could only write to her as her lover till she married, from which time he would be her faithful friend, and that alone.

"*O my dear Henry*," he cries in English, but passing immediately into French, "if I wrote all that to her it is because duty forced me to do it, for I love her more violently than ever, and it would have been so sweet not to break this illusion yet, to begin again the beautiful days of that love which made me so happy."

After some warm expressions of affection for Reeve, he ends: "I am an enemy to tirades of friendship, but I will only say these few words: I am your friend for life and till death[1]."

He tells his friend how in the midst of his agitations

[1] *Correspondance.* Krasinski to Reeve. Florence, Nov. 18, 1830.

his only calm moments were when he betook himself to the contemplation of the Medici Venus:

For she is perfect beauty; and beauty, whether it be of marble or flesh and blood, is always an anodyne in hours of anguish, and, at the same time, a stimulus in hours of apathy.

He entered Rome with indifference as he relates in the same letter: "because strong emotions age the soul, as strong shocks age the body." But the conclusion of the letter changes to the more natural note of the young Pole looking for the first time on the grandeur of the Eternal City. With Mickiewicz, then in Rome, he visited St Peter's, which moved him religiously not at all. His great moment came to him in the Coliseum. At the sight of the ruined amphitheatre, in Krasinski's day a scene of the most poetical desolation, which to the Pole was the enduring testimony of the triumph of an oppressed cause against an empire's power, inspiration flooded the youth's soul. Polish art has represented the Anonymous Poet dreaming within the walls of the Coliseum: for it was in its moonlit arches that Krasinski conceived the idea of *Iridion*, and there that he places what is not merely the crisis of his mystical drama, but the great spiritual keynote of the theory of salvation that he built up for his people.

" On a beautiful moonlight night," thus the letter to Reeve, "I entered under those arcades which have seen so many generations, and have not crumbled away under the weight of either men or time."

He heard in fancy the discordant cries of the Circus, the "soft and tremulous" hymn of the Christian martyrs.

At this moment the moon appeared on the walls of the Coliseum, as though she rose from a tangle of ivy which fell in festoons from the summit of the building. Columns, arcades, porticoes, the seats of the Caesars, of the senators, of the populace, stood out, pallid and in ruins. The arena was laid bare. In the centre rose a cross of black wood. To me that cross is worth the Cathedral of Milan and the church of St Peter's. That cross was persecuted in this spot, many centuries ago, when the Coliseum represented all the might of those who had built it. And that cross...to-day stands erect where it was trampled underfoot, and the superb Coliseum which proudly beheld its humiliation is now being consumed to dust around it. But it has no aspect of pride in its triumph. In silence it stretches its black arms to the two sides of the building, and seems to cast a shadow of peace and benediction on the earth where persecutors and persecuted sleep.

Let him who does not believe in Christ go to the Coliseum on a fine night; and if he does not fall on his knees before the symbol of faith that man, I say beforehand, has neither soul nor heart[1].

News travelled slowly in those days, and when Krasinski penned these words he was ignorant of what had happened in his country. Before his next letter, written a week later, all Europe rang with the news that the Polish nation had risen to arms. That gallant struggle, with its tale of heroism, of failure and of martyrdom, broke out in Warsaw on the night of November 29, 1830.

[1] *Correspondance.* Krasinski to Reeve. Rome, Dec. 9, 1830.

CHAPTER III

THE SACRIFICE
(1830–1831)

For the next ten months Poland was the battle-field of a
nation fighting unaided for her life. The Rising of 1830
cannot correctly be called an insurrection. It was a war
for rights that had been guaranteed by a European
treaty, which all the powers of Europe had signed. It
was waged by a small but national army, swelled by
the rally to its banners of men and women of every class
and condition, who fought side by side with a passion
of patriotic abnegation. Brilliant victories marked the
first months of the war. For a time it seemed as though
Poland were about to secure her freedom.

The news of the November night was as the call
of the trumpet to the youth of Poland. In intense
agitation, Krasinski wrote off to Reeve. By way of
safeguard in case his letter should be opened by others
he wrote in English[1]. His father who, it must be remembered, held a high command in the Polish army,
was in the thick of events, of which Krasinski, far from
the scene, could gain no accurate information.

" The day-break is peeping...but at present we do not know
whether it is the dawn of new life, or the glimpse which
appears when a nation is about to be destroyed. I am in great
anguish. The newspapers are full of obscure words. A thousand thanks to God! I have been assured that my father

[1] I always give Krasinski's English entirely as it stands, only correcting
what are obvious slips of the pen.

escaped the dangers of the 29th of November "—when the first fighting began—"and that he sent his resignation to the Emperor ; but what will happen further ?...No human strength or aid can help us in this desperate cause, but the same God who has said : ' Let there be light,' and light appeared, may now say : ' Let Poland be,' and Poland will grow gigantic and free. Write to me instantly what Zamojski thinks of doing. I am in the greatest incertitude. Write to me very soon, for every day may change my position and throw me forward to fields of blood and death."

He then alludes to an English friend of his own and of Reeve in Rome to whom Krasinski says he will give his last remembrances for Henrietta before he sets out for the war. He assures Reeve that :

As often as I shall be able to give you news of me, I shall. You, however, can still address me at Rome ; for I must remain here until I receive certain instructions from my father. Pardon me, I write in such a miserable manner in English, but I am now troubled and agitated with fever in brain and body... I must tell you that I am in a strange and difficult position. The cause is too long to be explained in this letter, but if you remember our talk on the subject you will understand fully the devilish position in which I am. It always seems to me that a fatal destiny hangs over my head as the sword of Damocles. Heaven grant that it may be removed or that it may fall soon ; oh ! soon, for to live amid tortures is to begin hell on earth.

It is evident that Krasinski was already racked with the misgiving that was to become a certainty. Even if he did not—and he probably did—strongly suspect that Wincenty Krasinski was not preparing to throw in his lot with the national cause, his apprehensions that his father would prevent his going to the war gave him no rest. He adds several despairing pages, "mad and troubled," as he says himself, feeling that he " was born to defend my country, for I love it with the impassioned love of the patriot, and my breast burns when I hear its name," equally convinced that to his eternal shame in the eyes of his fellow-Poles, he was to remain inactive[1].

A month passed. The son waited in vain for his father's summons to the field of action. Young Zamojski, whom Krasinski had wished to join in Geneva and thence accompany to Poland, hurried to his country. The boys who had sat with Krasinski in the school and University benches joined the national ranks. He alone was left behind, eating his heart out in rage, suspense, despair. By this time, he probably knew that there could be only one reason—when Polish mothers willingly gave up their only sons to face death for their nation —why his father withheld the permission to his son to follow the traditions of his patriotic and famous house. Apart from the outrage to his patriotism, the proud and too sensitive boy, the descendant as he was of one of the noblest families of Poland, was stung to the quick by the disgrace of his position. Some adverse criticism of both himself and his father appeared in *Galignani.* Whether this was written by an enemy, perhaps Łubienski[2], or whether it was the work of a well-wisher of Krasinski, who, aware of his difficulties, intended by this means to give him the advice he could not offer in person, Zygmunt could not tell[3]. Half frenzied, after Reeve had sent him the paper he wrote to his friend a wild letter, which afterwards he begged Reeve to burn and forget, or to keep it if he wished to see " what extremities can drive a mind to, when tortured by pain": the words are in English. Besides that letter several others that passed between Reeve and Krasinski in these

[1] *Correspondance.* Krasinski to Reeve. Rome, Dec. 18–22, 1830.
[2] J. Kallenbach, *Zygmunt Krasinski.*
[3] *Correspondance.* Krasinski to Reeve. Rome, Jan. 22, 1831.

days are missing. Probably both boys burnt communi-
cations that at this time of Krasinski's life were too
painful and too intimate to risk their being seen by
other eyes. But those that remain show us how Krasinski was able to reveal to Reeve's sympathizing ears
the tortures of his soul which, even if he had not been
entirely cut off from them by the Rising, he could not
for his father's sake have confided to Polish friends.

"I am nailed to Rome until the moment when my
father writes to me to come," he tells Reeve in the
midst of his abandonment of anguish at sitting still
while others were dying for Poland, and at the thought
of how those who loved him, "and Henrietta herself,"
would be upbraiding him.

"The minister has refused me my passports; I have no
money: materially it is impossible for me to move...I pray,
for it is my only resource. My father will soon write to me to
join him. He is as good a Pole as any in Poland, and braver
than any of them. Yes," protests the son, refusing to look his
forebodings in the face, "he will send me the order to come,
and then I shall start."

He breaks out again into English after that single
paragraph in French which, referring directly to his
father, is obviously written in a strain quite foreign to
the rest of the letter in case it should be opened in the
post by some other than Reeve.

"But it is impossible for another to suffer what I
do. I never leave my room except to visit Leach"—
the English friend referred to above:

I read, or rather I endeavour to read, in my lonely room. My
eyes, either filled with tears or dry with rage, cannot follow the
black letters upon the white paper. Oh! my dear Henry,
when rowing with you on blue Leman, when talking of love,
of hope, of future happiness, I never thought there would arrive
an hour in which I would see my fame stained and my honour

gone, without being able to make the least endeavour to re-cover them. Never, when I was happy in my love, when I had many presentiments of future glory, did I think that I would be obliged to dream while others are awake, to write while others fight, to drink wine while others drink blood, and to linger in a dungeon while others arise to freedom and light.

Then, clinging to his forlorn hope, he tells Reeve that even yet a few weeks may see him riding in the charge, and he speaks enthusiastically of Zamojski, the friend by whose side he had longed to fight, and whose exploits in the war he always followed with generous admiration[1].

Reeve wrote his answer, full of sympathy and of somewhat tranquil advice ; seeking to reassure Zygmunt with the fact that, from private letters, " I know that an European war is inevitable," and "if so, Poland is saved": urging Krasinski to control his "unbridled enthusiasm"; and hinting broadly that against every obstacle he had better make for Poland[2].

In the early months of 1831, Rome was in a state of panic, revolution having broken out in Italy. Orders came from the Russian ambassador, bidding all Poles who were natives of the Kingdom of Poland to quit the Eternal City. Krasinski therefore went to Florence.

" I do not know what I shall do," he told Reeve, writing in bad English, as he sat at his window, looking down on the Arno. " I have no news neither from my father nor from my friends in Poland."

It appears from what follows, and from a passage in the above letter from Reeve which crossed one of Krasinski's, and in which Reeve begged him not to heed what he—Reeve—had written, that in some letter

---

[1] *Correspondance.* Krasinski to Reeve. Rome, Jan. 22, 1831.
[2] *Op. cit.* Reeve to Krasinski. Geneva, Feb. 5, 1831.

which Krasinski must have destroyed Reeve had used expressions that had deeply wounded Krasinski, while Krasinski in his turn had offended Reeve. Krasinski declares passionately that Reeve is mistaken, that when Zygmunt wrote to him whatever he did write he was in mental delirium, broken-hearted. The strength of the friendship that demanded perfect frankness was proof against such misunderstandings on either side, for which Krasinski's condition of mental overstrain, apparent in the whole tenor of his reply to Reeve, was probably responsible.

"Your last letter," says he, "proves to me that I have gone down in the estimation of my friend. Thank you for your frankness. But you have never been in the position in which I am, and you cannot allow for the influence on me of the events, the cares of every day, of the want of hope and the violence with which my soul is agitated within me. When a man feels that he has just begun his career of misfortune, he must resign himself to everything, arm himself with active courage to hurl himself against obstacles, and with passive courage to endure every torment, to expect the jeers of men, the reproaches of his friends, the insults of mankind which so much delights in insulting...

"I still write sometimes; but when I do I nearly always play on the theme of some old legend concerning the fight of man with the old enemy of the human race. I have begun to read the Bible in English. Sublime! *Manfred* has also become my favourite." To a certain extent it influenced his *Undivine Comedy*. "When the world casts us off, we must seek something above, and I have always loved the world of spirits. Perhaps one day, when you hear it said: ' He is dead,' you will no longer think what you thought of me when you wrote your last letter. That letter pierced my heart...You let yourself go in all the bitterness of mocking at a man who is your best friend. I do not love you less, my dear Henry; but you know I never hide what I feel[1]."

Shortly after Krasinski wrote thus, he returned to Geneva. For a little while he and Reeve were once

---

[1] *Correspondance.* Krasinski to Reeve. Florence, Feb. 20, 1831.

more together : but Reeve was soon on his way to
England.

Wincenty Krasinski had by now taken the line
which sundered him from his countrymen, and covered
his name with ignominy. He had no sympathy with the
Rising. He had no belief in its efficacy, in which opinion,
it is only fair to add, he was not entirely alone. But his
conduct in 1828 had never been forgiven or forgotten
by his fellow-Poles : and on the night that the Rising
broke out the crowds in the Warsaw streets pursued
him with threats and execrations. His life was only
saved by two of the Polish leaders standing in front of
him to protect him from the populace. He resigned
his command, and informed the national government
that so long as the war lasted he would live in retire-
ment on his country estate. Then Nicholas I summoned
him to Petersburg. Convinced as the General was of the
ultimate failure of the Rising, his wounded vanity and
thirst after success seized the chance of advancement
in the good graces of the Tsar[1]. He betook himself,
while his country ran red with the blood her sons were
shedding for her, to the capital of Russia, and accepted
favours from the sworn enemy of Poland. Bitter regrets,
fruitless grief for the country that he never ceased to
love, henceforth ravaged his life.

And, while his father was already in Petersburg,
Zygmunt was still waiting in Geneva. The news rang
in his ears of victories on the Polish battle-fields. Tears
of rage filled his eyes when, instead of the Polish trumpets, he was reduced to hearing the Swiss soldiers
exercising on the Geneva squares[2]. At last, on the

[1] J. Kallenbach, *Zygmunt Krasinski.*
[2] *Correspondance.* Krasinski to Reeve. Geneva, April 4, 1831.

fourteenth of May, after six months of harrowing suspense, his father's answer came. He was forbidden to fight for Poland. He was to remain where he was.

Then began the terrible, protracted struggle of the son with the father whom he passionately loved, and whose conduct he could only despise and condemn.

" Dearest father," he wrote on the same day that he received the General's letter and, with it, the death-blow to his hopes. Through what conflict with himself he passed as he framed that most difficult of answers only his own heart knew. We must bear in mind as we follow him here that he was still only a boy, under age, entirely dependent on his father, living, moreover, in days when parental claims were much more insistent and far more respected than they are in ours.

"On the fourteenth of May I received my dear father's letter, and I watered it with my tears. Up to now I have been waiting every day in suspense for news of you and, my hopes disappointed, every day I grew more sad.

"Thank God, I am out of that state of suspense. You ask me, dearest father, what I have been doing since the sixteenth of December. I have spent the time in a ceaseless fever, in ceaseless waiting, in ceaseless sufferings of every kind...I was thinking always," he tells the General, after mentioning the Italian cities he saw with his heart far away from them, " of dear Poland and my dear father."

Then, describing how he waited on and on at Geneva for the letter that still delayed :

"Now when that letter has come, when I have read there your explicit will, I beg you for a hearing, for attention, for forbearance with your son, for your mercy, love and blessing.

"You cannot doubt, dearest father, that I love you more than any other, that I am ready to sacrifice all ties for you... but certainly my father also cannot doubt that I am his son, the descendant of Bishop Adam "—Adam Krasinski, one of the leaders of the Confederation of Bar that rose in the defence of Polish nationality in 1768—"and a Pole. I wrote in my letter to you…that I hate the people who rose against you in Warsaw, but I wrote at the same time that I love Poland and that when her national affair came on nothing could keep me back.

"The same thing I repeat to-day.

"Our age is the age of consecration and penance.

"It is a sacred duty, commanded by God, to make the sacrifice of oneself. All the delusions of youth have fallen from my eyes—the hopes of bright days of earthly happiness. I have never felt happy from the time I was conscious of life. I was not happy in love…I know equally well that fame, besought for by men, terminates in a few acclamations, and afterwards in nothing. I used to dream about it, now I promise it to myself no more ; but it is borne to the depths of my soul that I am bound to fulfil a sacred duty from which no one on earth can free me. There are certain duties in the world, which only lie between the creature and the Creator, which allow of no third person between them. The serving of one's country is one of those duties.

"You write to me, dear father, to travel, to study, to cultivate my mind, and to go out into society. It would be difficult for me to do so in the state in which I am. Suffering has eaten deep into my heart; I am in an unbroken fever; I sometimes feel as if my brain would turn ; I would wish no one such days and nights as are mine. I can neither read nor write; I can hardly finish the conversation that I begin.

"And then to travel, to stroll among foreigners, when at the other end of Europe my father is overwhelmed with misfortunes, my grandmother dragging out her last years in sadness, and my countrymen fighting to die or conquer, is a thing not only impossible for me to do, but which would bring a blush of shame every moment to my cheek.

"And who would even wish to speak to me ? to press my hand ? to know me ? when they find out that I am a Pole, travelling for amusement and education at a time when Poles are dying every day for Poland ? I cannot endure such a state. I am dying bit by bit. By God! It would be better to die at once, and not suffer like this.

"But these are more or less egotistic reasons—for it is possible to make an oblation of oneself and to bear disgrace as a sacrifice. I am ready to undertake such an oblation, though I know what would be its result after a few months : death or madness. But that is not the point. I now go back to what I said above, to the sacred duty which stands above all others, and which calls me to Poland, to join the ranks of my brothers.

"I have now reached the solemn moment. I am forced to tell the father whom I love and have always loved above all things, that I shall go against his will, that I shall try to return to Poland, that from to-day this has become the only aim of my thoughts and actions.

"Dear father! May God judge me, and do not you refuse me your blessing.

"Mr Jakubowski, to whom I have said this, has told me that he will try by every means to keep me here. I respect him the more because he is doing his duty. So I must be at war with the man who for two years has given me daily proofs of his affection. My lot is full of bitterness, but I trust in God.

"Within the next days I will try to get to Paris, and from there as quickly as I can to Warsaw. I will write to you from every place I can.

"It is done! I still feel on my face your tears when you said good-bye to me at Błonie. My heart is torn on all sides. Wherever I look I see the future dark.

"How am I to finish this letter? What am I to say further?

"On my knees I beseech you, remembering the picture of my mother, the anniversary of whose death I kept for the tenth time a month ago in Geneva, I beseech my father for his forgiveness and blessing. The sufferings which I shall still cause you are imaged in my soul—I already bear their load upon my conscience...When I think of you I shudder all over and recoil before my resolution.

"But when Poland rises to my mind strength returns to me again, I remind myself again that when a child I often vowed before my dear father that I would always, always love her.

"I will keep that vow. I entreat you for your forgiveness and your blessing. God in His infinite mercy will permit me some day to receive that blessing at your feet.

"Dear father! Do not turn your face away from your son. I firmly believe that I am doing what I ought to do. Forgive me. He Who died on the cross forgave His murderers in the hour of death. I beg you for your forgiveness and your blessing[1]."

But there was little to hope from the father who understood his son so imperfectly that he could expect him to travel and seek amusement while Poland was battling for her right to exist. Something of the indig-

[1] Given by Dr Kallenbach, *Zygmunt Krasinski*.

nation, lurking behind the unhappy boy's enforced outward respect for an unworthy father, flashes out when in
answer to the trite question, "What had he been doing
with himself since December?" he hints at the misery
that had been his history during those long months.

To this letter Krasinski added a postscript a few days
later to the effect that the tutor, Jakubowski, had closed
all the doors of escape for him[1].

Krasinski was now face to face with the dilemma
from which there was no way out, that was the tragedy
of his life—the choice between his love for his father
and his love for his nation, his duty to his father and
his duty to his nation. He had now to make his choice
whether he would be at open war with the father who
had nothing left except his son, or whether he would
turn his back upon the country that was dearer to him
than life, in the hour when she called upon all her
children to save her.

The months that followed this appeal to his father
hurried a boy of nineteen by sheer agony of mind into
a premature, darkened manhood. The tears he shed,
as he wept in despair and grief, injured his eyes for life
and brought him again and again as the years went on
to the verge of blindness. Dr Kallenbach does not
hesitate to declare that it was Krasinski's mental suffering during that spring and summer that sent him, worn
out in body and soul, to his grave before his time[2].

Devotion to his country had been instilled into
Zygmunt Krasinski's soul from his earliest childhood.
It was the tradition of his house, his strong inheritance
through generations of ancestors. With the Pole, pa-

---

[1] Given by Dr Kallenbach, *Zygmunt Krasinski*.
[2] J. Kallenbach, *op. cit.*

triotism is no vague abstraction that, till some great call stirs it to active being, scarcely enters under normal circumstances into the working day of a man or woman. In Krasinski's time, as in our own, the Pole's existence was a hand to hand and unceasing conflict to preserve faith, language, nationality against an oppression endeavouring to crush out every vestige of Polish race possession. The ideals of nationalism are those that most deeply affect the Pole's life : the love of Poland was Krasinski's master-passion. With the exception of his love poems, and even these are constantly interwoven with the thought of Poland, Krasinski has written scarcely one line that does not palpitate with his passion for his country, that is not given to her sorrows, that is not sung for her sake. In those heart to heart outpourings, which make up his letters to his friends, it is the sufferings of Poland, it is his hopes for Poland, that tear words of fire from his lips. And that this devotion was not merely the ripe growth of his manhood, although naturally it deepened and mellowed with the course of events, but was the inmost fibre of his soul when yet a boy, we see clearly enough from his youthful letters to Reeve, even before that desolation had overtaken Poland which caused her sons to mourn for her as for a bereaved mother.

And on the other side, Krasinski's father stood for all that was home. His mother was dead. He had neither brother nor sister. His father was mother, brother, sister to him : and the waters of many afflictions could never drown that son's affection. He could not prove his fidelity to his country without sinning against his father. If he remained faithful to his father, he was faithless, so it would seem, to his nation.

Then, too, that pride of race, that profound sense of noble obligation, which was rooted in Krasinski's character, and of which we see proof after proof in his letters, asserted itself in the support of patriotism, and called him to the battle-field at any cost. A youth's generous instincts, the inherited impulse of a soldier's son that beat strongly in Krasinski's small and weakly frame, his passionate recoil before disgrace and dishonour—all were there, spurring him to act in direct defiance to his father.

Krasinski, as we have seen, wrote his intentions to the General. Then a wall of obstacles rose around him. Jakubowski watched over him like a jailor; cut short the money supplies without which he could not move; and warned the Geneva authorities to be on the look out if he attempted to leave the city[1]. Unable to endure the prospect of resorting to a step that would not only break his father's heart, but dishonour him yet further in the eyes of his nation by the public spectacle of his only son openly taking sides against him, Zygmunt addressed passionate appeals to the General, imploring for his consent. While, as the weeks went by, he waited for the answers in an agony of uncertainty how to act, Reeve kept writing from Paris, proposing plans, each wilder than the last. He begged Krasinski to escape from Geneva, no matter how; regretted that he had not carried him off somehow with himself and his mother; suggested that Zygmunt should start without a passport on purpose to get himself arrested, and then slip off on foot over the frontier for Paris, which was crowded with Poles on their way to the front. Convinced that for everybody's sake Krasinski must join

[1] J. Kallenbach, *op. cit.*

the Rising, full of sympathy both for his friend and for
the Polish cause, Reeve carefully passes on to Zygmunt
all the opinions on the latter's duty that he could
gather from the lips of Poles.

"One of them," says he, "told me that he doesn't
know you, but that he believes you to be a good sort
of boy and a good Pole[1]."

I ought to have brought you with me at any price. However, in spite of the fact that, to use Morawski's expression,
each day that goes by is an eternity of loss for you, all is not
lost. It is not too late yet. They have known here for a long
time that your father is at Saint-Petersburg; but the colonel
told me yesterday that he is utterly broken-hearted, that he
will not see anyone, but weeps all day.

Reeve assures Krasinski that the best he can do
for his father is to take his share in the Rising. "I love
you as I have never loved a man before, and as I never
shall love one. That is why I am urging you on." And
with greater zeal than tact he adds: "I told Morawski
you are ill. 'If he is not dying,' he said to me, 'he can
still go, and if he is dying let him have himself carried
to die on the free soil of Poland[2].'"

All this Zygmunt knew only too well.

"Ah! my friend," he answers, "you have plunged the dagger
straight, straight to my heart...Yes, I know it, my salvation is
in Paris. If I don't go there I am lost...But listen to my
voice yet once more, that voice that you sometimes loved to
hear. I am alone, and everything is an obstacle to me, nothing
is a help. My father is dying, as you say, weeping; the son can
well die, gnashing his teeth. Have you considered what you
write to me, advising me to get myself arrested? Do you believe me capable of adding one stone to the heap that has
stoned my father? Do you want me to go promenading
through France the disgrace of the man who won such glory
there? Do you want me, a hero with the gendarmes, to read

[1] *Correspondance*. Reeve to Krasinski. Paris, May 24, 1831.
[2] *Ibid.* May 25, 1831.

in a newspaper two days later epithets of infamy lavished on the name of my father, sprinkled with a few praises for myself? Yes, I say openly, but only to Henry Reeve, and to none other in the world, my father has committed a grave, a terrible fault; it is not my place to call him to account for it.

"I shall wait at Geneva for my father's answer. If it is satisfactory, I go; if not, I go all the same; because then my duties, though not cancelled, will be lightened. After all, think what you will; say that there is a want of energy in my soul, that I speak, and do not know how to act, that I am weak, irresolute. Good! Be as unhappy as I am, and then judge me."

His brain obviously unhinged for the moment under his mental tortures, among which not the least was the conviction of his everlasting disgrace, he continued:

Do not attempt to defend me any more, to uphold my reputation. I do not ask you to answer: "No," when they tell you I am "a wretched creature"; but think it only, that will be enough for me. Shut deep in your heart the friendship you have for me. If your face lets it out it will compromise you. Carry to the post on the sly the letters you write to me; disguise your handwriting. Let nobody suspect that Henry Reeve has any relations with Sigismond Krasinski.

But he has still a flicker of hope that "one hour can change all, and then they will know who I am":
and if that hour never comes, then at all events his best loved friend, Reeve, will know it.

"At least, during the days of uncertainty that are floating between my past and my agony, do not forget me, write to me every day...Remember that if fate and men are against me, you at least ought to remain neutral...that if, at the end, all is for ever lost to me, name, glory, father, country, there must still remain between us something in common—if only the thought of Chamonix"—where they had been together—"and the memory of the tears of Saint-Cergues"—where shortly before they had said good-bye to each other[1].

A mutual friend chanced to be in the room as Zygmunt closed this packet. He added a few words below Krasinski's signature, describing the violent agi-

[1] *Correspondance.* Krasinski to Reeve. Geneva, May 28, 1831.

tation into which Reeve's last letters had thrown Krasinski, and how the latter, at the moment that the friend sat and wrote, was hurrying with wild steps up and down the room.

Reeve, now in England, scorned the idea of concealing his friendship ; tried at Krasinski's request to find Henrietta Willan, whose silence her lover ascribed to contempt for him; and told how his heart failed him at the thought of going to a dance the evening that his friend's outburst of misery lay in his pocket.

"Your part is taken," said Reeve. " The choice is terrible, because that choice had to be made. Now that you have decided to remain a son, pray, suffer, and love what is left to you[1]."

But Krasinski, who bore his burden unflinchingly all his life long, in these early days doubted his strength to carry through his sacrifice.

"You know me," he answered Reeve. "I am by no means a being made for resignation. Fiery impulses, even if they were to fling me into an abyss, cost me nothing ; but perseverance in good, as in evil, is supremely difficult to me.

"Skrzynecki [the Polish commander-in-chief] has had a defeat...Nothing is lost." It was the beginning of the end. " She will be born again, that beautiful Poland[2]."

At the same time he wrote the following letter to a favourite cousin, Stanisław Krasinski, who had been wounded in the war.

This letter will find you on the bed where you are suffering for Poland. With pride that I am related to you I read in the papers that in an attack on a Russian battalion you were seriously wounded. If my voice still counts for anything with you, if you have not by now forgotten him who promised to love you and always to wear your ring, accept my good wishes...You alone are now a Krasinski. The rest

[1] *Correspondance.* Reeve to Krasinski. London, June 6, 1831.
[2] *Ibid.* Krasinski to Reeve. Geneva, June 12, 1831.

of our glory has departed—but let our name disappear if only Poland stays. Although appearances may be strong against me, although I am now rotting far away from Poland, although perhaps before long disgrace will fall and hang over my head, believe that Zygmunt's heart is Polish, and will not cease to be so till its last moment. Love me if you can still love one who is remaining in Geneva while his brothers die. Believe, if you still care to believe me, that the obstacle on my way must be a weighty one when so far I have not been able either to remove it or pass over it. Good-bye, Staś. Good-bye. Perhaps God will give me such a blessing that before long I shall be crying out at your side: "Hurrah, and death to the Muscovites." Good-bye. I love you and adore your courage[1].

Krasinski was now completely unnerved by the suspense he suffered in his father's silence, and by mental conflict[2]. He confided to Reeve how "in the silence of the night" he was preparing himself for the hour, when, with the arrival of his father's letter, his decision must be made; an hour "more terrible than that of death, because a decision is preceded by a struggle that exhausts the soul, and death is merely a victory gained over us[3]."

In the intervals of grappling with his own problem, in his ever increasing sadness as the news from Poland grew worse, Krasinski took to his writing and excessive reading to deaden grief. The sufferings of his mind were now telling upon his body. Racked with pain, he spent the nights over his pen and books, with fatal injury to his eyes, already half blinded by weeping. He told Reeve that the only hours in which he could be said to live were those in which he poured out his sorrows in the figure of an autobiographical story.

This story—*Adam le Fou*—is only known to us from

[1] Given by Dr Kallenbach, *Zygmunt Krasinski*. See Appendix to Vol. II, pp. 435, 436.
[2] J. Kallenbach, *op. cit.*
[3] *Correspondance.* Krasinski to Reeve. Geneva, June 21, 1831.

the scraps of French translations from the Polish that
Krasinski enclosed in his letters to Reeve. It presents
an idealized picture of Reeve as Lord Henry Gram ; a
Marie who stands for Henrietta Willan ; while Krasinski himself is represented as Adam, maddened by his
fate, Adam being one of Krasinski's own names.
Couched in a Byronic vein, it runs on the same lines as
the personal confidences that fill Krasinski's letters to
Reeve during the Rising. Adam sees himself despised
as a coward by the girl he loves ; his name contemned,
his friends estranged. There seems to have been some
vague hope in Krasinski's mind that this story might
in a future day vindicate his honour by showing those
who held him cheap what his inaction in the war had
cost him[1]. But his idea came to nothing. Reeve
clamoured for it in vain : the Anonymous Poet would
never consent to divulge his name, or drag his father's
conduct into the public gaze[2]. The work breaks off
unfinished. Its remembrance of the Coliseum that had
so deeply affected Krasinski was afterwards ennobled
and purified in *Iridion*.

"I dreamt among the ruins," says Adam. "The ancient
world overthrown at my feet before a wooden cross...the
memories of my enslaved country, ran together in my brain.
I was comforted to contemplate Rome lying low in clay and
mud ; for in my childhood I had sworn vengeance on another
Rome, and, as I trampled on the first, I thought that some
day I would trample on the second." (*Adam le Fou.*)

Discussions on literary topics with Reeve afforded
Krasinski's overstrained mind some relief. He gave
Reeve a little lecture that proved to be strangely ap-
propriate, not to Reeve, but to Krasinski himself.

[1] "Perhaps one day it will be the only proof that will witness in my
favour." *Correspondance*. Krasinski to Reeve. Geneva, July 25, 1831.
[2] J. Kallenbach, *Zygmunt Krasinski.*

You ought not to hurry to finish your poem. Wait from day to day now; life will become harder for you and, in proportion to the load, your powers will grow...Laocoon, you will wrestle; and from the struggle and the fight stars will burst forth, I mean thoughts, unknown flights, stronger, more gigantic, to the beautiful and sublime, because you will be surrounded by baseness and ugliness...Till now, Henry, you have only been a man in your moments of poetry, while you walked in the circle of a child. But now, when your circle is enlarged, when you are a man among men, struggling every minute, you will be above man in your poetry, for to be a poet is to carry his present reality to the past or future...to heaven or hell[1].

Then the Anonymous Poet, whose inspiration was now clamouring for release, tells the friend, whom he still believed possessed of gifts far greater than his own, that at last he is convinced that he too has:

a spark of poetry in my bosom, very imperfect, it is true, as rhythm is wanting in me. The proof is that, without any hope of men ever reading me, I write and write...What is it to be a poet if not to have a superabundance of thoughts which rush in torrents over the surface of the soul, and which boil there until they find an outlet? It matters little to him if this outlet reaches the ears of men or the void, so long as he rids himself of that fire which burns him, and gives him not one moment's breathing space[2].

On a July afternoon there is a glimpse of Krasinski for once, in the thick of his troubles, at play. He went to the garden of Reeve's adored Constance to steal a rose for his friend.

In the road which passes the garden hedge I met the Sautter father talking to a neighbour, while a string of oxen plied before him. Between my teeth I murmured a *Damn* and tied my horse to a little gate behind. Then I paced up and down the road in the attitude of a man who awaits his adversary to fight a duel. At last he [Sautter] came towards me, and appeared to be considering me. I gave him back look for

---

[1] *Correspondance.* Krasinski to Reeve. Geneva, June 23, 1831.
[2] *Ibid.* July 13, 1831.

look and, seeing that he wouldn't learn any more about me, he went off in the direction of the cornfields. I thought the opportunity favourable, and I leaped the hedge. But at the same instant two enormous dogs rushed out of a thicket, and attacked me. I drew out my dagger and, thanks to the blade that I presented at their heads, I made an honourable retreat as far as the gate where I jumped on my horse. But there *behold!* there was father Sautter, who reappeared among the ears of corn on the other side. Caught between two fires, I behaved with an astonishing presence of mind : for I pacified the dogs by whistling and making friendly signs to them. As for father Sautter, when I saw him passing out on my right ten steps away from me, I stretched myself out on my saddle, I laid my head on the neck, my feet on the back of my horse, and I made as if I were going to sleep. The lawful proprietor of Bourdigny passed by, looking at me with a smile, as if I had given him the impression of being an oddity, then he retreated to his house, leaving me for company his two amiable Cerberuses...Like a falcon dying of hunger I swooped upon a rose and another flower which I arranged in my pocket-book, and that I shall send you as soon as they are dried.

This letter was still open when the courier came in from Petersburg.

" What can I say to you, my dear Henry? My distress only grows worse. My father writes to me with a heart-rending tenderness. He tells me he is ready to make a sacrifice of himself and his child to his country ; but he implores me to wait, and declares that he will shortly join me. Henry, what would you do if you were in my place? Ah! what need have I to ask another what he would do? I see that I am ruined. I am a fool, I am a coward, I am a wretched being, I have the heart of a girl, I do not dare to brave a father's curse. I expected an imperious, violent, forcible letter, and I was prepared for a decisive, terrible, forcible struggle too...But when yesterday's letter arrived ; when instead of threats, I found prayers; instead of fury, I saw blessings; instead of commands, supplications ; instead of sentiments at the thought of which I shuddered, a love of Poland piercing through each word, all my strength *melted into tears* "—these three words are in English. " I had prepared my arm to strike a blow; and, when it fell, I found no resistance...I am touched to tenderness, full of affection for my father, for his bitter misfortunes, and I have no longer sufficient strength to decide. That is my condition.

You can cast on my head the curse of a friend; but I tell you I am no longer myself. I have, however, answered, promising nothing, still saying that if the opportunity presents itself I shall go to Poland. But where is that opportunity?...I have just seen in the last few days a Pole...who informed me that prince Gagarin told him in Rome that all the Russian embassies have my description, and the order to arrest me and send me straight to Saint Petersburg if I try and escape from Geneva. That's nothing. When it is the case of duty one faces everything. But my father, my father, he who once powerful, rich, loaded with flatteries and glory, saw himself the first man in Poland[1],...to-day he is beaten down, he has lost everything, and has only me in this vast universe. If this last support fails him, what will become of him? It is not death I fear for him. It would be a benefit to us both, but it is those long years of old age, full of heart-breaking recollections, disgust and bitterness; it is his heart broken above my tomb; it is the look that he will cast around him without finding one who will stretch out a hand to him...Yet I have a ray of hope remaining that he will fight for Poland, and I at his side...

"However, I am in the most complete incertitude. The advice of men can do nothing for me. I hope for inspiration only from the Mother of God; and when that inspiration comes I will follow it...

"And that thought of suicide that still hovers in my brain, it is odd it no longer has the effect on me of a crime. On the contrary, it seems to me that it is a thing which is permitted... But when I reason I see truly it is a crime. Oh! if to die were to sleep for ever! Eternity? Oh, well, you will see, we shall have new toils, new troubles, in that eternity. We shall curse it one day as we curse the earth...Rest! Rest! Sleep! but no dream! or rather dreams, sometimes, but those of a child...

"What a madman am I! What a fool! Judge by this where I have got to. I, I am setting up for a materialist! I, I already desire annihilation! Ah! how suffering beats down the wings of the soul[2]!"

Krasinski's every mood and emotion, and his con-

---

[1] Here Krasinski's filial feelings led him to a considerable exaggeration of his father's former position.

[2] *Correspondance.* Krasinski to Reeve. Geneva, July 8, 12, 1831. The letter quoted before this is obviously wrongly dated, having been written before Krasinski heard from his father.

tradictory impulses, flowed out in unchecked streams
to the ear of the only person to whom he could then
speak freely : so the weakening of religious faith of
which he speaks in this last letter may be taken as only
the wild words of a boy of nineteen, half beside himself.
Yet possibly they were the first steps towards the agony
of doubt which came upon him later.

Side by side with his confessions to Reeve, who, still
busy over mad plans on his friend's behalf, answered
in genuine, if somewhat sentimentally worded, sympathy, Zygmunt continued to wrestle vainly with his
father.

"I would give my life if I could see you somewhere else," he
wrote to the General, "and to embrace you once more before
I die....I love, oh, I love my father, and with folded hands I
stay far from Poland. Have pity on me!"

He reminds his father of the forty wounds the latter
bore on his body for Poland, and implores him to consider what comfort can the son ever have in the remaining years of his life, the son who remained behind
when his country summoned him? He has in his heart
that which no argument can pacify or destroy :

I allude to that desire to fight for Poland, that deep conviction that it is my duty, to that terrible fear that I shall be
cursed by men and God for sitting quietly here.

Carrying that fiery coal in my bosom, I have not one, not
one moment of peace. Lethargy and fever—those are the two
states which master me by turns. Two days of fever, two days
of lethargy—that is my life! Take pity on me, dear father!...
I repeat again, that feeling of duty and the fear of disgrace
torment me so much that sometimes I go out of my senses
when I think about it. I am unhappy! In the past I used
to say that from Romanticism; to-day, alas! it has become
reality[1].

The father's move was to appeal once more to the

---

[1] Given by Dr Kallenbach, *Zygmunt Krasinski.*

son's affections and to assure him that the Rising was no national movement, but the work of a few revolutionaries. His eyes opened to the fact, bitterer to him than death, that his father in Petersburg was listening to the enemies of his country, belittling a conflict that all Europe regarded as a national war, Krasinski retorted by a noble defence of a great cause, prophetical of the Anonymous Poet's future philosophy.

It is the war of the weak against the mighty, of those consecrated to death against their old aggressors, of men mindful that they have had great ancestors...And the more Poland is covered with blood, flames, corpses, the more holy does her cause become to my heart, the more do I see in this cause the finger and the Providence of God, for to those whom He protects He is not wont to give victory without toil and sorrow. Those, on the contrary, whom He sends for the punishment of the human race, those, I say, He surrounds with ease and benefits without labour; but, for those whom He has charged with any great work of redemption, He places obstacles in the way, He bids them suffer and die, for, by the fault of men themselves, it is one of the laws of this unhappy world that there can be nothing beautiful or salutary without suffering and pain...To save the world the death of God was necessary. To save one nation, how much more are necessary human deaths and afflictions[1]!

So the duel dragged on between father and son during the summer months of 1831: the son writing to his father, with tears in his eyes and rage in his heart[2], the letters that were a torment to write, passing through crises that, so he tells Reeve, took years from his life. The while, defeat after defeat in Poland were telling plainly of the end. To Reeve, who com-

---

[1] Given by Dr Kallenbach, *Zygmunt Krasinski*.

[2] "Though I am in a very bad moment for criticizing, though I have just finished a letter for my father and I have tears in my eyes and rage in my heart, let us speak of *Maria*," a poem by Reeve. *Correspondance.* Krasinski to Reeve. Geneva, Sept. 18, 1831.

plained that he could not love his own country, the Pole replied :

Henry, do not imitate Byron. If you hate the men, adore the land...Wait till your country is unhappy. Wait for the day when the tears of your sisters will be mingled with the ocean, when the groans of your brothers will prevent you from closing your eyes, when you see your country ravaged...entangled in chains, shamed by her degradation; and then you will love your country more than you love the inspiration of poetry, more than your mother, more than everything that could awaken in you a feeling of affection, friendship, love.

" Better to perish in the first battle than to live far from one's country," the writer mournfully said, as he gazed out on the lake and mountains of Geneva, and thought of the Polish plains, where war was raging[1].

Out of that acute shame in his own position, which is scarcely ever absent from his correspondence during the Rising, sudden insight flashed upon the poet who chose to remain anonymous and unknown.

I now know that at the bottom of the heart every noble soul possesses something more holy than glory : it is the idea of *sacrifice ignored* [he underlined the words], dumb, silent, of the duty to be accomplished for one's own interior glory, and not for the fame that goes forth from the same mouth as calumny[2].

As he watched his country's doom closing on her, he added :

If Poland is going once more to perish, I feel no longer the strength to remain upon this earth. The day that Warsaw surrenders will be the signal to a Polish soul to leave the body[3].

It was in these September days that Poland's last desperate stand was made. After a heroic defence, Warsaw fell on September 7, 1831. The Rising was over.

[1] *Correspondance.* Krasinski to Reeve. Geneva, August 24, 1831.
Ibid. Sept. 2, 1831.   [3] *Ibid.*

"Warsaw has surrendered": so, under the first shock of the blow, Krasinski wrote to Reeve, who was awaiting almost with terror its effect upon his friend.

How I now adore that land, bleeding, sacred with so many sorrows and disasters, bathed in the blood of martyrs...All for her, my life, my endeavours, my days, my nights, my sadness, my joys! All for her, my sword, my lyre, all, to my last sigh[1]!

Again he wrote in an outburst of passionate grief:

Henry!
Have you heard it, the last cry of my great nation? Has the iron of the victorious horses resounding on the pavement of Warsaw reached your ears? Have you contemplated in a dream of despair the Satan of pride and crime rushing through the ranks of an appalled crowd, making his entry into the streets of an expiring city? For death is there where liberty is no more. Such then had to be the end of that noble Poland...I speak no more of the future, of hope...We have become again what we were before, men with no attribute of humanity, beings destined...to see, in their ripe age, the oppressor gather the harvests on the fields they watered with their blood in the days of their youth; to speak low and bow their heads...to break the strings of our lyre, the blades of our swords, and to sit beside them in silence...

This nightmare of delirium, this nightmare of a year, is broken to shivers; so many sorrows and so many hopes, so many strong emotions and such great enthusiasm, have come to their end. I have no longer to struggle against obstacles; for the road that I should have followed has crumbled into the abyss. Where is she? Where is she, that Poland of a moment, that meteor of a country? Do you hear the pass-word of the Russians on the walls of Warsaw?

Nothing, nothing attaches me to this world any longer, neither H., nor you, Henry, nor the tranquil happiness that certain men promise themselves when a revolution is ended, nor the hope of seeing my father again—nothing, nothing!

And, I tell you, in days when crime triumphs many souls doubt God.

He himself was for the sake of his country's sorrows to know that doubt.

---

[1] *Correspondance.* Krasinski to Reeve. Geneva, Sept. 25, 1831.

Of course those are not the elect, but weaker men—and yet men with high souls, men who many times adored God and invoked Him in the hour of danger...I shall never doubt; for each drop of blood shed only reminds me of that of Golgotha; but I shall say aloud, " The human race is cursed for its iniquities, and the penalty involves the innocent and the guilty. Death and agony must be to counterbalance impiety and bad faith. The Poles have perished."...

"Now my *rôle* begins," goes on the Anonymous Poet; "and if it is to be more obscure, perhaps it will not be less unhappy. Remember these words; and if, one day, you hear that I have been dragged off to Siberia, raise your eyes on high, and thank your God for having permitted your friend for once at least to show that he was a good Pole."

Telling Reeve he can write no more because his heart is too heavy, he transcribes an article by Lamennais on Poland[1], of which the last words:

made me start. Again it seems to me that all is not lost, that from these ashes and these bones will soon spring forth a dawn more lasting than that which has just been quenched...It is not said in God's thought that a people must perish, until the moment when that people itself accepts death. And we will never accept it; because from the death of so many victims has sprung forth a new moral life that for long will animate my country. Let us walk from sacrifice to sacrifice, from sorrow to sorrow, and always in silence. At last, we will reach the term of expiation. At last, we shall hail a horizon unveiled before us. And if not, if the generation to which I belong must again perish full of glory and young in years, or must slowly wither away and go out unknown, so be it! as long as our last thought is a thought consecrated to Poland.

This is all very fine; but, in one word, they are in Warsaw, Poland has fallen, I am in Geneva[2].

The downfall of the Polish Rising of 1830 ends the most painful chapter in Krasinski's history, and the most decisive.

With the full knowledge of all that it entailed he

---

[1] Mickiewicz said of Lamennais that his tears for Poland were the only sincere ones he saw in Paris.

[2] *Correspondance.* Krasinski to Reeve. Geneva, Sept. 21, 1831.

chose the sacrifice which ruined his life. For his father's sake, he lost friends and well-wishers. For his father's sake, he bore the disgrace of his name, the fiery trial, intolerable to a proud and patriotic youth, of the imputation of indifference to his country. For his father's sake, says, after Zygmunt's death, one who had greatly loved him, "he denied himself the liberty of saying what he thought, acknowledging what he wrote, or showing to whom he was attached[1]." All the dreams of literary fame that had been his as a brilliantly gifted boy he now renounced. Were it only for his father's relations with the Russian authorities, it was impossible for him ever to disclose his authorship of the most impassioned utterances of nationalism that exist in the Polish language. From the time that he was a boy of nineteen to his death nearly thirty years later, the life of Zygmunt Krasinski was maimed and stunted. He could never again live in his own country. Each hour that he stayed there was to him a martyrdom, an insult to his patriotism, dwelling as he must under the roof of a father, throwing in his lot to all outward seeming with that father, who was the recipient of honours from the hand that was inflicting the most unrelenting of persecutions upon his nation[2]. Only

---

[1] See the letter of Count Ladislas Zamojski to Henry Reeve. J. K. Laughton, *Memoirs of the Life and Correspondence of Henry Reeve.*

[2] What a mortal pang the favours conferred on his father by Nicholas I carried to Krasinski's heart is illustrated by a letter to Reeve, in reply to the information volunteered by that tactless youth shortly after the fall of Warsaw, that Wincenty Krasinski had been decorated by the Tsar. "I know it, I know it, Henry. Why speak to me of the Tsar and his gifts? Hamlet said as he went into his mother [quoted in English]: 'I will speak daggers to her, but use none.' And I permit anyone to plunge a dagger of steel in my heart, provided that he spares me what you have not spared me...You have the right to tell me everything; it is not you that I blame,

under compulsion when the Russian government withdrew his passports, and threatened confiscation of the family estates unless he showed himself in the Kingdom on the appointed day, even if he were on a sick-bed at the moment, did he from time to time go back to Poland. Watched closely by the Russian authorities, who marked against him the names of those with whom he consorted, and whose spies opened his private correspondence, he wandered, homeless, abroad, seeking in vain for the health that the events of 1831 had shattered, rent by grief for his country, battling against despair[1].

But during those years of Poland's history between 1831 and the eve of the sixties, when the Russian

but my destiny. But let us say no more on the subject, for there are words that a woman never utters, and also things of which a man never speaks." *Correspondance.* Krasinski to Reeve. Geneva, Dec. 26, 1831.

[1] See *Letters of Zygmunt Krasinski to Stanisław Koźmian*, Lwów, 1912 (Polish), p. 131. Krasinski encloses an official letter from the conqueror of Warsaw, Paskievich, to his father, in which Paskievich states that the suspicions of the Russian government have fallen on Zygmunt by reason of his relations with a body of Polish priests, the Resurrectionist Fathers, in Rome, whose crime in the eyes of the Russian rulers of Poland was the spiritual work that they carried on for their country. The whole letter is an open threat, informing Wincenty Krasinski that his son is regarded with disfavour by the government, and that not even the elder Krasinski's "many merits" can save the son if the latter compromises himself further. This missive throws light on the extreme circumspection with which Krasinski was obliged to walk. The fact of spies reporting upon him and overlooking his letters accounts for the precautions that he takes when writing to his friends. To each of them he signs himself by a different name, in allusion to some common joke, to his address at the moment, his passing mood. With Gaszynski he is "Era Piper," in memory of their boyhood in the Krasinski palace. His mystifications when referring to his work, knowing that unbidden readers could discover and report his authorship to Petersburg, thus most seriously involving his father and bringing Siberia upon his own head, are even more elaborate. He speaks of his writings under feigned titles: *Iridion* is "the Greek," the *Psalms of the Future*, "embroidery," and so on ; or else he mentions them dispassionately as the compositions of other men.

G.

5

government was avenging the earlier Rising and driving a maddened nation into another ; when the youth of Poland, debarred from every national heritage, could only learn the teaching of their country in a literature as magnificent in its art as uplifting in its ideals, in a poetry, persecuted and proscribed, that was read in hiding at the peril of life and liberty throughout all Poland, there arose a nameless poet[1]. He spoke out of the silence tragically imposed upon him what his own grief taught him, a message so noble and so inspiring that it remains to our own day among the greatest of Poland's and indeed of the world's spiritual possessions. No one except a handful of intimate friends, sworn to secrecy, knew that the Anonymous Poet was Zygmunt Krasinski, thus consecrating his life and genius to the country he was forbidden openly to serve.

[1] For details of this period of Polish literature see my *Adam Mickiewicz*, and my *Poland: a Study in National Idealism.*

CHAPTER IV

THE SOWING OF THE SEED
(1831–1834)

Krasinski was now at grips with the problem that to him and his nation meant life or death. There now began for him the years of his long search after the word that would clear the enigma of Poland's fate, and, by so doing and thus justifying an inexplicable Divine ordering, save his people and himself from moral destruction.

"He emerged from the year 1831," writes Dr Kallenbach, "as from a severe illness, with his health ruined, his imagination strained to its last limits, tortured and restless, his heart seared, and the more painfully, because it was wounded by a father's hand[1]."

He spent the end of 1831 and the beginning of 1832 quietly in Geneva. For himself he had no hope of happiness; but faith in the future of his nation woke again after the first shock of her defeat.

"For us," writes this boy whom suffering had unnaturally matured, "for us, contemporaries panting in anguish, delirious with fear and hope, a partial defeat seems a lost cause; for, when an event is delayed beyond our grave, for us it is already an affair of eternity and no longer an affair of time. But, by the order of things, this is not so; because as great things, noble and holy things, call for an enormous amount of pain in order to be effected, in order to reach their ends, only one generation, and sometimes even several, cannot be enough.

[1] J. Kallenbach, *Zygmunt Krasinski.*

To resign oneself, then, is a law; it is another one to make every effort to add our drop of sacrifice, of bitterness, to the ocean of pain whose waves shall one day demolish the throne of the unjust and the oppressor[1]."

Then he, when the Rising had but just sunk to its close, foretold the fate of Poland under the vengeance of the Tsar; words that were fulfilled to the letter, both during Krasinski's lifetime, and until the day when we saw the fall of the Russian empire.

There shall be sledges that will depart for Siberia, spies denouncing, prisons gorged, young men made privates in the army for life, geniuses exiled or crushed, hearts which will be frozen, which will be broken by dint of persecutions, not violent, not obvious, but clandestine, secret, persecutions every day, every morning, every evening, insults of every nature, vexations each moment...Laws will be mutilated, institutions overthrown, schools forbidden...They will protect the corruption of morals, they will make a scarecrow of holy religion to disgust noble hearts with it, vileness will be rewarded with crosses and honours...They will brutalize the people by dint of brandy...Remember this prophecy when they speak to you of the magnanimity of the Emperor of Russia[2].

But it was far from Krasinski's scheme of things to sit passive either in lamentation or the smugness of content. He continually urged upon Reeve to bestir himself and act. " There is weakness where there is no struggle," he told him. " Where there is struggle there is strength and nobility[3]."

To think of happiness as an aim is pure childishness. You will never gain anything by that; you will always lose. I too cradled myself in those mad ideas, and I thank my God for having got out of them both pretty quickly and pretty early. The only thing that man can hope for...to which he can steer his soul and the emotions of his soul, is greatness, that is to say, superiority in any direction. And I maintain that...this continual struggle between obstacles and men can bring about

---

[1] *Correspondance.* Krasinski to Reeve. Geneva, Oct. 2, 1831.
[2] *Ibid.* Oct. 16, 1831.   [3] *Ibid.* Sept. 29, 1831.

noble and radiant moments, instants of joy. But to ask for
calm is to ask dew of the deserts of Sahara...Why do I write
all this?...Because I want to pursue your ideal of calm into the
furthest recesses of your soul, because I want to drive it for
ever from your soul. For, if you keep it...you will descend
instead of mounting, you will sleep when everything around
you will be awake, you will go on shooting partridges, but
never will you be either a man or a poet...To-day, when for
me all is finished, when my name is destined not to rise above
the waves of the abyss, I want you to be celebrated. If you
give yourself up to calm, you will go down both in my eyes
and in my love[1].

But, although Krasinski had parted with his hopes
of fame, he continued writing. Soon after the news had
reached him of the loss of Warsaw, he sent to *La
Bibliothèque Universelle* what he told Reeve was his
"funeral hymn for Poland," *Une Étoile* : a pathetic
little prose poem, in which Poland is the falling star
that will again rise. In October he wrote, also in
French, one of his fanciful stories on the cholera and
a demoniacal youth who disseminates it. He drew here
on his own excessive impressionability, recalling the
moments when, in the midst of his struggle with his
father, Asiatic cholera appeared in Europe, and he, with
his nervous system wrecked by his troubles[2], had made
sure that it would carry him off[3]. He wrote the story
"from ten in the morning to eight in the evening,
without leaving the table except to light a cigar. When

---

[1] *Correspondance.* Krasinski to Reeve. Geneva, Oct. 20, 1831.

[2] J. Kallenbach, *Zygmunt Krasinski.*

[3] Krasinski arranged the whole programme of his dying, so to speak,
on this occasion ; settled to write in his last hours to Reeve and Henrietta
Willan, and drew up a will in which he left all his French and English
manuscripts to Reeve, and which he concluded with the words: "The
only regret that I have in leaving this earth, in the century of bankers and
oppressors, is not to have fallen on a Polish battle-field, and to have none
of my English friends at my death-bed." *Correspondance.* Krasinski to
Reeve. Geneva, July 13, 1831.

I got up I was half mad¹." Traces of *Le Choléra* appear in the *Unfinished Poem*². In this same autumn, too, was begun *Agay Han*, the first of Krasinski's published work that is of any importance. The young Pole found solace for his patriotic grief in picturing to himself the reverse of the shield, the hour in Poland's history when she placed a Tsar on the throne of Muscovy.

It is with admiration and wonder that the reader dwells upon Krasinski's *Iridion* as a noble summons to the heights of pardon, written by a Pole under the most cruel national circumstances. What was the fiery struggle through which Krasinski, beset by storms of not only patriotic, but personal, hatred, passed before he gained the victory we know in part from letters that he wrote to Reeve at the end of 1831, five years before *Iridion* was given to the Polish nation. In October, 1831, Krasinski received a visit from Łubienski, the youth who had mortally outraged him in the University. Łubienski came with the intention of effecting a reconciliation and readmission to Krasinski's friendship. Krasinski, taught by suffering, as he tells Reeve, to be hard and reserved for the first time in his life, would not forgive one whose overtures he distrusted, and whose character—certainly no heroic one, for Łubienski, free to fight for his country, had not done so—he despised. As they parted, Krasinski heard the other's voice, broken by tears, calling after him a last good-bye. A moment of what he describes as "terrible hesitation" rent Zygmunt's soul. Then he remembered that it was

---

¹ *Correspondance.* Krasinski to Reeve. Geneva, Oct. 30, 1831.

² J. Kallenbach. Preface to *Correspondance de Sigismond Krasinski et de Henry Reeve.*

by the doing of this sometime friend that, as he says, his father had been often calumniated, he himself driven from Poland, hated, so he believed, by his compatriots, regarded by them as an unpatriotic Pole. He bade Łubienski a dry farewell, and turned his back upon him[1].

Reeve had already sent Krasinski a candid rebuke for the spirit of hatred that breathed through his every mention of Łubienski, saying plainly that Krasinski's lust for vengeance, which Reeve had always deplored, was the dark side of his moral character, and could not be justified by the sophisms with which Krasinski attempted to defend it.

To this Krasinski replied in the above quoted letter, adroitly turning the point of the young Englishman's easy reproach by his appeal to what he, the Pole, had seen and known.

Your letter is beautiful; it is sublime, Henry. In other moments I would have bowed my head before it. To-day I admire it as a work of art, but it does not reach my heart...You, a free man, a man born free, you cannot understand the feelings of a man whose ancestors were as free as you, but who, himself, is an oppressed slave. You have never seen a young and beautiful woman weeping hot tears for the loss of her honour, torn from her by the brutality of a conqueror. You have never heard the chains quivering around the arms of your compatriots. In the night, the sounds of lamentations have not made you start from your sleep, you have not risen on your pillow, you have not listened, half asleep, to the wheels jolting on the pavement, the wheels of the cart that carried your relation, your friend, one of your acquaintances to the snows of Siberia. In the day you have not seen bloody executions, nor a tyrant in uniform scouring public places like lightning, hurling his four Tartar horses at full gallop against the passers-by : the passers-by were my compatriots, he was a Russian. You have not been forced to hear a hard and harsh language imposed on a people who did not understand a word of it.

[1] *Correspondance.* Krasinski to Reeve. Geneva, Nov. 18, 1831.

You have not felt the degradation that slavery brings in its train. You have not caught a glimpse of the haggard faces of your brothers through the grating of a prison. Round the winter hearth, they have never told you how such a one disappeared, how the other was condemned, how this village was burnt, that town sacked, and all Praga drowned in the blood of its inhabitants, children flung palpitating on the frozen, stiff breasts of their mothers...You have not followed on the map the desolation of your country, how it has grown shrunken, impoverished, how at last it has been overwhelmed under the weight of the oppressors...In tranquility you were born ; in tranquility your childhood passed; everything...has spoken of, and inspired you with, peace, happiness, forgetfulness, dreams. That is why hatred appears so hideous to you. I speak no longer of Łubienski. He has gone. He and his father are unhappy. That is enough to make me forget even the word *vengeance*. But I only want to explain to you, to justify, the feeling, the passion rather, of that hatred that is in me. I hated with all the strength of my little heart before I loved either woman or friend. It is an element that has mingled with my nature, which has become a part of all that I am. For a man who hates a whole nation as unrestrainedly as I do, it is a small thing to hate an individual[1].

Along with this moral battle, the precursor of *Iridion*, Krasinski's deep intellect was wrestling with the social problems of the future, poring over history and philosophy, mainly as they affected the fate of his country. To his thinking everything pointed to that cataclysm that he was to paint with such mastery in his *Undivine Comedy*; even such an episode as the gift of tongues claimed by Edward Irving, because, as he wrote to Reeve, "souls are strained to the last degree" in "the instinct of the great catastrophe[2]." To his father he addressed similar language.

It is obvious that the fall of the present society of Europe is rapidly approaching...that something new, unknown, of which we do not even dream, is struggling to emerge and encompass this world.

[1] *Correspondance.* Krasinski to Reeve. Geneva, Nov. 18, 1831.
[2] *Ibid.* Nov. 25, 1831.

We are in a condition like that of Rome, perishing under the invasions of the Barbarians. And then civilization had reached a high level, and then men were satiated with everything to the utmost of their desire and satisfaction...Therefore they sank into weariness and weakness. We of to-day proceed differently as to form, but the same as to spirit...

To us men of the present generation life has become difficult indeed. We are suspended between the past and the future. We love the past because we are its children, and everything is tearing us from it and driving us to the future which we shall never see, for, before its confirmation, certainly several generations must suffer and struggle and fall in the midst of the battle. The only shield here is faith in Christ, and courage, for all our life will be a tempest...We are not born for happiness, but for the sweat of blood, for the continual war, not only external, with circumstances—that matters little— but internal, with our contradictory feelings, memories and hopes which will never cease to clash, to oust each other from our souls[1].

But in the immense convulsion that he foretold, Krasinski, even at this early stage of his philosophy, saw hope in the acceptance of pain, regeneration in the abjuration of materialism.

"Note well," says he to Reeve, "this eternal truth that the happier a man becomes the more he degenerates. Only in suffering are we truly great...But all these noble sentiments have perished in Europe to-day": he alludes to the desire for moral glory and for national independence triumphing over material pleasure and mental comfort.

A native country no longer plays any part. Material happiness is everything. Those who possess it desire peace; those who have it not desire war to acquire it...So I believe in a vast desolation. Everything must crumble into ruins... and then only I hope for regeneration, but not before.

He adds he is not far from the conviction, which became his national faith, that his nation shall bring

---

[1] Given by J. Kallenbach, *Zygmunt Krasinski.*

new life when there "is nothing left in Europe except silence and ruins[1]."

During his solitary rambles, Krasinski continually pondered over these matters. One day, entering a wretched inn near Geneva to clean his pipe, he talked there to two peasant girls of the workmen's riots then going on in Lyons. He told Reeve the profound impression made upon him by the class hatred of one girl, driven to rage by hunger, and by the terror of the other, a gentle and timid soul, at the prospect of the bloodshed that must come. This occurrence strongly influenced certain scenes of *The Undivine Comedy*.

Now begins with sad reiteration Krasinski's apologies for breaking off abruptly in his letters : these he will repeat all his life. The pain in his eyes will not let him write, he says; or he is nearly blind. Reeve joined him in the February of 1832 ; but the joy of their meeting was soon shattered by Wincenty Krasinski's summons to his son to join him in Poland. "God only knows what may happen[2]," wrote Reeve to his mother in well founded apprehension : for the position was fraught with peril to a youth like Krasinski, devoured with patriotism, incapable, as he had written months ago to Reeve, of bearing in silence the spectacle that awaited him of his nation ground down under the fate of the conquered. "I cannot dissimulate," he had said, "and from Warsaw the road is all ready, all macadamized to Siberia[3]." Although he wrote to his father what a son was obliged to write, that he longed to see

[1] *Correspondance.* Krasinski to Reeve. Geneva, Dec. 1, 1831.

[2] J. K. Laughton, *Memoirs of the Life and Correspondence of Henry Reeve.*

[3] *Correspondance.* Krasinski to Reeve. Geneva, Oct. 7 (wrongly dated for November, Dr Kallenbach points out), 1831.

him and the home of his childhood, he told him frankly that when outside the doors of his country house only pain awaited him, and that he shuddered at the prospect of beholding the misery which had overwhelmed Poland. The real confidants of his heart, Reeve and Gaszynski, knew that the thought of his return to his country was agony which, were it not for his father's command, he would have refused to face[1]. Gaszynski especially must have understood, without the words that Zygmunt could not bring himself to utter, what life in Poland would henceforth mean to the son of Wincenty Krasinski.

Gaszynski now re-enters Zygmunt's life, never again to leave it. The two had been completely cut off from each other by the Rising : Krasinski had in vain endeavoured to find out through his father what had become of his old schoolfellow. Exiled from Poland, Gaszynski joined the Polish emigration in Paris ; and in the spring of 1832 was at last able to communicate with Krasinski. When Zygmunt saw once more his friend's familiar handwriting, he wrote back :

> It is long since I have shed one tear. I believed that their source had dried within me, for my brain is long since parched ; but to-day I wept when I received your letter, when I read the writing of a friend.

That friend, as Krasinski reminds him, had been his defender in the University scene. He had shared with him the sports and studies of their boyhood, gone, Zygmunt mournfully asks, whither ?

Then, sadly and tersely, so tersely that Dr Kallenbach ascribes this unusual restraint to the state of the

---

[1] See the letter to Reeve above quoted, where Krasinski states plainly that he will not go back to Warsaw, even if his father returns there.

writer's eyesight, Zygmunt gives his friend the account
of his year and a half of silence.

> If you hear them calumniate me, do not defend me, but
> think : "It is a lie." You know me. Know me still. I have lived
> out bitter moments. As I unhappily began life, so it continues
> still in that same fashion...All this time I have been driven
> mad, I suffered to extremity, I sickened again and again. I
> used every means to reach you [to fight with Gaszynski in the
> war], but obstacles stronger than my strength closed the way
> to me...In the beginning I spent the days and nights in fever,
> later in madness...In two months I must return where fetters
> clank, "to the land of graves and crosses." Siberia awaits me.
> I shall find compatriots there.
>
> Now tell me, Konstanty, what do you think of doing?
> Do you need anything? Money? I have not got much, but
> what I have is at your disposal[1].

The generosity with which Krasinski gave financial
assistance to his brother-Poles, whether friends of his
or no, was always a marked feature in his character.
Later in his manhood, when in command of great wealth,
he had but to suspect that a Polish poet or some other
Polish exile was in need, and, even if the relations between himself and the man in question were not cordial,
he at once sent help. He always handed over these
sums of money anonymously, generally through the
intermedium of one of his friends. Not only his own
delicacy of feeling, but the peculiar difficulty of his
position among his fellow-countrymen, impelled him to
the same unbroken secrecy in his contributions to either
private or national causes that ruled over every other
department of his life[2].

The conviction of which he speaks in the above
letter, and of which he had often written to Reeve, that

---

[1] *Letters of Zygmunt Krasinski to Konstanty Gaszynski.* Geneva,
March 9, 1832.

[2] Preface to *Letters of Zygmunt Krasinski to Stanisław Małachowski*,
Cracow, 1885 (Polish).

every journey of his to Poland meant one longer still, and for ever, to the mines, now haunted Krasinski's mind. The fear of Siberia, where, should his authorship have been discovered, he would in all probability have been sent, became one of the nightmares of his life. Every time he set out for his country, he bade farewell to his friends as one on the eve of an eternal parting.

"I have changed much, Konstanty," wrote Krasinski again to the friend who had last known him as an ambitious, wayward boy. "I have despaired of happiness." Summarizing in a few words the ideals of greatness he had learnt in suffering and his loss of love and glory, he tells Gaszynski who, in the past, had been his literary sponsor :

I have written a great many things this year, all stamped with fever and despair ; but now the time is coming to betake myself to the poetry of deeds...I have not sufficient strength of soul to become a Cooper spy ; but I will be what God created me, a good Pole, always and everywhere.

"I am half blind, I scarcely see my letters " : but he scrawls a few more words of deep thankfulness that Gaszynski still loved him and had not misjudged him[1].

A few days later he wrote with the same difficulty, repeating to Gaszynski what was now his fixed idea.

Do not be so carried away by hope in happiness and faith in success. A great work is never accomplished in a short time. Thousands of sufferings are needed to save a nation...There is nothing good, nothing noble in this world without long pain, without long toils.

"Konstanty,write often to me,"he adds in a transport of pain, hinting at what he would not say openly of the meeting between him and his father, and his future position in his country. "Oh! if you knew what I have suffered, what I suffer, what is

[1] *Letters of Zygmunt Krasinski to Konstanty Gaszynski.* Geneva, March 17, 1832.

the fate that is awaiting me, what weariness, what difficulties ; but I trust in God that the day will come when you will know that my love for Poland did not end in words[1]."

His mournful anticipations preyed upon his mind and body with such injury to his eyesight that the doctors cut him off from his two chief solaces, reading and writing.

"You are happy," he tells Gaszynski in his letter of April 2nd, " to have escaped the sight to which I must hasten back ;...you will not gaze on the tears and execrations of the vanquished. To one used to live a European life it will be terrible to return again...to dissimulation, to the concealment of one's thoughts.
" If it is possible to write anything in Poland, I will write. I feel the source throbbing in me, and I could inundate the hearts of my countrymen by many a wave of poetry, but under the censure, but amidst constraints, I cannot write. The poet must have freedom[2]."

Yet the Anonymous Poet was inspired with *Iridion* in Petersburg and with his first *Psalms* in the Warsaw palace.

"God saved all the world by His own sufferings," he says a few days afterwards, returning again and again with the reiteration of one sick at heart to the only thought in which he could find comfort in his grief for Poland.

We will save our country by our sufferings. It seems that this is the eternal law, and that salvation cannot be without suffering, without pain, without blood. And when yearning falls on you, when sadness burdens you, when on a foreign soil it befalls you to curse your fate and to sigh for Poland, think : God also suffered for us ! And that thought will reconcile you with the world, not with that transient, little world which passes away before our eyes, and each moment can sink from beneath our feet, but that great, only world, embracing all the order of creation, spirits, man and the Creator Himself. And then you will feel that you are walking towards immortality,

---

[1] *Letters of Zygmunt Krasinski to Konstanty Gaszynski.* Geneva, March 22, 1832.   [2] *Ibid.* April 2, 1832.

that your aim is suffering and greatness on this earth, but on the other side of the grave greatness and happiness.

But because I am preaching you a sermon, do not think that I have reached that rest of which you speak. On the contrary, each day I sink deeper into rage and despair...I have sought and I have not found, I have dreamed and have gained nothing by my dreams[1].

In May, with Reeve as his companion for part of the way, Krasinski started for Poland. His father had ordered him to present himself at Turin to Carlo Alberto, his cousin, at which, writes Reeve, "he is much annoyed and I much amused...I shall grin on seeing him return from an interview with the man who betrayed Santa Rosa and sought to hang Prandi and Co.[2]" Reeve, however, did not enjoy this spectacle, for the interview failed to come off. In a condition near blindness, Krasinski made the journey by slow stages, halting at Venice for an unsuccessful treatment on his eyes. He parted with Reeve at Innsbruck. It was the farewell of their youthful friendship[3]. They still corresponded for a few years longer, with as great affection as before—on Krasinski's side at all events : all Reeve's letters from this time are missing, probably destroyed by Krasinski for caution's sake—but with ever increasing lapses into silence. They met each other again ; but they were never more to each other what they had once been. Propinquity had been the chief motive of their intimacy in Krasinski's young loneliness ; but the life of Henry Reeve, the successful politician, the prosperous man of affairs, and that of the Polish poet, working for

[1] *Letters of Zygmunt Krasinski to Konstanty Gaszynski.* Geneva, April 6, 1832.

[2] J. K. Laughton, *Memoirs of the Life and Correspondence of Henry Reeve.*

[3] "I never lived in his intimacy again" : thus Reeve, *op. cit.*

his nation in secrecy and pain, drifted too far apart for the affection of their youth to be able to survive[1]. In all likelihood, even before they said good-bye at Innsbruck, the months of mental torture that Zygmunt had endured during the Rising had already morally parted him from the young Englishman who had known no struggle : for Krasinski, writing from Vienna to Reeve, prophesied that the latter would end by falling into materialism, and complained that he had become very English [2]—which we regret was not intended as a compliment.

For several weeks Krasinski remained in Vienna under the oculist. Unable to read or go out until his evening drive, he sat the whole day in a darkened room, a prey to all his old griefs and harrowing anticipations. On the eve of his entry into his country where, under the iron rule of Nicholas I, all correspondence with the exiles of the Rising must cease, Krasinski wrote his farewells to Gaszynski, brief by reason of his suffering eyes, begging him in the uncertainty whether they might ever meet again never to doubt that he was his friend and a true Pole.

He reached Warsaw in the August of 1832. He had left it in 1829. He returned to find the Cossacks and Russian police in the streets where three years ago he had seen the Polish uniforms he would never see there again : to be reminded at each step that the Poland he had lived in as a boy was gone from him for ever. He went on at once to his country home, where his father awaited him. Reading between the lines of

[1] J. Kallenbach, *Zygmunt Krasinski*. See also Dr Kallenbach's Preface to *Correspondance de Sigismond Krasinski et de Henry Reeve*.

[2] *Correspondance*. Krasinski to Reeve. Vienna, July, 1832.

a short note in English which Krasinski wrote from Warsaw to Reeve, it is apparent that he looked forward with
dread to a meeting, the pain of which must have far
outweighed any joy it could have brought him. Upon
what passed between him and his father when they saw
each other again he kept absolute silence : only telling
Reeve of his father's tears and blessing when he embraced him, and of the affection that had prepared every
comfort and luxury for the son who had been long
absent.

Amelia Załuska was also at Opinogóra. Henrietta
Willan was by now little more than a memory for Krasinski, and, with the impressionability of his nature, his
love for the woman who had fascinated him as a boy
re-awoke. He hung upon her music, and wrote his
usual style of fragments in poetical prose, addressed to
her. But he was only permitted to be a few weeks at
his home. His father intended to spend the winter in
Petersburg, and insisted on his son accompanying him.
Nothing could have been so ill judged as to expose a
half blind boy, whose nerves and health were shattered,
to the rigorous winter of the Russian capital, to the long
journey by carriage over the bad roads at so late a
season, and still more to the false and intolerable position of residence under the shadow of Nicholas I, among
those to whom the misery of Poland was a triumph.
Whether Wincenty Krasinski, who from first to last
never succeeded in understanding his son's character,
decided upon this proceeding with the ambition of
securing for Zygmunt some post in the Russian government[1]; or whether, as Count Tarnowski surmises, the

[1] Stanisław Małachowski, *Short Sketch of the Life and Writings of
Zygmunt Krasinski* (Polish). Being privately printed, I have been unable

General had received a mandate from the Tsar, to dis-
obey which meant Siberia[1], is a matter of conjecture.
It was one step further in the road that the Anonymous
Poet trod for his father's sake.

All Krasinski's letters to Reeve from the moment
that he crossed the frontiers are worded with great caution. With his correspondence opened by the Russian
police, he could say no word of any Polish matters, of
the things that most went to his heart. In a letter to
Reeve, sent after he had started for Petersburg, he
writes, with irony pointed to deceive those through
whose hands the words might pass, both a covert warning to the Englishman to be careful what he wrote to
him[2] and his own vow to be ever faithful to Poland.

> If you ask me "What shall you do there?" I will answer:
> *I don't know* [in English]. However, you know me, and you
> know that I love eating, drinking, etc., and that nothing in this
> world can make me change my opinion on that point, nothing,
> nothing[3].

Krasinski spent five months in Petersburg, too ill
to leave his room. He passed his time between his bed
and walking restlessly about his luxurious apartment,
hung with green and silver tapestry, which looked out
on a courtyard and a sky heavy with snowclouds. His
solitude was only broken by the visits of his father who,
says he to Reeve, was "an angel" to him, and by the
occasional calls of the few uncongenial acquaintances he
had in the city. His eyes were on fire, and the doctors
doubted whether they could save them. He was obliged

to see the original, and in this instance quote Dr Kallenbach's reference.
J. Kallenbach, *Zygmunt Krasinski*.

[1] St. Tarnowski, *Zygmunt Krasinski*.
[2] *Correspondance*. Dr Kallenbach's note, Vol. II, p. 10.
[3] *Ibid*. Krasinski to Reeve. Knyszyn, Sept. 22, 1832.

to live with closed eyes, to dictate his letters, to employ a secretary to read aloud. In later years he confided to a Polish friend that these months in Petersburg were the saddest of his life; practically blind as he was, in acute fear of totally losing his eyesight, alone in his singularly painful position, cut off from all to whom he could unburden his mind[1]. But that dreary winter of moral loneliness was filled for Krasinski with one absorbing occupation : thought.

"I have learned to think," he wrote to Reeve[2]. Utterly cast upon the resources of his own soul, he not only collected clearly his thoughts on the strife between past and present that were to become *The Undivine Comedy*, but it was during this winter that *Iridion* took being. Dr Kallenbach points out the analogy between the two great Polish poets, Adam Mickiewicz and the Anonymous Poet, whose genius rose above the same conditions of slavery, and who were, by those very conditions, inspired to speak under a veil the words for their nation that could not be said openly[3].

"A few days ago," Krasinski told Reeve, "during the night the idea of a poem came to me, a great idea. I leapt from my bed, and cried : *Anch' io sono pittore*[4]."

This idea was his *Iridion*. Three months later he tells Reeve in a dictated letter that his Iridion Amphilochides is "a Greek in Rome : *et dulces moriens reminiscitur Argos*[5]." More he dared not say.

That the motive of *Iridion* was already sufficiently

---

[1] St. Małachowski, *op. cit.* Quoted by Count Tarnowski and Dr Kallenbach in their monographs on Krasinski.

[2] *Correspondance.* Krasinski to Reeve. Petersburg, Nov. 1, 1832.

[3] J. Kallenbach, *Zygmunt Krasinski.*

[4] *Correspondance.* Krasinski to Reeve. Petersburg, Oct. 22, 1832.

[5] *Ibid.* Jan. 20, 1833.

developed for the play to be begun proves what point Krasinski had reached in the conflict between his craving for revenge and what was to the young Pole, watching his country's agony, the hardest word of Christianity. Three years more passed before *Iridion* was finished: its creator wavered before he could attain to his sublime conclusion at the foot of the cross in the Coliseum. But the fact remains that it was in the heart of the Russia of Nicholas I that the Anonymous Poet of Poland began to work out his conviction that love and purity of soul only can save an oppressed nation, and that her revenge can but bring about her own destruction. As a son of the conquered race in the enemy's city, Krasinski was in moral kinship with the Greek Iridion, gazing on the triumph of Rome. He fought his battle out in the silence and solitude of his room, while, as a relief from the monotonous snows of the northern capital, his memory returned to translucent blue Italian skies, to the roses of the Palatine, the glowing colours of classical Rome among which walks Iridion[1].

While he was thus developing in Petersburg the problem of *Iridion* he also reflected on those that, touching the innermost emotions of his heart less intimately, were, as we see from his letters to Reeve, fast ripening for expression in *The Undivine Comedy*.

Reeve had made a new friend in an Englishman, who, as the man of the future, evolved into the Pankracy of *The Undivine Comedy*. Krasinski mistrusted him.

Henry! every man, if he be weak, finds his Mephistopheles like Faust. [These words show how Krasinski's conception both of the Mephistopheles in *Iridion* and of Pankracy was seething

[1] J. Kallenbach, *Zygmunt Krasinski.*

in his brain.] It begins with enthusiasm, it finishes with disgust or despair. There is nothing to fear from a heart we love; but the ascendancy of a strong head is a very different thing. For some time we struggle, then we become a slave[1].

There are two parts in man: thought and action [writes the creator of Henryk]: one as noble as the other, and dividing life turn and turn about between them. Those who never act are called fakirs; those who never think and always act are called machines; those who think and work are called men. It is obvious that in this last class there are individuals in whom the element of thought predominates, in others that of action. But if there is to be greatness or beauty there must always be a proper quantity of both one and the other[2].

I know better than anyone there must be a future. I understand the triumphal procession of that future...I know that we will all pass to dust, having admired nothing, loved nothing real, hated much. And, if we do love something, it is only a world of dreams, of emptiness: the past.

When I consider the matter as a philosopher, I see only an admirable and eternal order; but when I consider the matter as a man who has the heart of a man, the feelings of a man, ties on this earth, I see only disorder...Then, when we have perished, let them arrange the earth in their own way, as they like; and here I think that a day will come when love will again prevail. For God is justice and beauty, the universe is harmonious, and I am immortal[3].

Before Krasinski left Petersburg he told Reeve that since he had last seen him he had thought so deeply that the work of several years seemed to have taken place within him.

God forgive me for having reached a conclusion degrading to humanity. It is that the masses have nothing but appetite, and never make use of reason; that *man* is everything, and that by *him* all things are done, and that *men* are nothing. Still the man is always obliged to sacrifice himself for men, and never to sacrifice them for him. Even though he himself be convinced that happiness is impossible on this earth, he ought to believe in it for others and walk with all his strength to that chimerical end[4].

---

[1] *Correspondance.* Krasinski to Reeve. Petersburg, Nov. 17, 1832.
[2] *Ibid.* Nov. 21, 1832.   [3] *Ibid.* Jan. 6, 1833.
[4] *Ibid.* Feb. 5, 1833.

Though Krasinski was barely twenty-one, by now his youth seems far behind him. He reminds Reeve of the "fabulous time of life" when they both dreamed and hoped, and had faith in men.

Formerly we wanted to become poetical beings; to-day we must become moral beings, live in the bosom of reality, that is to say, sustain each moment a struggle that burns by slow fire, a struggle which is waged between our ideas and facts, which produces the modification of our ideas, the concessions that our soul, formerly absolute and superb, is forced to make to the world of matter, action, interest, etc. etc.

He sees in that very conflict poetry ; but the poetry of duty done in darkness, of work unrewarded save by the sentiment of personal dignity[1]. This is the language of one who is no more young. There is in these letters of Krasinski a growing pessimism. At this time he began the study of German philosophy that for years contributed to darken his spiritual outlook. In the first letter he was free to write to Gaszynski after he had left Russia he told him that he still wrote : "but not with a like faith as of old. Where are all my faiths gone[2]?"

One significant incident cut across the manner of Krasinski's life in Petersburg. He was presented by his father to Nicholas I. He stood face to face with the man at whose hand the Polish nation suffered a fate that has made the history of Poland the tragedy of modern Europe; whose treatment of the vanquished was one of such pitiless cruelty that Mickiewicz could find no greater blasphemy to place on the lips of his Konrad, driven mad by the tears of his people, than the taunt that God was no father to His creatures, but

---

[1] *Correspondance.* Krasinski to Reeve. Petersburg, Jan. 25, 1833.
[2] *Letters to Konstanty Gaszynski.* Vienna, July 7, 1833.

their Tsar¹. Krasinski, being the son of a Pole who
had thrown in his lot with Russia, was received by the
Tsar with a graciousness that was in itself the bitterest
affront to a Polish heart, and offered a post at court or
in the diplomatic service. The danger of the moment,
when a refusal might have involved the gravest consequences, was only averted by the condition of Zygmunt's health that won him the imperial permission to
leave Russia for a better climate.

These details of his interview with Nicholas I
Krasinski probably confided long afterwards to the friend
who has related them². In his as yet published correspondence we have no word upon the subject. But an
echo of what it had meant to him may be found, in
veiled figures, in another place—in a prose poem, called
The Temptation, that he wrote four years later for a
young compatriot who was about to be confronted with
the moral ordeal of a Pole's life in Petersburg.

He left Petersburg in March, 1833. He stopped for
a short time in Warsaw on his way to Vienna. Dictating
from there a letter to Reeve, he apologizes for a long
silence. He had had no one to write his letters for him,
and could only during his journey trust to the kindness
of any chance person who would take down his dictation.

There are ineffable delights for the artist [he proceeds with
reflections that are the key to Henryk's character in *The Undivine Comedy*]: but also he is fated to suffer more than anyone
else in this world. In truth his egoism is sublime; but it is
always egoism. And what will he do when he finds himself in
positions where, to be happy, he must forget himself? He will

¹ Adam Mickiewicz, *The Ancestors*, Part III. See my *Adam Mickiewicz*, where I have given a translation of the scene in question.
² Stanisław Małachowski, *Short Sketch of the Life and Writings of
Zygmunt Krasinski*, quoted by Count Tarnowski, *Zygmunt Krasinski*,
and by Dr Kallenbach, *Zygmunt Krasinski*.

never know what the love of a woman really is ; because, for him, everything is himself. He loves his masterpieces ; but he loves nothing else. That is why reality is poison to him. That is why he can find nowhere any fulfilment of his desires, any end to his dreams. Everything that is not himself disgusts him and drives him to despair...So long as he is alone he is happy ...That is why a great artist is never either a good husband or a good father...One pays dearly for having been admitted to the secrets of the gods. One only drop fallen from on high on your brow renders you incapable of living here below[1].

In our dreams [writes the idealist, tormented by the eternal quest], in those sublime conceptions which yet must often seem ridiculous to the masses, we never feel the most simple difficulties, our courage is ready to brave the thunderbolt of heaven ; but if we have to take but two steps, say a few words, approach, in fact, earthly life in its daily occurrences, we sink with fatigue...To dream is to be of another world, but it is not to be ignorant or mad. There is only madness if we think we can apply the laws of our dreams or of our synthesis to the analysis of life down here ; but everyone is obliged to fall into that mistake in the beginning. Some stay in it, and those are feeble, incomplete beings, but full of gentle poetry and misfortunes. Others, having recognized their youth, and not understanding this sublime warning of Heaven, imagine that all is finished ; that the true world is wretchedness and analysis. These are also feeble and incomplete beings, who end by the corruption of materialism. There are few men who have strength enough to bear difficulties and obstacles, to decide to enter practical life by facing it—the only one that leads to some results—and to keep at the same time an unshakable faith in the promises that were made to them in the day of their delirium, when they caught a glimpse of luminous spheres that they have never since been able to attain. They only will do something[2].

Konstanty Danielewicz, the friend who had stood by Krasinski when he was mobbed at the University, joined Zygmunt in Warsaw, and went on with him to Vienna. From this time Danielewicz, until his death, was the devoted companion of Krasinski in his wan-

---

[1] *Correspondance.* Krasinski to Reeve. Warsaw, April 4, 1833.
[2] *Ibid.* April 7, 1833.

derings, and the one that the poet seems to have loved best of all his friends. The misfortunes of his life were a bond that knit Krasinski, with whom to pity was to love, very closely to him. His philosophical intellect strongly influenced, not altogether for the good, the trend of Krasinski's mind during the years that they lived together. He was a finished musician, though no poet ; and in his playing, Krasinski, who was passionately fond of music, found inspiration for the struggle of the spirits in *The Undivine Comedy* over Henryk's soul[1]. His somewhat severe candour, and a certain want of sympathy with Zygmunt's nervous and highly strung temperament, never chilled their friendship, or diminished the enthusiastic admiration that Krasinski, an idealist in his affections as elsewhere, lavished upon him.

Krasinski spent the summer in Vienna with Danielewicz, undergoing medical treatment. He was in wretched health, and the days went by for both youths in external monotony, but, for Krasinski, in creation. He and Danielewicz sat talking for hours of the social problems which were at the time convulsing Europe : and it was then that Krasinski, only able to write a few words at a stretch in his blind condition, committed to paper *The Undivine Comedy*. To antedate the words he wrote to Gaszynski, with their foreshadowing of the promises of *Dawn*, soon after *The Undivine Comedy* was completed :

> I know that our civilization is nigh to death : I know that the times are near when new crimes will come to punish the old, and themselves be condemned in the sight of God—but I know that they will create nothing, will build nothing. They will pass like the horse of Attila, and, after them, silence. Then

[1] J. Kleiner, *History of the Thought of Zygmunt Krasinski.* Lwów, 1912 (Polish). See also *Correspondance.* Krasinski to Reeve. Warsaw, April 9, 1833.

only, that which neither you nor anyone knows or understands will come upon us, rise from the chaos, and build the new world from the Divine Will, from the predestiny of the human race; but then both your and my bones shall be somewhere dust[1].

In the October of 1833 Krasinski published under false initials his *Agay Han.*

He had begun this story in Geneva. The Tartar page, Agay Han, is in love with Maryna, the widow of the false Demetrius. After her husband's death, Maryna has taken refuge in a castle, where the Muscovite boyars capture her, and cast her into prison. She is rescued by the page; but she gives her hand to Zarucki, who had defended the castle before it fell. Panting for revenge, Agay Han follows them with Russian troops, slays the husband, and drowns both Maryna and himself.

This, the last work of Krasinski's immaturity, lacks interest. Begun when the author's nerves had gone to pieces during his sufferings in Geneva[2], the style of the first part is weak and over coloured. Before the story ends the errors of manner are pruned away, and after the earlier chapters the rest of the work, says Dr Kallenbach, shows a decided step forward in the poet's powers[3]. There is, however, so great a gulf between *Agay Han* and its successor—the masterpiece of matured genius which as *The Undivine Comedy* will live with the Polish language—that it is hard to realize they were written, and with no intermediate degrees, by the same hand.

In the autumn Krasinski wandered, still with

---

[1] *Letters to Konstanty Gaszynski.* Rome, Jan. 17, 1834.
[2] J. Kallenbach, *Zygmunt Krasinski.*
[3] *Op. cit.*

Danielewicz, by slow stages from Vienna through Italy, till he reached Rome. We find this journey with its memories of Krasinski's dead companion in the *Unfinished Poem*. *The Undivine Comedy* was finished during the halt at Venice. In a letter written from Rome to Reeve, between whom and Krasinski some cause of coolness had arisen which had put an end to their correspondence for several months, Zygmunt details the plot of the play. To Gaszynski he wrote telling him that he was sending him the manuscript, to which he first gave the name *The Husband*, charging him by everything that was holy to guard the secret of the authorship, to get it published in Paris if possible, and to accept as a friend's gift whatever financial gains came of it. But for some reason Krasinski changed his mind, and left the manuscript alone. More than a year after he had told Gaszynski that the work was ready, he wrote, speaking darkly for fear of unwarranted eyes discovering his identity:

If you should find in Paris a recently published work, *The Undivine Comedy*, tell me your opinion of it...Then I also will give you my remarks and observations[1].

But psychologically *The Undivine Comedy* belongs to the year in which Krasinski wrote it. Therefore we have now reached that chapter of the poet's life.

[1] *Letters to Gaszynski.* Naples, March 29, 1835.

CHAPTER V

THE UNDIVINE COMEDY: THE DOMESTIC DRAMA

The Undivine Comedy is the drama of a perishing world. It was written little more than forty years after the French Revolution, at a time of widespread social upheaval and universal unrest. A Polish boy of twenty-one voiced the problems and apprehensions which are still ours with the penetration of genius that places *The Undivine Comedy* amongst the masterpieces of the world's literature.

The Undivine Comedy is written in prose, the finest that ever came from Krasinski's pen. It stands alone among his creations. The gravity and restraint of the style, its strange terseness, unique in the work of one whose tendency is to over elaboration, have been in part ascribed to the conditions under which Krasinski wrote the play, forced as he was by practical blindness to concentrate much into brief phrases[1]. We never, says Mickiewicz, see the *dramatis personae* full figure. The situations and characters are not developed: they are only indicated[2]. Yet such is the strength of the

[1] J. Kallenbach, *Zygmunt Krasinski.*
[2] Adam Mickiewicz, *Les Slaves.* Paris, 1849. Vols. IV and V, the former of which contains the fine analysis of *The Undivine Comedy*, have been republished in one volume by the Musée Adam Mickiewicz, Paris, 1914.

few strokes with which Krasinski draws them that they stand out sharp, living. The nurse speaks once: and in her one cry over the blind child the Polish peasant, with her simplicity, her piety, her devotion to her nursling, is in the flesh before us[1]. To the godfather falls a part that does not fill a page; but how well we know him and his stupid, pompous complacency! The whole story of the wife, who has nothing except the limitations of a woman's heart to pit against the restless egoism of a poetic genius, is played out in scarcely half a dozen short scenes, as remarkable for their power and unswerving truth to human nature as for their reserve.

The atmosphere of the play is profoundly pessimistic. Its gloom is unrelieved. The domestic tragedy, the ruin of a wife and son, is the theme of the first part: the universal tragedy, where the war of class against class, past against future, ends also in ruin, but the ruin of all the world, is the theme of the second. Although by birth and tradition, and, to a certain extent, conviction, which was however not nearly so pronounced in his youth as later, Krasinski belonged to the aristocratic party; yet in *The Undivine Comedy* he gauges each class alike with icy impartiality, or, to speak more correctly, with a severity that effectually withholds the reader's sympathy from either. His aristocrats are wholly without moral fibre: decadent, flabby inheritors of a doomed cause. Their opponents, revenging themselves for years of oppression, are not demons—the colour of the drama is not lurid or stained with crimson, but grey: they are merely brutalized human beings taking the heads of their tyrants in cold blood. The champion of the past, or of the aristocracy, plays his

[1] J. Kallenbach, *op. cit.*

part without conviction out of a heart no longer capable
of nursing any spark of the living fire. Faith and enthusiasm are wanting likewise to his antagonist, the
leader of the revolution. In *Iridion* we have the martyrs of the catacombs, the lovely lineaments of Cornelia, grandeur in the figure of Iridion himself, who,
although he sinned, sinned because he had "loved
Greece." But in *The Undivine Comedy* there is no one
even approaching heroic proportions: no one for whom
we can feel a spark of whole-hearted admiration. The
fact that these morally negative men and women are
not abnormal, but human characters whom we have
met in our daily lives, is among the most painfully
true aspects of *The Undivine Comedy*.

For the sadness of *The Undivine Comedy* is not that
of a young pessimism. There is no touch of youth about
the drama. It is the work of one who had passed
through a rude shock, a bitter awakening. The tragedy
of Poland was too recent, his own wounds were too
fresh, for the Anonymous Poet to be able as yet to
speak the language of *Dawn* and *Resurrecturis*. As
Dr Kallenbach observes, *The Undivine Comedy*, with
its brooding melancholy, its presages of woe, was one
of the first fruits of the disastrous Polish Rising[1].

"I know nothing more painful than all this drama," said
Mickiewicz, speaking in Paris to his audience of Poles and
Frenchmen, who were all ignorant as to who the author of *The
Undivine Comedy* might be. "The poet who composed it could
only have been born in the bosom of a nation that has suffered
for centuries. Grief is not exhaled here in pompous phrases.
I have no tirades to quote. But each word is a drop drawn
from one great mass of suffering and pain[2]."

Beyond the fact that it is written in the Polish

[1] J. Kallenbach, *op. cit.*   [2] Adam Mickiewicz, *Les Slaves.*

language *The Undivine Comedy* is not national. There is no mention, even indirectly, of Poland. There is no indication of place except that to the last rampart of the besieged nobles is given the name of an old fortress of the heroic days of the Polish Republic. Were it not for the nurse's invocation to " Our Lady of Czenstochowa," and the typical characteristics of the servants who are at once recognizable as Poles, whereas all the other personages in the play are cosmopolitan, not Polish, types, we should not know that the scene of *The Undivine Comedy* is laid in Poland. All Krasinski's later work was spoken directly to his people, and through them to the world. His earliest, the first that gave him his rank among the great poets of his race, is spoken to the world, and then to his nation.

In front of each of the four parts into which Krasinski divides the play he places a short preliminary prose poem, by way of introduction. The first is the surest indication of the unyouthful despair which filled Krasinski's heart at this time. He writes, says one of his biographers, in the flower of his age a work of genius unique of its kind in Europe ; and his opening is the antithesis to the rapture and sublime faith in self of a young poet. It is the bitterest curse on poetry[1].

There are stars around thy head [he addresses poetry]; the waves of the sea beneath thy feet. Before thee the rainbow runs on the waves of the sea, and cleaves asunder the darkness. What thou beholdest is thine...The heavens are thine. There is nought equal to thy glory.

Thou playest to strange ears of unconceived delights... Thou drawest forth tears. But thou thyself, what feelest thou? What dost thou create? Through thee floweth a stream of beauty, but thou art not beauty. Woe unto thee! The child

---

[1] St. Tarnowski, *Zygmunt Krasinski.*

that weeps on its nurse's bosom, the flower of the fields that is unconscious of its own fragrance, have more merit before the Lord than thou.

Whence hast thou arisen, empty shadow, that givest to man to know the light, and knowest not the light thyself, hast not seen it, shalt not see it? Who created thee in irony or wrath? Who gave thee thy futile life, so false that thou canst feign an angel's moment, ere thou wallowest in the mire, ere as a serpent thou goest to crawl and stifle in the slime? Thine and the woman's is the same beginning[1].

Yea, but thou dost suffer, albeit thy pain shall create nought, shall avail nought...Thy despair and thy sighs sink to the earth, and Satan gathers them and, rejoicing, adds them to his lies and deceptions—and the Lord will one day deny them, as they denied the Lord.

Not that I complain of thee, poetry, mother of beauty and salvation. Only he is unhappy who, in worlds in womb, in worlds that are to die, must remember or foresee thee: for thou only destroyest those who have consecrated themselves to thee, who have become the living voices of thy glory.

Blessed is he in whom thou hast dwelt, as God dwelt in the world, unseen, unheard, mighty in each member, great, the Lord, before whom creation humbles itself, and saith: "He is here." Such a one shall carry thee as a star on his brow, and will not depart from thy love with a chaos of words. He will love mankind, and come forth as a man among his brethren. But he who keepeth thee not secretly in his heart, who betrayeth thee before the time and giveth thee forth as an empty delight to men, upon his head thou shalt scatter a few flowers and turn away, and he amuseth himself with withered flowers and weaveth a funeral wreath for himself through all his life. His and the woman's is the same beginning.

If poetry, for art's sake, had once tempted Krasinski, as, from his boyish letters to Reeve, we know that it had done, it did so no more. He was himself a poet: and he saw the danger, the false outlook on life and its

---

[1] The meaning is that woman, a being of the earth, rises high only to sink low. J. Kleiner, *History of the Thought of Zygmunt Krasinski.* Lwów, 1912 (Polish). The aspersion Krasinski here casts upon women is very unlike him, for his ideal of woman was a singularly high and spiritual one. It illustrates again the pessimistic condition in which *The Undivine Comedy* was written.

ruinous consequences, engendered by poetry taken as the worship of form and the dramatization of emotion and passion, without the soul's stern realities behind them. "For him," to quote Mickiewicz, "poetry is not an art, not an amusement." It is:

a serious inspiration...True poetry, among the Greeks themselves, signified nothing else except action. What does the Polish author ask? That the most initiated souls, the highest, the strongest, those that communicate with the Divinity, should reserve all their strength to act instead of speaking...He has painted here the picture of poetical power, the power of a soul which flings itself entirely into its imagination...and which believes it possesses all things, but is lost because it uses this gift of heaven for its own pleasure[1].

This brings us straight to the conception of Henryk and the first part of *The Undivine Comedy*.

Henryk is a poet who, setting out with some noble aspirations, has consumed his life in poetic dreams and worship of the imagination. He has toyed with his emotions so long as a thing of art that, by the time the drama opens, his heart is little more than a worn-out husk. Genuine passion is dead: he poses, unaware that he is posing. Believing he has at last found the woman of his fancies, he decides to "descend to earthly marriage." On the eve of his wedding, an angel flying over his house with the message, "Peace to men of good will," utters the warning: "Blessed be he among creatures who has a heart. He may still be saved," and promises Henryk salvation in his fulfilment of a husband's and father's duties. At the same moment a chorus of evil spirits make ready to capture the soul that will be an easy prey, under the guises of poetic love, ambition, and nature. The third of these Krasinski never worked out.

[1] Adam Mickiewicz, *Les Slaves*.

The wedding feast takes place with high rejoicing. The bride, half fainting with fatigue in the dance, but lovely in her pallor, is gazed upon with rapture by her poet husband.

"Oh, eternally, eternally thou shalt be my song," he tells her; to which she:
"I will be thy faithful wife, as my mother told me, as my heart tells me."

She implores him to let her leave the dance, for she is weary to death. No, he entreats her to remain, and to go on dancing, so that he can stand and feast his eyes on her beauty.

For a short time the husband lives more or less contentedly. Then comes the inevitable reaction. His old poetical longings seize upon him. Krasinski symbolizes them by the figure of the evil spirit that, clothing itself in the form of the ideal woman of Henryk's dreams, appears to him at night while he is asleep.

Husband (waking up). Where am I? Ha! by my wife. This is my wife. *He gazes at his wife.* I thought you were my dream, and behold! after a long interval it has returned and is different from you. You are good and agreeable, but the other—— Oh, God, what do I see?
The Maiden. Thou hast betrayed me. *She disappears.*
Husband. Cursed be the moment when I married a woman, when I forsook the beloved of my young years[1].

The wife wakes, sees something amiss, and, supposing her husband to be ill, entreats that he will take this or that remedy.

Husband (starting up). I must have fresh air. Remain here. For God's sake don't come with me.

He escapes to the moonlit garden. Loathing for

---

[1] All through *The Undivine Comedy*, long after the wife has disappeared from the scenes, it is always as the "Husband" that Henryk is introduced. In like manner, Marya is always the "Wife."

the domestic fetters that have taken the place of poetry
in his life fills his being. He abhors the thought of the
clinging, loving wife, in whom he can find no fault except that the soul of a poet is wanting in her.

Since the day of my marriage I have slept the sleep of the
torpid, the sleep of a German shopkeeper by the side of a
German wife. I have gone about after relations, after doctors,
in shops; and because a child is going to be born to me I have
had to think about a nurse. *Two o'clock strikes from the church
tower.* Come to me, my old kingdom, subject to my thought.
Once the sound of the night bell was your signal. *He walks
about and wrings his hands.* God, is it Thou Who hast sanctified the union of two bodies? Thou Who hast decreed that
nothing can part them, though their souls discard one another
and leave their bodies like two corpses beside each other?

Again thou art near me. Oh, my own, my own, take me
with thee.

Maiden. Wilt thou follow me in whatsoever day I come
for thee?

Husband. At each instant I am thine.

The colloquy is cut short by the sound of the window
being thrown up in Henryk's house, and the wife's
voice begging him to beware of the night cold and to
come back.

By the next scene the child has been born. It lies
asleep in its cradle. Henryk reclines on a chair, his
head buried in his hands. Dry " Thank you's " fall from
his lips as his wife deluges him with the tiresome details
of her preparations for the christening feast. Krasinski's whole depictment of this injured woman, sweet,
lovable, and weak of soul, has a truth and tenderness of touch that is remarkable in a youth of his age.
She is, indeed, the only sympathetic figure in the
drama: yet hers too is that same want of staying power
that is hurrying her class to their doom. She can make
no stand against the misery of her marriage save by

the disordered imagination that destroys herself and her child.

Caressing her baby, soothing her "little one, her pretty one," to sleep, her husband's morose gloom as he sits apart attracts her attention. She seats herself at the piano. Her hands run vaguely over the keys. She can bear her fears in silence no longer.

Wife. To-day, yesterday, ah! my God! and all the week and now for three weeks, for a month, you have not spoken a word to me—and everyone I see tells me I look ill.
Husband. On the contrary I think you look well.
Wife. It is all the same to you, for you don't look at me any more, you turn away when I come in. Yesterday I went to confession, and called to mind all my sins—and I could find nothing that could have offended you.
Husband. You have not offended me.
Wife. My God! My God!
Husband. I feel I ought to love you.
Wife. You have given me the finishing stroke with that one: "I ought." Ah, it would be better to stand up and say: "I do not love you." At least I would then know all—all. *She starts up and takes the child from the cradle.* Do not forsake him, and I will sacrifice myself to your anger. Love my child—my child, Henryk. *She kneels down.*
Husband. Don't pay any attention to what I said. I often suffer from bad moments—ennui.
Wife. I ask you for only one word, only one promise. Say that you will always love him.
Husband. You and him too.

He kisses her; and as she throws her arms about him a peal of thunder rolls through the room. Then wild and strange music is heard; the demon maiden appears, luring Henryk to follow her. Calling on the name of Mary, the frenzied wife, clasping her child to her breast, clings to her husband. Where she sees a horrible ghost and smells the foul air of the grave, he sees the beautiful incorporation of his poems. In vain is her cry of anguish and terror. Her husband turns savagely upon her. She is nothing more to him than the "woman of clay and mire," while the apparition is the heavenly ideal for whose sake he will cast off his home. He disappears with the demon. His wife, shrieking out his name, falls senseless.

The guests assemble for the christening. They whisper and wonder. Where is the father? Why is the mother so pale and wild? Krasinski's Polish critics rank this scene as one of the most powerful of the drama for its concentrated bitterness, for the irony with which, in a few words, the author exposes the characters of each of the spectators who are to be the defenders of the world against the coming deluge. An idle curiosity is the only sensation of the men and women who watch the unhappy mother. The priest, as Mickiewicz notices, confronted with grief where surely a minister of God might have offered some word of spiritual comfort, contents himself with performing the function for which he was summoned, and there his part ends[1].

First Guest (*under his breath*). It's a queer thing where the Count has got to.

Second Guest. He is gaping about somewhere or is writing poetry.

First Guest. And Madam is pale and looks as if she has not slept. She hasn't said a word to anybody.

Fourth Guest. I have left a charming princess. I thought there would be a good lunch, and instead there is, as the Scriptures say, weeping and gnashing of teeth.

The Priest. George Stanislas, dost thou accept the holy oil?

Godparents. We do accept it.

One of the Guests. Look. She has got up, and walks as if in her sleep.

Second Guest. She has stretched out her hands in front of her, and, tottering, is going up to her son.

The Priest. George Stanislas, dost thou renounce Satan and all his pomps?

[1] Adam Mickiewicz, *Les Slaves.*

Godparents. We do renounce them.

The Wife (laying her hands on the child's head). Where is your father, George?

Priest. Please do not interrupt.

Wife. I bless you, George, I bless you, my child. Be a poet so that your father may love you and never cast you off. He will be pleased with you, and then he will forgive your mother.

Priest. Have respect for the things of God, Madam.

Wife. I curse you if you are not a poet. *She faints and the servants carry her out.*

The Guests (all together). Something unusual has happened in this house. Let us go away.

They retire with haste. The christening proceeds. When it is concluded the godfather makes over the cradle a speech that has obviously been made very often before, and as obviously will be made very often again[1].

George Stanislas, you have just been made a Christian and entered human society, and later you will become a citizen, and by the efforts of your parents and the grace of God an eminent holder of office. Remember that you must love your country, and that it is fine even to die for your country.

So he speaks who in the end of the play is the first to leave the sinking ship.

In the meanwhile, Henryk has been pursuing his will-o'-the-wisp in the mountains. She decoys him to a precipice she bids him leap, and there shows herself in her true form, a hideous fiend. The devils are thrusting him down over the brink: and even in that dread moment Henryk's cry is rather that of the actor's monologue than of a human soul about to face its eternal fate. He is falling without a struggle, for his is never a moral conflict. Invariably he yields without a stand. Then the angel guardian rises over the sea. Henryk has thrown away the chance of salvation the

---

[1] Adam Mickiewicz, *Les Slaves.*

same angel had offered him on his marriage eve. He
is now given another: "to return to his house and sin
no more; to love his son."

He goes home. His wife is there no longer. The
servant falters out that she has been taken to the mad
asylum. And now the husband realizes what he has
done.

> "All that I have touched I have destroyed," he cries, "and
> I shall destroy myself in the end. On what pillow will she lay
> her head to-day? What sounds shall surround her in the night?
> The howls and songs of the insane."

So he raves on.

A voice from somewhere. Thou composest a drama.

That voice, says Count Tarnowski, is not an external voice: it is the voice of Henryk's conscience[1].
For even now Henryk must poetize. He—and his
son—are the only two who ever talk poetically in a play
where stern simplicity is the rule. The son's poetry
is spontaneous, as the song of a bird: but it is patent
that Henryk has always his eye on an imaginary audience. He reproaches himself for his wife's madness:
but his language does not convey that sense of agony
and measureless remorse which would have been evoked
from another man in the like circumstances. How
much of it is real sorrow, how much of it the pose that
is now an integral part of the nature of a man who has
for years used emotion as the tool of poetry, who has
lived as an actor greedy for dramatic settings, the
speaker himself is incapable of telling[2]. It is part of
the genius of Krasinski's creation that, except in one
later episode, the reader with no explanation of the fact

---

[1] St. Tarnowski, *Zygmunt Krasinski.*   [2] *Op. cit.*

remains perfectly cold when Henryk holds forth, however passionate to outward semblance his utterances may be: while on the other hand Marya's words, simple, unstudied, dictated by love and grief, speak straight to the heart.

Henryk rushes to the asylum. Klaczko and Dr Kallenbach dwell upon the mastery with which Krasinski treats the scene in the madhouse. One shade less restraint would have overstepped the bounds of tragedy and turned it into the grotesque: but all is grave and moving[1]. Krasinski unites his personal impressions of a madhouse, where he had visited a friend, with the great world convulsion for which the first part of *The Undivine Comedy* is preparing us. We are conscious of uneasiness and dark forebodings as within these lugubrious walls Henryk, sitting by his wife's couch, hears resound from the rooms above, the rooms below, the rooms on either side, mad cries: one blaspheming, another clamouring for the heads of kings and the liberties of the people, a third shrieking that the comet is already flashing in the skies which is to bring "the day of terrible judgment."

Here Henryk's eloquence leaves him. We feel that he is more or less genuine, constrained and inefficient as he is in an ugly situation that can appeal to no poetic sense, but only to the strength of soul that is not in him.

Husband. Do you know me, Marya?
Wife. I have sworn to be faithful to you to the grave.
Husband. Come, give me your hand. We will go away.
Wife. Let me have a few minutes more, and then I will be worthy of you. I have prayed three nights, and God has heard me.

[1] J. Kallenbach, *Zygmunt Krasinski.*

Husband. I don't understand you.

Wife. From the time I lost you a change came over me. "Lord God," I prayed, and beat my breast. "Send down upon me the spirit of poetry": and the third day in the morning I became a poet.

Husband. Marya!

Wife. Henryk, you will not despise me now. I am full of inspiration. You will not forsake me now in the evenings.

Husband. Never, never.

Wife. Look at me. Have I not made myself your equal? I understand everything, I will give it out, I will play it, I will sing it. Sea, stars, storm, battle. Yes, stars, storm, sea—ah! something still escapes me—battle.

She breaks into doggerel lines.

Husband. The curse! the curse!

Wife (*throwing her arms round him and kissing him*). My Henryk, Henryk, how happy I am!

Seeing his gloom, she tells him what will surely drive the cloud from his brow, namely, that his son will be a poet.

At the christening the priest gave him for his first name—Poet, and you know the others, George Stanislas. I did this. I blessed him, I added a curse—he will be a poet. Ah! how I love you, Henryk!

Then the wildness of the prophecies that are ringing from every side of the asylum while she and her husband talk together falls upon her also. She babbles incoherently, but ever gently, of what would befall the world if God went mad; soon returning to her favourite thought of the poet child who will bring joy to his father. Her brain gives way: and she dies, happy, says she, because it is in Henryk's arms that she dies.

Here ends the first part of the domestic drama. How much of its peculiar dreariness may be ascribed to the shadows of Krasinski's own childhood we can but conjecture; but possibly the picture was, if only subconsciously, coloured by a sensitive and observant child's impressions of a home where there had been little sympathy between husband and wife.   Certain it is that George, the son of Henryk and Marya, is to a great extent Krasinski himself.

There is a further point to observe in this unsparing portrayal of a poet's marriage, or, in other words, of the dreamer mated with reality.   Krasinski spoke here not merely out of his knowledge of human nature in general, but out of his knowledge of his own self.   The marriage of Henryk is the curious foreshadowing of Krasinski's marriage.   Krasinski was to be the indifferent husband whose heart when he married was turned with passion in another direction.   The resemblance does not end there.   Morbid introspection, love of a situation, a tendency to self-dramatization, were the chief faults of Krasinski's character.   Henryk is, in fact, Krasinski at the latter's potential worst—but a worst that he never reached : for Henryk erred through want of heart, Krasinski through too much.   Yet in Henryk we have the clear vision of what the Anonymous Poet might have been, and what his innate nobility of soul withheld him from becoming.

Henryk's marriage, then, thus wretchedly ends. He has failed as a husband; but he is still a father.

With the son something of the ruthlessness of Greek tragedy enters the play.   The poetical prologue to the second part is entirely devoted to this strange child. He gazes to the skies and sees something, hears something, that no one but himself knows.   His father looks at him in silence, with eyes that fill with tears.   A gypsy refuses to reveal what she reads in his hand, and goes away, wailing.   Beautiful, pure, mysterious, he is like some flower in Eden before the fall of man.

Thus the introduction. The figure of the sad child who never plays like other children, whom his father's friends visit and to whom they promise some great future, whose nerves destroy his fragile body, is Krasinski's recollection of his boyhood in his father's house, told poetically as he tells all such scraps of his autobiography. And, passing beyond Krasinski's childhood, not only is the blindness of George the blindness in which Krasinski wrote the play, but, says Dr Kallenbach, "all this second part is full of personal memories and personal sorrows." So openly does the Anonymous Poet expose in these few pages the wounds of his heart, his sacred domestic tragedies, that this were alone sufficient to account for the elaborate precautions which he took so that the authorship of *The Undivine Comedy* should never be discovered[1].

The action opens with Henryk and George praying at the mother's tomb. This beautiful and artistic scene is the reminiscence of Krasinski's visits in his childhood with his father to his mother's grave[2].

Husband. Take off your hat and pray for your mother's soul.

George. Hail, Mary, full of grace, Queen of heaven, Lady of all that flowers on the earth, in the fields, on the banks of streams.

Husband. Why do you change the words of the prayer? Pray, as you have been taught, for your mother who died ten years ago at this very hour.

George. Hail, Mary, full of grace, the Lord is with thee. Blessed art thou among angels, and each of them, when thou passest by, plucks a rainbow from his wings and casts it at thy feet.

Husband. George!

George. But those words rush on me and pain my head so much that, please, I must say them.

---

[1] J. Kallenbach, *Zygmunt Krasinski.*   [2] *Op. cit.*

Husband. Get up. A prayer like that does not reach God. You do not remember your mother. You cannot love her.

George. I see Mother very often:

and he tells his father that she appears when he is between sleeping and waking, and that the last time she was white and wasted, and sang to him this song :

> I wander everywhere,
> I enter everywhere,
> In the confines of the worlds,
> Where there are angels' songs:
> I gather up for thee
> The throngs of countless forms,
> Thoughts and inspired words,
> Oh, little child of mine!
>
> And from the highest souls,
> And from the lowest souls,
> Colours and shadowings,
> Sweet sounds and rays of light,
> I gather up for thee,
> That thou, my little son,
> Shalt be like those in heaven,
> And by thy father loved.

Husband (leaning on a pillar of the tomb). Marya, would you destroy your own child, burden me with two deaths? What am I saying? She is in heaven, tranquil and peaceful as she was during her life on earth. The poor child is only dreaming.

George. And now I hear her voice, but I see nothing... from those two larches on which the light of the setting sun is falling.

> I'll give thy lips to drink
> Of sound and power,
> I will adorn thy brow
> With ribands of bright light,
> And with a mother's love
> I'll wake in thee
> All that is beauty called
> By angels in heaven and man on earth,
> So that thy father may
> Love thee, my little son.

Husband. Do the last thoughts at death accompany the soul even when it reaches heaven? Can a spirit be happy, holy and mad at the same time?

George. Mother's voice is growing faint. It is nearly dying away behind the wall of the charnel house. Oh, there—there —she is still repeating:

> So that thy father may
> Love thee, my little son!

Husband. God, have pity on our child to whom it seems Thou in Thy wrath hast destined madness and an early death. Lord, tear not reason away from Thine own creation. Look on my torments, and do not give this little angel up to hell. Me at least Thou hast endowed with strength to bear up against a throng of thoughts, passions, and feelings, but Thou hast given him a body like a spider's web which each great thought shall tear asunder—oh, Lord God! oh, God! For ten years I have not had one day of peace. Thou hast sent down upon me a hail of sorrows and evanescent images, feelings and dreams. Thy grace has descended on my brain, not on my heart. Grant me to love my child in peace, and let there be harmony henceforth between the Creator and creature. Son, cross yourself and come with me. "Eternal rest."

This is the one moment, says Dr Kleiner, when it seems as though Henryk's heart were for once to guide him[1]. Henryk is no monster. He is not abnormal. His character throughout is drawn with the truth and consistency that give *The Undivine Comedy* its terrible power. Henryk is the idealist whose ideals remain on his lips, and who is ignorant of the struggle that, as Krasinski said in another place, of itself ennobles. Krasinski was too great an artist to drive Henryk into the unnatural extremity of a man without love for his one son[2]. He was also too close an observer of human nature to lend himself to such a situation. The indifference of a man of Henryk's stamp to his wife was a foregone conclusion: but the son was flesh of his flesh, the inheritor of his name. There is egoism, there is pose, in Henryk's intercourse with his son: but there is unfeigned love. His cry of anguish, when he calls

[1] J. Kleiner, *History of the Thought of Zygmunt Krasinski.*
[2] *Op. cit.*

upon the doctor to tell him if all hope is gone, rings true enough. And in this presentment of a father's love for the son whose life he yet ruined, Krasinski draws very tenderly upon his own father's relations with himself: the only intimacy of family affection that he who, as he once told Reeve, scarcely remembered what it was to have a mother, had ever known. Yet such paternal sentiment as is Henryk's cannot save him. In it he seeks himself, not his son. Self-dedication to a child suffering for the father's sin is no part of Henryk's programme.

We gather that in the years which are supposed to succeed the scene in the cemetery Henryk seeks for mental rest in the study of philosophy, and fruitlessly. Then we see him once more wandering in the mountains. The desires of his heart are returned in bitterness to his lips. His wife's prayer for her son is granted: the child is a poet, in whose madness the father must ever gaze upon the curse of poetry, the disordered adjustment of mental perception, that have ruined the lives of husband, wife and son.

"For many years," thus complains Henryk as he walks among the hills, " I have worked at the discovery of the last end of knowledge, thought and pleasure, and I have found— the emptiness of the grave in my heart. I know every feeling by name, and there is no desire, no faith, no love left in me. Only a few presentiments cross the waste—that my son will be blind, that the society in which I have grown up will be dissolved. And I suffer in the same way as God is happy, alone in myself, alone for myself."
Voice of the Angel Guardian. Love the sick, the starving, the despairing, and thou shalt be saved.

He does not listen. He still wanders, lamenting, in carefully picked words, that his child "for the sins of the father, the madness of the mother, is destined to eternal blindness." The demon, in the form of a black eagle, sweeps upon him, bidding him gird on the sword of his fathers and fight for their honour and power: promising him that his enemies, his "mean enemies," will crumble to dust before him. Here is the anticipation of the war of the universe, in which Henryk is to be the champion of his class. This is the lure of all others most calculated to ensnare him.

"Be thou what thou mayest," cries he, his vanity on fire: "false or true, victory or destruction, I will believe in thee, emissary of glory."

He flings away a viper that crosses his path.

"Go, mean reptile," says he contemptuously, regarding it as the emblem of the lower orders that are to rise against those who have held them in thrall. They shall be crushed, and perish unmourned and ingloriously even as this adder.

But before Henryk takes up his part as a soldier and leader of men, his domestic drama, together with the curse that has fallen upon the child, must be worked out. The short remaining scenes of this division of the play could not have been what they are were it not that Krasinski put into the figure of the blind, distraught child two facts of his own life. Almost blind himself while he was writing *The Undivine Comedy*, and under the terror of the lifelong and total darkness that then threatened him, Krasinski describes George's blindness from the internal evidence of personal experience. The other point, the son's inheritance from his mother of a sick brain, touched him closely also, although in the play he presented it under dimensions that were never approached in his own case. He, too, inherited from his mother an overstrained nervous fancy, that was the cause of intense suffering to him, and against which he was strongly warned by his father as against a hereditary disease. *The Undivine Comedy* may be looked upon, apart from its many other aspects, as a painful study of heredity.

The father has summoned the doctor to examine George's eyes. This doctor, with his formalism and his dry want of sympathy with what he considers merely an interesting case, is of a piece with the other personages in the grey world of Krasinski's drama.

Husband. Nothing has done him any good. My last hope is in you.

Doctor. I am greatly honoured.

Husband. Tell the gentleman what you feel.

George. I can't see you, father, or this gentleman any more. Sparks and black threads are running before my eyes[1]. Sometimes a thing like a little, thin snake comes out from them—and then it becomes a yellow cloud. The cloud flies up, then falls down, a rainbow breaks out of it. And that doesn't hurt me at all.

Doctor. Stand in the shade. *He looks at his eyes.* Now turn to the window. (*To George*) You can laugh at this. You will be as sound as I am. (*To the Husband*) There is no hope. There is an entire failure of the optic nerve.

George. A mist has come over everything—everything.

Doctor. His brain has ruined his body. Catalepsy is to be apprehended.

Husband (*leading the doctor aside*). All you ask—half my fortune.

Doctor. Disorganization cannot be reorganized.

Husband. Have pity on me, do not leave us yet.

Doctor. Perhaps you would be interested to know the name of this disease?

Husband. And is there no, no hope?

Doctor. It is called in Greek: amaurosis. (*He goes out.*)

Husband (*clasping his son to his breast*). But you do still see something?

George. I hear your voice, father.

[1] In letters to his friends Krasinski described his own blindness in exactly similar terms.

Husband. Look at the window. There is the sun, the beautiful weather.

George. A crowd of figures swarm between my eyes and eyelids. I see faces I have seen, places I know, pages of books I have read.

Husband. Then you do still see?

George. Yes, with the eyes of my soul, but the others have gone out.

The Husband falls on his knees. A moment's silence.

Husband. Before whom have I knelt? Where can I demand the redressal of my child's wrong? (*Rising.*) Rather let us keep silence. God laughs at prayers, Satan at curses.

Then again is heard the unknown, inexorable voice: " Thy son is a poet. What more dost thou desire?"

Now reappears the godfather, pompous and banal as ever. The years since we last saw him have left him unchanged. His type does not change.

"Certainly it is a great misfortune to be blind," is his brilliant remark to the doctor who has been called in to investigate the strange mental condition of the boy. " He had always a delicate constitution, and his mother died rather—rather—a bit cracked."

Husband (*entering*). I must apologize for calling you at such a late hour, but for some days my unfortunate son has waked about midnight, got up and talked in his sleep.

Doctor. I am very curious to see this phenomenon.

They go to the bedroom. The relations gather round to look on at another curious family spectacle and to comment on it in almost the same terms that they had used when watching the child's mother.

A Relation. Hush.

A Second. He has awakened, and doesn't hear us.

Doctor. Pray do not speak, gentlemen.

Godfather. This is a most extraordinary affair.

First Relation. How slowly he walks!

Another. His eyelids do not flicker. He scarcely opens his lips, and yet a shrill, long-drawn out voice comes from them.

Servants. Jesus of Nazareth!

George. Off from me, darkness! I was born the son of light and song. I will not yield myself to you, though my sight has fled with the winds and wanders somewhere in space: but it will one day return, rich in the rays of the stars, and will set my eyes aflame with its fires.

Godfather. He babbles, not knowing what he says, just like his dead mother. This is a very remarkable sight.

Doctor. I agree with you.

Nurse. Our most holy Lady of Czenstochowa, take my eyes and give them to him!

George. Oh, my mother, I beseech you, send me thoughts and pictures so that I can live within my soul, so that I can create a second world within myself, equal to the world that I have lost.

A Relation. Do you think, brother, this requires a family council?

George. You do not answer me. Oh, mother, do not leave me!

Doctor (to the Husband). It is my duty to tell you the truth.

Godfather. So it is. It is a duty—and the virtue of doctors.

Doctor. Your son's senses are disordered. He has conjointly an abnormal excitement of the nerves which often causes, so to say, a condition of being asleep and awake at the same time, a state similar to that which we see here.

Husband (aside). Oh, God, he seeks to explain Thy judgment.

The room is cleared. George wakes, hearing the confused goodnights of the departing guests. His father soothes him, tells him that the doctor has promised the return of his sight, and leads him back to bed with a tenderness he never showed his mother. The boy sleeps: and Henryk pours out over him the lamentation, partly sincere but partly turned with an artist's eye for effect, that brings the history of his private life to an end.

Let my blessing rest on thee. I can give thee nothing more, neither happiness, nor light, nor fame: and the hour has struck when I must go to war, when I must act with a few men against many. Where wilt thou take refuge, thou, alone, blind, powerless, child and poet in one, sad singer with none to listen to thee, thy soul living beyond the confines of the earth, and thy body chained to earth—oh, thou unhappy, unhappiest of angels, oh, thou my son?

CHAPTER VI

THE UNDIVINE COMEDY:
THE SOCIAL DRAMA

The second division of *The Undivine Comedy*, consisting of Parts III and IV, is devoted to the great upheaval of which we have at intervals caught the ground-swell in the foregoing scenes. The storm has burst, with no transition from the normal to the deluge: a transformation, the truth of which none of us who have witnessed the greatest cataclysm in history can deny.

In the third and fourth parts of the drama the world is nothing but a battlefield between the opposing classes of humanity. The representatives of the old order of things, or the aristocrats, with such dependents as care to remain with them, have been driven into their last stronghold, the fortress of the Trinity. The leader of a dying and rotten society is Henryk. We have called one division of *The Undivine Comedy* the domestic, and the other the social, drama: but in reality there is no cleavage between them. Henryk still figures under one name only, that of the "Husband." The curse of his marriage is always with him. The man who failed in every branch of his intimate life will fail in the mastery over other men. The poet who, to quote Klaczko's expression, " sought impressions, not truth[1]," will break down when confronted with the crisis. He plays the

[1] J. Klaczko, *Le Poète Anonyme de la Pologne.*

part he has longed to play, that of the commander of an army. Well-sounding phrases fall as usual from his lips; but he has none of the conviction of the justice of his cause that either sweeps all before it, or that takes the sting from defeat. He fights, knowing that his side is doomed, without the grandeur of a forlorn hope. At least he will be the chief actor on the world's stage till the curtain goes down for ever. More—he is a poet: and the picturesque trappings of tradition are with the past. There is no artistic beauty in a future represented by a mob of infuriated men and women, haggard with toil and want.

The opponent to Henryk is the man of action, Pankracy. Where Henryk is the impersonation of imagination without heart, Pankracy is that of cold reason, equally without heart. With no family ties to sweeten life, he has dragged himself up from childhood in poverty and misery. His strength is in his will and brain, in the compelling and ruthless mind that no softer influence can bend aside. That such a man will gain the day over Henryk is self-evident. His triumph is doubly assured from the character of their respective followers. Henryk's party consists of mere inert decadents, whereas the revolutionaries have behind them the strength of rage and ferocity. But in Krasinski's system the heart is the creative and life-giving power of humanity. Without it, the mind can only bring forth inefficiency and destruction. Therefore like Henryk, Pankracy has neither faith nor fire. The grandeur of a noble ideal and its wholehearted service is looked for in vain from *The Undivine Comedy*. Were it there the play would be false to its name and intention. This is in part the explanation of Pankracy's secret moments of vacillation: but also, as Mickiewicz remarks, how many great leaders have not known doubt of their own cause at given instants[1]!

The prologue to the third part, the least happy of the four prologues, gives a sketch of the revolutionary camp and a short description of the person of Pankracy, of his icy face and his strange magnetism over his followers. Here we see too one of his Jewish adherents. These, in reality, are only biding their time to turn with fury against their new masters. When the third part begins, the bloody work of Pankracy's camp is in full swing. Certain of these scenes are based on those of the French Revolution. This part of the drama has also for a foundation Krasinski's ideas on the logical conclusions of Saint-Simonism. Knives are being sharpened for the massacre of the nobles, cords prepared by which they shall swing on the gallows. Pankracy has despatched a Jew to treat with Henryk for a secret interview. Leonard, the youth who alone of all the personages in *The Undivine Comedy* is possessed of true ardour, brutal as it is in its manifestations, enters Pankracy's tent and reproaches him with his inaction.

What is the use of these half measures, these negotiations? When I swore to admire you and to listen to you it was because I held you for the hero of latter times, for the eagle flying straight at his aim, for the man staking himself and all his on one card.

Pankracy. Silence, boy.

Leonard. All are ready. The Jews have forged weapons and woven cords. The crowds are shouting and calling for the command. Give the command, and it will run like a spark, like lightning, and change into flame and pass into a thunderbolt.

Pankracy. The blood is mounting to your head. It is the consequence of your age, and you do not know how to cope with it, and you call it enthusiasm.

[1] A. Mickiewicz, *Les Slaves.*

Leonard. The feeble aristocracy have shut themselves up in the Trinity, and are awaiting our arrival like the knife of the guillotine. Forward without delay, and have done with them!

Pankracy. It is all the same. They have lost their physical strength in pleasures, their mental strength in sloth. To-morrow, or the day after to-morrow, they must perish.

Leonard. Of whom are you afraid? Who is keeping you back?

Pankracy. No one. Only my will.

Leonard. You are betraying us.

Pankracy. Like a refrain in a song, so treason comes in at the end of every speech of yours. Don't shout, because if any-one overheard us—

Leonard. No spies are here, and what if they were?

Pankracy. Nothing—only five balls in your breast, because you dared to raise your voice one note higher in my presence. Believe me. Be at peace.

Leonard. I confess I was carried away: but I am not afraid of the penalty. If my death can serve as an example, and add strength and weight to our cause, command it.

Pankracy. You are full of life, full of hope, and you believe sincerely. Happiest of men, I will not deprive you of life.

Pankracy has set his mind upon meeting Henryk in a private conference, ostensibly to win him over to his side, in reality because if he can convince the one man who stands in opposition to him he can convince himself.

"Why," so he soliloquizes in solitude, "does that one man stand in the way of me, the leader of thousands? His strength is little in comparison with mine—a few hundred peasants, blindly be-lieving his word, attached to him with the love of their domestic beasts. He is a wretched being, he is a cypher. Why do I long to see him, to lure him over? Is it that my spirit has met its equal and has halted for a moment? He is the last obstacle against me in these plains. He must be overthrown, and then —My mind, why canst thou not deceive thyself as thou de-ceivest others? Shame on thee, for thou knowest thine aim; thou art mind—the ruler of the people. In thee is gathered the will and power of all, and what is a crime for others is thy glory. Thou hast given names to mean, unknown men. Thou hast given a faith to men without feeling. Thou hast created a new world around thee; and thou thyself wanderest and knowest not what thou art. No, no! Thou art great."

Meanwhile, Henryk is in his element. He is in a

position to attract all eyes. He goes to the war not from any sense of honour or obligation, but as to a wild and romantic poem[1]. He re-enters the scene, disguised in a heavy cloak, with the red cap of liberty on his head, compelling a Jew to guide him through the hostile camp and show him all there is to be seen. This journey where the poet is led by a double-faced traitor through what Dr Kallenbach calls the Walpurgis-night of a brutal, revolting humanity is, says the same writer, an ironical travesty of Dante's pilgrimage with Virgil in *The Divine Comedy*, and the motive of Krasinski's change of title from the original one, *The Husband*, to that of the comedy that was not divine[2].

Henryk and the Jew are concealed in a wood, near a meadow where a gibbet has been erected. Tents are pitched. Camp fires are blazing. The bottle passes from hand to hand. One by one, bands of the different classes of men and women who have been victims for centuries of tyranny and greed, come out and dance around the gibbet, singing and clamouring for blood.

Bread, money, wood to burn in winter, rest in summer! Hurrah! Hurrah! God did not have pity on us. Kings did not have pity on us. The lords did not have pity on us. To-day we will return thanks to God, kings and lords for our service.

Husband (*to a girl*). I am glad you are so rosy and merry.

Girl. Well, and it's because we've waited long for such a day. I was always washing plates, scouring forks with a dish-cloth. I never heard a kind word. And now it is time, time, that I myself should eat, I myself should dance.

Husband. Dance, citizeness.

Jew (*softly*). For pity's sake, your illustrious lordship. Somebody might recognize you.

Husband. If anybody recognizes me, then you will die. Let us go on further.

---

[1] J. Klaczko, *Le Poète Anonyme de la Pologne.*
[2] J. Kallenbach, *Zygmunt Krasinski.*

It is the turn of the lackeys. One boasts he has killed his old master, another is looking for his to inflict the same punishment upon him. "Citizens,"cries a valet, "we, bent over a boot-tree in sweat and humiliation, polishing boots, trimming hair, we have felt our rights."

With wild, hoarse cries a troop of butchers comes next, clamouring for blood, no matter whose it is, whether that of cattle slaughtered for the lords, or that of the lords slaughtered for the people. And in the world revolution that Krasinski foresaw it is not merely the savage instincts of the human race that are let loose: moral shackles must also go. A woman boasts to Henryk that she is free at last, and that she owes society a debt of gratitude for having released her from her husband, who was "my enemy, the enemy of freedom, who kept me in bonds."

She is left behind: and there is the brief episode of the *condottiere* of the people, Bianchetti, absorbed in his plans for taking the fortress of the Trinity. He refuses to confide them to Henryk, his apparent comrade in arms. "Though you are my brothers in liberty," he says haughtily, "you are not my brothers in genius."

"I advise you to kill him," Henryk says to the Jew, "because every aristocracy begins like that." These few lines show how barren of its end the revolution will be. One aristocracy will perish; another, if even of a different order, will rise in its place.

Into Henryk's words breaks a piteous cry from a poor, broken old man, a silk weaver.

Cursed be the merchants, the directors of factories. My best years, when other men love women, fight on the open field, sail on the open seas, I spent in a narrow room, bent over a silk-loom.

Husband. Empty the bottle you hold in your hand.

Artisan. I have not got the strength to do it. I cannot raise it to my lips. I have scarcely been able to crawl here, but the day of freedom will not dawn now for me. Cursed be the merchants who sell the silk and the lords who wear the silk. *He dies.*

"Where are your fine words now," says Henryk with contempt to his despised companion, "your promises—equality, the perfection and happiness of the human race?"

It is for the satisfaction of his curiosity and by way of doing a daring thing that Henryk is in his enemies' camp, not for any military purpose. An unmoved spectator, he stands and looks on at his brother nobles being dragged off to the gallows by the crowds of peasants who have suffered wrong at their hands: unmoved, because, by his own showing, he despises his own class and hates the one below him. No thought of sympathy crosses him for the oppressed whose sufferings once meant something to him. After *The Undivine Comedy* was published, Krasinski wrote a species of prose drama which he was never able to complete, in which we are given the history of Henryk's youth. There he is an enthusiastic dreamer, who is led on a pilgrimage through the sorrows of the world which it is his hope one day to relieve. The intermediate stages are missing: till in *The Undivine Comedy* we have the mournful indication of the gulf between the idealist's beginning and his end.

From the power and the pathos with which Krasinski represents the unhappy toilers of the earth who have had nothing out of life save grinding and uncheered labour, hour in, hour out, we see clearly enough that it was neither from aristocratic prejudice, nor from any lack of the deepest compassion for the misery of the poor, that Krasinski could find only matter for dread in the coming revolution. In that revolution he foresaw, not the amelioration of suffering, but the annihilation of moral law. He foresaw it as a necessity before the dawn that at this time he only dimly, in comparison with his later vision, perceived would rise behind it. The laws of religion and morality must first run riot: and hence the scenes watched by Henryk and his guide of the orgies ushering in new and degraded rites on the overthrowal of Christ's altars, which Krasinski based on what he considered the logical consequences of the teaching of Saint-Simonism.

"Eagle, keep thy promise," murmurs Henryk, as he hears the blasphemies around him, and gazes on the horrible profanations which, led by Leonard as the high-priest of the new religion, are being perpetrated in the ruins of the last cathedral to fall beneath the axes of the rebels, that have swept away every church from the face of the earth. "On their shoulders I will raise a new church to Christ." In the spectacle of unspeakable outrage on which he has been gazing Henryk has found another stepping-stone to his ambition. He will restore God's Church, not as her son but as her patron.

I will express this new, mighty world in one word. That word of mine shall be the poetry of all the future.

And again the voice he has heard before rings above his head: "Thou composest a drama."

The day is dawning. Henryk turns to leave the enemy's camp. Unearthly lamentations of the spirits who have "kept guard over the altars and monuments of the saints, who have carried the echo of the bells on their wings to the faithful, whose voices were in the music of the organs," follow him.

We weep for Christ...Where is our God? Where is His Church?

Husband. Faster, faster to the sword, to battle! I will give Him back to you. I will crucify His enemies on a thousand crosses. Jesus and my sword!

Voices in the bushes. Mary and our swords! Long life to our lord!

Husband. Follow me! Follow me! Jesus and Mary!

And henceforth Henryk becomes the champion of Christianity. Often before this scene the language of some sort of piety has been surprised on Henryk's lips ; and yet it might have seemed as though a man of his stamp would have rather chosen a species of refined agnosticism as his appropriate setting. Had Krasinski adopted this perfectly obvious treatment part at least of the terrible truth with which he presents Henryk would have been sacrificed. Henryk's is the type of a lip religion. He talks in exquisite phraseology of the sacred things which have no bearing on the conduct of his daily life. He will freely utter the old Polish battle cry of *Jesus and Mary* or the name of God when the poetry of the situation demands it: as his defence against moral fall, never. Religion in his conception adds beauty to the world. It is picturesque. It is, besides, his aristocratic inheritance that descends to him with his great name and estates. His pose is to be something in the nature of a crusader. Atheism he leaves to Pankracy, to the vulgar. For one moment we saw him take a poetical excursion into the regions of scepticism when rebelling against his son's fate: but this was obviously one of his situations, and holds no particle of the agony that broke the heart of Mickiewicz's Konrad when grief for his nation drove him into blasphemy.

The hour has struck for the secret midnight interview

between Henryk and Pankracy. Henryk awaits his opponent in a palatial hall of the castle, drawn from Krasinski's memories of his own home. The portraits of Henryk's ancestors hang around the walls; his armorial bearings shine on a pillar; silver goblets and tankards glitter on the tables.

" In a moment will stand before me," soliloquizes Henryk to imaginary spectators, " the man without a name, without ancestors, who rose from nothingness, and perchance will begin a new epoch if I do not thrust him down into nothingness. My ancestors, inspire me with what made you the rulers of the world !...Let descend upon me a blind, inexorable, burning faith in Christ and His Church, the inspiration of your deeds on earth, the hope of immortal glory in heaven: and I will slay the enemies, I, the son of a hundred generations, the last inheritor of your thoughts and deeds, your virtues and your errors. (*Midnight strikes.*) Now am I ready."

Pankracy is led in, and he and Henryk are left alone together.

Pankracy. I greet Count Henryk. That word "Count" sounds strangely in my throat. (*He fixes his eyes on the pillar where the coat of arms hangs.*) If I am not mistaken, those red and blue badges are called coats of arms in the language of the dead. There are ever fewer such little dots on the surface of the earth.

Husband. With the help of God you will shortly see thousands of them.

Pankracy. There is my old nobility—always sure of themselves, proud, obstinate, flourishing with hope, and without a farthing, without a weapon, without soldiers, believing, or pretending that they believe, in God, because it would be difficult to believe in themselves. But show me the thunderbolts sent down in your defence, and the regiments of angels from heaven.

Husband. Laugh at your own words. Atheism is an old formula, and I expected something new from you.

Pankracy. Laugh at your own words. I have a stronger, mightier faith than yours. The groan torn by despair and pain from thousands of thousands, the hunger of artisans, the misery of peasants, the shame of their wives and daughters,

The Undivine Comedy   125

the degradation of humanity: that is my faith and my God for
to-day.

Husband. I have placed my strength in the God Who
gave the rule to my ancestors.

Pankracy. And all your life you have been the plaything
of the devil. But I leave the rest of this discourse to theo-
logians if some pedant of that trade still exists in the country.
To business! I came here, because I wanted to know you, and,
secondly, to save you.

Husband. I am obliged to you for the first. The second,
leave to my sword.

Pankracy. Your sword is glass, your God is a dream. You
are condemned by the voice of thousands, you are hemmed
round with the arms of thousands. A few spans of earth
remain yours that will scarcely suffice for your graves. You
cannot defend yourselves twenty days. Where are your cannon,
your stores, your provisions—and, finally, where is your
courage?

His insults, says Henryk, escape with impunity only
because the aristocrat has given his word that the
leader of the people shall leave his roof unscathed.

"Knightly honour has come upon the scene," sneers
Pankracy. "It is a worn-out rag on the banner of humanity.
Oh! I know you. You are full of life, and you ally yourself
with the dying, because you want to deceive yourself, because
you still want to believe in caste, in the bones of your great-
grandmothers, in the word 'my country': but in the depths
of your heart you know yourself that the penalty is owing to
your brethren, and after the penalty, oblivion."

Husband. And what else is there for you and yours?

Pankracy. Victory and life. I recognize only one law. It
is your destruction. It cries by my lips; "Decrepit worms,
full of food and drink, yield to the young, the hungry and
the strong."

Pankracy then speaks of the new epoch that is to
be born from his word, when the earth shall be rich
and flourishing from pole to pole, man free, great and
happy. But that the true fire is not in him we gather
from Henryk's rejoinder: "Your words lie, but your
unmoved, pale countenance cannot counterfeit inspira-

tion." Still Pankracy knows how to appeal not only to the ambition of the poet, but to that in him which was once, long ago, noble.

" If you would attain immortality," he says, "if you love truth and have sought it sincerely, if you are a man in the pattern of humanity, not in the fashion of nursery fables, do not throw away this moment of salvation. Not a trace will remain to-morrow of the blood which we will both shed to-day. If you are what you once seemed, forsake your house and come with me."

For the first time Henryk wavers. His wish to see the man of those dreams that had once been his was not mere curiosity : it was a desire to gaze, as it were, upon his own marred face[1]. Pankracy's words recall to his memory the visions of a long past day. The higher voices to which he had listened in his now doubly dead youth call faintly to him once more. He rises. He paces the room, murmuring to himself in broken whispers: "Vain dreams! Who shall fulfil them ? Progress, the happiness of the human race—and I once believed in them." Is there here an undertone of real, if fruitless, regret for his ruined self? Pankracy, watching the transitory struggle as the caustic spectator, congratulates himself that he has " touched the nerve of poetry"; proof that for his part his language had not been actuated by sincere and passionate faith.

Both Pankracy ànd Henryk, as is apparent from their respective taunts, know that his adversary is doubting within himself. No spark of truth, says Klaczko, comes out in either[2]. In the midst of what appears an out-burst of real emotion Pankracy betrays himself by the admission that he has succeeded in playing upon Hen-ryk's poetical fancy. The duologue must end where it

---

[1] J. Klaczko, *Le Poète Anonyme de la Pologne.*   [2] *Op. cit.*

began. *The Undivine Comedy* is not to tell of success, but of failure, of negation. With contempt Henryk rejects Pankracy's proposal, and makes mockery of his base birth. With equal contempt, Pankracy points to the portraits of Henryk's ancestors, and rakes up the scandals of each. The interview concludes merely with a mutual bandying of words. The final issue will be played out on the ramparts of the Trinity.

Part IV opens with a short prose poem descriptive of the morning breaking over the doomed castle. Mickiewicz, himself a master of word painting, likens its effects of light, mist and cloud to a canvas of Salvator Rosa[1]. In preparation for the last struggle Henryk is solemnly blessed as the leader by the Archbishop, while choirs of priests sing, and Henryk's brother nobles watch coldly and grudgingly.

First Count. See with what pride he looks on us all!
Second. He thinks he has subjugated the world.
Third. And he only got through a camp of peasants in the night.

All swear in reply to his harangue—the usual one on such occasions—that they will be faithful to him till death. Yet where will such resolution be found in this effete band? Krasinski's loss of faith in the society of his generation and his sense of its demoralization are openly expressed in these closing scenes of *The Undivine Comedy*. Yet Krasinski himself was a son of one of the most courageous races in Europe, and when he wrote *The Undivine Comedy* the spectacle was still recent of Polish men and women shedding their life-blood, parting with every joy in life, for their country's sake. The craven, time-serving aristocrats of *The Undivine*

[1] Adam Mickiewicz, *Les Slaves*.

Comedy are not Polish types. As we have said before there is nothing national in the play. Indeed the absence of Polish colouring in the depictment of character is the one reproach that Mickiewicz makes against *The Undivine Comedy.*

All hope of victory is gone. The nobles gather round Henryk. One whispers to him :

What, is all lost then ?
Husband. Not all—unless your hearts fail you before the time.
Count. What time ?
Husband. Death.
Baron (leading him to the other side). Count, you have probably seen that dreadful man. Will he have if only a little mercy on us when we fall into his hands ?
Husband. I tell you truthfully that none of your ancestors ever heard of a mercy like that. It is called the gallows.
Baron. We must defend ourselves as best we can.
Prince. Two words with you in private. All that is good for the common people, but between ourselves it is obvious that we cannot resist. You have been chosen leader, and therefore it is your business to open negotiations.
Husband (turning to the crowd). Who mentions surrender will be punished by death.
Baron, Count, Prince (all together). Who mentions surrender will be punished by death.

Although Henryk knows that his doom is close upon him, he still delights in his lordship. The sinking sun, as he watches it from the towers of the fort, seems to him the fiery and fit ending to his life in the wild glory of which he had always dreamt.

I stand here on the boundaries of the eternal sleep, the leader of all those who yesterday were my equals.

And on these words breaks once more the avenger of that past from which the husband and father cannot escape, the witness to his eternal failure—the blind boy. He has heard without fear or interest the sounds of the

The Undivine Comedy
129

battle raging round the walls of the fortress. His heart
is not with outer things, it is in his visions: and it is
there that the delicately strung soul, incapable of coping
with the tempests of the world, will take refuge[1].
Everything about this unhappy child is weak. Even
his religion, notes Klaczko, is not his mother's deep
piety. It partakes more of the nature of his father's
poetizing, a thin, sentimental stream from which he can
draw no strength either for himself or a battling world[2].
His very end is pointless. He falls a useless sacrifice
to a random shot[3].

He leads Henryk into the subterranean caverns of
the fortress.

Do you not hear their voices, do you not see their forms?
Husband. There is the silence of the grave, and the torch
lights but a few steps before us.
George. Ever nearer, ever clearer, they come from under
the narrow vaults.
Husband. In your madness is my curse. You are mad,
child: and you are destroying my strength at the moment I
most need it.
George. I see their pale forms assembling for the dreadful
judgment. The prisoner advances. He has wrung his hands.
Husband. Who is he?
George. Oh, father, father!
Choir. Because thou hast loved nought, because thou hast
worshipped nought but thyself, thou art damned—damned for
all eternity.

The eyes of the child then see the vision of Henryk
being tortured.

"I hear your groans," cries he, falling on his knees at his
father's feet. "Father, forgive me. In the middle of the night
my mother came to me and bade me "—*He faints.*
Husband. Only this was wanting. My own child has led
me to the threshold of hell. Marya! Inexorable spirit! There
begins the eternity of torments and of darkness. I must still
fight with men. Afterwards the eternal war.

[1] J. Klaczko, *Le Poète Anonyme de la Pologne.* [2] *Ibid.* [3] *Ibid.*

He leaves the vaults, while the spirit voices wail after him :

Because thou hast loved nought, worshipped nought save thyself, thou art damned—damned for all eternity.

The starving inhabitants of the besieged fortress throng round the leader, clamouring to him to make terms. The godfather, who has no mind to face extremities, has taken upon himself to treat with the revolutionaries.

All my life has been a true citizen's, and I do not heed your reproaches, Henryk. If I have undertaken the office of envoy, it is because I understand my century and know how to appreciate its worth.

Turning to the crowd, the baron, the prince and the rest of them who are all prepared to save their skins by going over to Pankracy, he tells them : " The great man who has sent me promises your lives on the condition that you join him and acknowledge the tendency of the age."

"We do acknowledge it," they cry. Yet it wants only a few words from Henryk, whose rôle is that of the glorious champion who will die but not yield, and the appearance of an armed band of his soldiers, and once more the waverers are more or less with him again. For the moment the enemy is driven off : but it is with the last shots of the defenders. Henryk's servant comes to tell him that there is no more powder, no more bullets.

"Then bring me my son," says Henryk, "that I may embrace him once again."

The servant leads in the blind boy.

Come, son. Put your hand in mine. Touch my lips with your forehead. Your mother's forehead was once as white and soft.

George. I heard her voice to-day, and she said : " This evening thou shalt be sitting with me."

Husband. Did she so much as mention my name?
George. She said: "This evening I expect my son."
Husband (*aside*). Will my strength fail me at the end of the road? Oh, God, permit it not! For one moment of courage Thou shalt have me as Thy prisoner for all eternity. (*Aloud*) Oh, son, forgive me that I gave you life. You will forget me among the angelic choirs. Oh, George, George, oh, my son!

A shot resounds, and George lies dead at his father's feet. The father seizes his sword and, shouting to his men, rushes into the hopeless combat. The enemy are in the castle. Henryk's followers are slain : the remaining defenders of the fortress fall on their knees before the victor, whining for mercy. Pankracy's soldiers run through the castle, looking for Henryk. Covered with blood, he stands on the angle of the bastion that overhangs the precipice.

I see it all black, floating towards me in spaceless tracts of darkness, my eternity without shores, without end, and in its midst God as a sun that shines eternally—and lights nothing. (*He takes a step forward.*) They are running. They have seen me.

And with the words : "Jesus, Mary!"—on his lips the romantic call to battle of his ancestors rather than the last prayer of the departing soul—crying, "Poetry, be thou cursed by me as I shall be cursed for all eternity," with his arms flung out as the swimmer about to take his plunge, he leaps into the abyss.

Pankracy is left apparently the conqueror of the field. He sits in judgment in the castle court, condemning to death each wretched survivor of the aristocrats as they appear before him in chains, in a scene that is the reflection of the revolutionary tribunals of the French Revolution. He then leads Leonard to the bastions and, standing on the spot where Henryk perished, points to the world he has won.

Gaze on those vast tracts. I must people those deserts, tunnel through those rocks, divide out land to each man.

Leonard. The god of liberty will give us strength.

Pankracy. Why do you speak of God? It is slippery here from human blood. Whose blood is it? We are alone, and it seems to me as if some third were here.

For now the hour of his defeat is upon him also. He points to the mountains, and cries in terror:

See you there on high—on high?

Leonard. I see over the rugged mountain peak a drooping cloud in which the rays of the sun are going out.

Pankracy. A terrible sign is flaming over it. Women and children have babbled fables that He shall thus appear, but not until the last day.

Leonard. Who?

Pankracy. Like a pillar of snow-white brilliance He stands above the precipices. Both hands lean on a cross as an avenger's on his sword. Of woven thunderbolts is His crown of thorns. From the lightning of that look he must die who lives. Lay your hands on my eyes. Smother my eyeballs with your fists. Part me from that look which shatters me to dust. Your hands are transparent as water—transparent as glass—transparent as air. I see still.

Leonard. Lean on me.

Pankracy. Give me if only a crumb of darkness.

Leonard. Oh, my master!

Pankracy. Darkness—darkness!

Leonard. Hey, citizens! brothers! democrats! Help, help, help!

Pankracy. Galilaee, vicisti! (*He falls into Leonard's arms and expires.*)

So ends this powerful and painful drama—ruin and failure are all that is left in a world whence every known landmark has been swept away. Krasinski discerned no hope for the future in either of the two hostile principles between which he saw mankind divided. He beheld a truth greater than either, and above both[1]. Therefore the leader of a cause that held no germ of life

[1] Adam Mickiewicz, *Les Slaves.*

in its bosom dies in a final act of despair. Therefore the leader of the opposing cause, at the moment of a triumph that could not endure because he had nothing to give the human race in the place of what he had taken from it, is struck down, witness to a power that had conquered his. And yet the final, scathing apparition of the Crucified, terrible to the eyes of the man who had denied Him, casting a light more lurid than that of the blood-red sunset over a ruined world, does not remove that impression of chaos, of universal desolation upon which *The Undivine Comedy* closes. Christ here appears an image of terror : an avenger, not a saviour. Still the fact that the drama ends with that last testimony to His triumph holds the link that would otherwise be hard to find between *the Undivine Comedy* and Krasinski's subsequent work—*Dawn*, the *Psalms of the Future*, *Resurrecturis*—where the weariness and pessimism of the Anonymous Poet's first great masterpiece are unknown.

"This poem," said Mickiewicz, "is the cry of despair of a man of genius who recognizes the greatness, the difficulty of social questions"; without being able to solve them[1]. At the moment that Krasinski wrote *The Undivine Comedy* socialistic dreams were widespread among the Polish youth, who saw in some universal social convulsion the only hope for their nation in the terrible conditions under which she was then labouring. Krasinski never shrank from boldly proclaiming what he deemed a salutary truth, however unwelcome : and thus in the midst of Utopian theories were heard the warning accents of an *Undivine Comedy*[2]. Years after

---

[1] Adam Mickiewicz, *Les Slaves.*
[2] J. Klaczko, *Le Poète Anonyme de la Pologne.*

it came out, with the strange impersonality of one who had spoken sinister prophecies because he was constrained to speak them, Krasinski in letters to friends pointed to the European revolutions through which he lived as the fulfilment of what he had foretold in his youth[1]. Klaczko has finely said that *The Undivine Comedy* is:

a farewell rather than a greeting addressed by the poet to humanitarian inspirations, a strong protest against the fatal illusion of the age which believes it can regenerate humanity without having first regenerated man, and establish universal right without having first strengthened the individual in his duties[2].

[1] Krasinski seldom in his correspondence alludes to his works, and when he does so it is almost exclusively under their moral and national aspect. The *Undivine* is that one which he most often mentions. There is a curious passage in one of his letters to Cieszkowski illustrating this impartial outlook upon his *Undivine Comedy*. In 1848 he was startled by hearing his little son repeating prophecies of great evil to befall France that he told his father he had heard from God during the night. " It reminded me," says Krasinski, "of the *Undivine* and George—and I went away sad." *Letters of Zygmunt Krasinski to August Cieszkowski*. Baden, Dec. 3, 1848. Cracow, 1912 (Polish).

[2] J. Klaczko, *op. cit.* There is in English literature a feeble reflection of *The Undivine Comedy* in Owen Meredith's *Orval*. Lord Lytton read a French rendering of Krasinski's drama, and made a species of transcription from it into English. The result is that while the plot and the arrangement of the scenes remain more or less the same, the English play, particularly in its utter loss of the stern conciseness that gives *The Undivine Comedy* its strength, is so unlike the Polish original that it cannot be considered even in the nature of a rough translation.

CHAPTER VII

IRIDION

Krasinski spent the winter of 1833–34 in Rome. He had destroyed in Warsaw all that he had already written of *Iridion*: but back in the Eternal City, where the ruins of an empire spoke with eloquence to the Pole's heart of the downfall of brute force, the figure of his Greek, nursing implacable revenge under the eyes of the Caesars, obsessed him: his "Thought," as he always called it.

"For a whole year it has given me no rest," he wrote to his father from Rome. "Here it has appeared to me. Here I have seen my Iridion, walking in the Forum ; I do not create him any longer, I only observe him. That man walks with me through all the ruins[1]."

He wrote thus in 1833 : but it was not until 1836 that *Iridion* was published. A disastrous passion robbed its author of the power to finish the play. In the early months of 1834 he met in Rome Joanna Bobrowa. She was a married woman, five years his senior and the mother of two children. His affection for Henrietta Willan and Amelia Załuska had been in the nature of a schoolboy sentiment : but now he fell headlong into the white heat of passion for her who, as he once told his father, had first loved him because he was unhappy[2]. Giving an account of himself to Reeve the summer

---

[1] Given by Dr Kallenbach, *Zygmunt Krasinski*.
[2] J. Kallenbach, *Zygmunt Krasinski*.

after he had first known Mme Bobrowa, he tells him
how he had that spring felt a wild craving for life and
action from which his physical health debarred him,
and that he had found them in his love[1].

At this time begins Krasinski's spiritual wavering.
We know from his introductory lines to *Dawn* that it
was the fate of his country that first shook his religious
faith : but his unlawful love contributed likewise to its
weakening. Both he and the woman who loved him
had too deep-seated a religious sense not to be torn by
bitter self-reproach. Krasinski's remorse and misery
increased with the lapse of time, especially after Mme
Bobrowa was compromised in the eyes of the world and
estranged from her husband. But at the outset it was
the impossibility of reconciling his passion for her
with the precepts of the Church to which he belonged,
and the fact that the tortures of conscience increased
both his, and in a still greater measure Mme Bobrowa's,
sufferings, that combined to turn him to a certain
extent against the faith in which he had been brought
up. Moreover, to justify the falsity of his own moral
position he was driven to warp those high spiritual
precepts in which he had once found strength.

" Physical pain," he writes to Reeve, " makes you return to
God...But moral pain repulses, separates, you from heaven...
You will be astonished, Henry, to hear the man speak thus
who formerly believed and hoped so much in God ; but I have
travelled fast on a fatal road. Oh! if you know where there
is a ray of hope, a new dawn, a faith young and able to fill my
heart, tell me[2]!"

Yet Krasinski's complex character is a mass of
contradictions. Not long after he had expressed him-

---

[1] *Correspondance.* Krasinski to Reeve. Wiesbaden, Aug 25, 1834.
[2] *Ibid.* Rome, Nov. 12, 1834.

self thus to Reeve, to whom earlier in the year he had written that : " For five months," namely, since he first loved Mme Bobrowa, " I have not said a single prayer : and yet I feel no remorse, so strong in me was that necessity for action which has driven me to love with all my faculties, to look for salvation where others find death[1]" ; he writes to Gaszynski :

> What I do congratulate you on from my heart is that you have returned to God. There is nothing else for man in the world than to believe and love...Since some time I have grown cold. My faith is not destroyed, but has slept[2].

The history of Krasinski's love was retailed in its fulness to neither Reeve nor Gaszynski[3], but to another Pole, Adam Sołtan, who, through the Radziwiłłs, was related to Krasinski. Belonging to a family that had distinguished itself for generations by its patriotism, Sołtan commanded a regiment during the Polish Rising, and was driven into exile at its close. The Russian government confiscated his estates, and took his five children from him. His young sons—the youngest a child of three years old—were carried off to Petersburg to be brought up by the Russian state. His daughters were placed in a convent of their own religion, where the Russian authorities kept them under supervision. Sołtan's father, already parted from his son, died of grief on the loss of his grandchildren. Sołtan himself

---

[1] *Correspondance.* Krasinski to Reeve. Wiesbaden, Aug. 25, 1834.

[2] *Letters to Gaszynski.* Naples, March 29, 1835.

[3] Krasinski's silence upon the subject in his correspondence with Gaszynski may be accounted for by Dr Kallenbach's conjecture that Gaszynski suppressed for publication all those passages relating to it; for, as Krasinski chose to tell Reeve with whom his friendship was fast waning part at least of what was filling his heart, it is very improbable that Gaszynski, one of his dearest friends to the last, was not confided in far more fully.

passed his years in exile, bereft of his children, forbidden to hold any communication with them, racked by anxiety for their fate[1]. His upright character, his peculiarly sympathetic nature, no less than his sorrows, gained for him Krasinski's undying affection. The sufferings of those whom Krasinski loved were as his own, their interests his. He spared no pains to use the General's influence in gathering for his friend every scrap of information that could be gleaned concerning the sons, and to give the children in their turn news of their father: and it was he who finally brought about the restoration to Soltan of the only daughter who survived. Krasinski's trust in this beloved friend was unbounded. To him he confided without reserve all that passage of his life which we have now reached. Meeting Mme Bobrowa in the summer of 1835, after the winter's absence: "perhaps," writes Krasinski to Soltan, " you will be pleased to hear that he who loves you has reached paradise, and writes to you from paradise[2]." Again to Soltan he wrote in a very different strain a month later when, the affection between himself and Mme Bobrowa having become the subject of public comment, Krasinski compelled himself for the sake of her good name to leave Ischl where she was staying.

I felt a sacred duty, the stern necessity of going away, so as not to injure her honour. She entreated me to stay, because above all things she loved. But it had to be: I left, cursing the

[1] St. Tarnowski, *Zygmunt Krasinski*.

[2] *Ibid.* Those letters of Krasinski that concern Mme Bobrowa are not printed in the published collection of the Soltan correspondence, *Letters of Zygmunt Krasinski.* Vol. II. *To Adam Soltan.* Lwów, 1883 (Polish). They are given in the first instance by Count Tarnowski in his monograph and are quoted also by Dr Kallenbach.

world and the base and wretched people who revenge themselves on those who feel, because they themselves feel nothing…I left her in despair: such, Adam, is the end of my paradise. I am as one damned. I never loved before: I did not know what love is…To-day I walk the scorched pavement of this town, and I would fain lie down on it and die, such pain does each moment without her cause me. If there were some faults, God will forgive us. It is hard to struggle as much as she does, to love and respect as much as I do[1].

And a little later, while she was in Trieste, he in Venice, he writes to Sołtan in similar language, execrating those who condemned the woman without knowing or caring how she had fought against herself, and acknowledging that he felt driven to suicide[2]. Then, shortly before the moment of parting:

You have no idea of what I have suffered. How happy I was likewise few could know. But it was that kind of happiness which destroys rather than augments strength. From all this has remained what is dearest to me, namely, the thought that there is no nobler woman on earth…Ah! what is poisoning my life is that she insists on returning to her house. Her husband knows all. She herself wrote it to him. So she knows what is awaiting her. But she considers it her duty to take her children to her husband and to suffer. She sees in this a species of expiation[3]."

Count Tarnowski here notices that, culpable as both had been, neither of these "suffering and struggling" human beings was wanting in nobility. The woman voluntarily chose her penalty. The man reverenced the action which destroyed his own happiness[4]. The short-lived rapture that Krasinski's love had brought him was now over. Until the final break in 1838 it was to be agony and remorse.

During this time Krasinski had written *Iridion*, "which," as he told Reeve, "torn up three times, ten

[1] St. Tarnowski, *Zygmunt Krasinski*.
[2] *Ibid.*   [3] *Ibid.*   [4] *Ibid.*

times broken off either by my sufferings or by my passions, for three years has not ceased to torture my brain[1]."

From Venice he went in the September of 1835 to Vienna. While waiting there with Danielewicz to see once more Mme Bobrowa on her way to her husband in Poland, before the emotions of those farewell weeks with her impeded him, aggravated as they were by the false position in which he stood and by the remonstrances of his friend, he finished the drama. Both it and *The Undivine Comedy*, which latter was written before he had known her, but published later, were dedicated to Mme Bobrowa : and it is said that she is the original of Cornelia in *Iridion*.

Iridion is the Anonymous Poet's first direct appeal to his nation. We have seen how the thought of it flashed across him when, mourning for his country's defeat alone in Petersburg, he remembered Argos. It matured through the years while he watched in bitter grief the tragedy of Poland, and behind the gallows and endless deportations to Siberia, behind the prohibition to a Pole of all Polish possessions, saw the danger to his country that he most dreaded : the moral degradation of hatred which such an oppression was calculated to engender. This thought, intensified by Krasinski's own intimate experience of the warring of the dictates of vengeance against a higher law, could, as he had himself expressed it, give him no rest until he sent it forth as a warning to his people. But if it were to reach Poland where Siberia was the penalty alike for the authors of the national Polish writings and their readers, it could only be told in some veiled form.

[1] *Correspondance.* Krasinski to Reeve. Florence, June 3, 1835.

Krasinski therefore allegorized it under the figure of the Greek, Iridion Amphilochides.

The keynote of the play is that the weapons of hatred will turn against those who use them, however sacred their object, and that evil means can bring nothing but destruction to the cause for which they are employed. It is evident from certain expressions in the prologue that Krasinski began the drama with the intention that the Greek who, to compass his end, has ruined everything he touched shall be eternally ruined himself. As the author closed the work he modified his idea, and we have the noble conclusion, the first step of the stairway that leads to the triumph and the unearthly glory of Krasinski's next great national song: *Dawn*.

In style Krasinski's second prose drama bears no resemblance to his first. Not only are the terseness and the reserve of *The Undivine Comedy* entirely absent from *Iridion* : but whereas in *The Undivine Comedy* we seem to move in an atmosphere of a heavy and oppressive greyness, there is the sensation throughout *Iridion* of the blue skies of Rome, the glittering marbles of the temples, the many-hued splendours of the Imperial City.

Krasinski places his drama in the reign of Heliogabalus when the Roman world was profoundly demoralized, and the fall of the empire seemed not far off. He saw, as we know, like elements of dissolution in the society in which he lived : and thus the application of his symbolized national thought to the present is evident. He pointed, in a few words of introduction, to the three systems which at that period of Rome's history stood side by side : paganism, barren of life and overlaid by alien religions from the East; Christianity, hidden and persecuted, but ever growing; and the barbarians, gradually pressing on Italy like a blinded and relentless force of nature. On these three elements the drama of *Iridion* is built: and all three are to be found represented in the character of Iridion himself; Iridion the Greek, who bears the second name of Sigurd from his Scandinavian mother, and who, to the Christians, is Hieronimus[1].

" The ancient world is now drawing nigh its end": so the drama begins in a prologue of stately prose that Count Tarnowski ranks among the masterpieces of the Polish language[2].

> All that dwelt therein is rotting, is dissolving, is demented.
> Amid the chaos I lift the song that is torn by violence from my bosom. May the spirit of destruction come to my aid! May my inspiration resound on every side, like the thunder of the tempest which is now rolling over the ages of the past and thrusting all life down into the abyss!—and then let it die away, even as thunder after its work is done. There, in the east, is the new dawn. But with that I have nought to do.

This chaos, observes Dr Kallenbach, does not refer merely to the historical background upon which Krasinski chose to found his secret thoughts[3]. It is also an allusion to the moral confusion in which Krasinski wrote the play, which was often put aside because the heart of its author was too disturbed and tempest-tossed to be able to work out his idea. Intrinsic evidences of this wavering of mental and spiritual outlook are distinctly traceable in the course of the drama.

[1] J. Klaczko, *Le Poète Anonyme de la Pologne*
[2] St. Tarnowski, *Zygmunt Krasinski.*
[3] J. Kallenbach, *Zygmunt Krasinski.*

Where, oh, Rome [continues the prologue], are the forms which of old so proudly and superbly trod thy seven hills? Where thy patricians, the sires of tribes, the oppressors of the plebs, the conquerors of Italy and Carthage? Where is the Vestal silently ascending the steps of the Capitol with the holy fire? Where are thy orators, standing above the waves of the people, encircled by the hum of murmured words and the storm of plaudits? Where the soldiers of the legions, sleepless, mighty, with visages lit up by the flash of swords? The past has gathered them to herself, and like a mother folds them in her bosom.

In their place rise forms till now unknown, strange, glittering with gold, with wreaths on their heads, with goblets in their hands.

Isis and Mithras have supplanted the gods of Rome. Barbarians stalk through the streets of the city.

From this world which writhes and dies I shall draw forth only one thought more. In it shall be my love, albeit it is the daughter of rage and the herald of destruction.

On, in your frenzy, gods and men, around my Thought. Be ye the music that sings an accompaniment to its dreams, the tempest through which like lightning it shall break. I will give to it a name, I will give to it a form, and, albeit conceived in Rome, the day when Rome shall perish shall not be its last. It shall live as long as earth and earthly nations—but there is no place for it in heaven[1].

The history is then given of the parentage of Iridion, the "son of vengeance," the symbolization of the mystic "Thought" of the Anonymous Poet. Iridion's father is Amphilochus, the Greek, his mother, Grimhilda, a Scandinavian priestess. This union of bloods in the person of Iridion is deeply significant. He must be the child of an oppressed race, and must also be linked with the force to which Rome ultimately succumbs.

---

[1] This phrase is one of the proofs that when Krasinski began the play he had no intention of finishing it as he did, and that *Iridion* was to have been the incarnation of vengeance only.

Some hint too of the north is requisite for the Thought
that the Anonymous Poet will send "to the north, the
land of graves and crosses."

Burning with hatred for the city that has enslaved
Hellas, Amphilochus carries the priestess from her
native land that he may learn from her inspiration how
to vanquish Rome. Iridion is brought up to the destiny
of avenging his nation, taught detestation of Rome
from his cradle. After the death of Amphilochus who
bequeaths the inheritance of revenge to his son with
his last breath, Iridion and his sister, Elsinoe, live
in the dead man's Roman palace, together with a
mysterious aged man, the guardian of their childhood,
Masinissa. With the stealth of the panther Iridion is
working towards the compassing of his end. He is not
concerned with the vision of a restored country. His
one desire is revenge: to see Rome humbled to the
dust. No sense of rectitude or of pity can stay his
hand. No means are too base if they can but bring
ruin on Rome.

When the play begins Iridion is about to carry into
execution the project which he has harboured for years,
namely, by giving his beautiful sister to Heliogabalus
to win through her the domination over the young
emperor that he requires for his schemes. The first
scene opens upon Elsinoe's last hours in her father's
house, as she awaits the moment when Heliogabalus's
slaves shall arrive to bear her to the imperial palace.
Never is Krasinski a greater artist than when he treats
episodes that for their horror seem beyond the range
of art. The delicacy with which he handles them, the
restraint that gives them their extraordinary power,
where no word too much is said, no word too little, are

nowhere more apparent than in this parting between the brother and the sister whose honour he has sacrificed. It passes in a hall in Iridion's palace. The fountain plays in the middle. Slaves are lighting the lamps. Iridion, sunk in anguish, has bowed his head upon the feet of his father's statue. His slaves, whispering to one another, reproach him for slumbering while his sister is weeping and swooning in her apartments. He summons her. She enters.

Elsinoe. Have the slaves come already?

Iridion. Not yet : but I would fain inspire thee for the last time with thy father's spirit.

Elsinoe. Oh, brother!

Iridion. Thou knowest that the Caesar insists in his passion, and the senate hath commanded thy statues to be placed in the temples of the city. Thou knowest that thou art not my sister, thou art not the bright-haired Elsinoe, the hope of thy natal house, the darling of my heart. Thou art the victim appointed for the suffering of many and for the shame of thy sires.

Elsinoe. Yea. You all have taught me this from my childhood, and I am ready. But not to-day, not to-morrow. A little later, when I have gathered strength, when I have listened to my fill to the teaching of Masinissa and thy commands, when I have drunk to the dregs of the chalice of your poison.

Iridion. Chosen maiden, prepare thee for thy fate. It behoves us to hasten on the road which we tread.

Elsinoe. Remember how I loved thee when we played on the grass-plots of Chiara. Oh, have mercy on me!

Iridion. Thou temptest me to pity.—In vain, in vain.

Elsinoe. Why so many prayers and lamentations? It befell in the olden times that men and gods might be bought off by death. Thy dagger flashes yonder, Iridion. Let us hasten annihilation for ourselves, Iridion.

Iridion. Thou blasphemest against my father's thought. Oh, sister, of old the life of one man sufficed for the salvation of nations. To-day the times are otherwise. To-day the sacrifice must be of honour. (*He clasps her in his arms.*) To-day thou shalt be wreathed with roses, thou shalt be decked in smiles. Oh, unhappy child, lay here thy doomed head.

For the last time in thy father's house thy brother presses thee
to his bosom. Take thy farewell of me in all the beauty of
thy maiden freshness. Never again will I behold thee young
—never, never again!

His heart faints within him. He cries aloud on
Masinissa : and at the entrance of the old man, majestic,
awe-inspiring, Iridion's hesitation is at an end, and
Elsinoe pleads no more. Serving girls carry in costly
robes, singing : "Even as Aphrodite, rising from the
azure ocean in the rainbows of the foam of the sea, so
shalt thou be. We bring thee roses, incense and pearls."
Masinissa and Iridion lead her to her father's statue,
where Iridion gives her his parting charge. Never
must she allow the Caesar to sleep in peace. She must
drop into his ear as a slow poison reports of plots for
his assassination, of treachery, till he is beside himself
with terror. Then the brother lays his hand on Elsinoe's
head :

Conceived in thirst for vengeance, grown to womanhood in
the hope of vengeance, predestined to infamy and ruin, I con-
secrate thee to the infernal deities of Amphilochus the Greek.

Elsinoe. The voices of Erebus resound on every side—oh,
my mother!

Choir of Women (surrounding her). Why tremble thy limbs
under the snowy veil, under the ribbons of purple with which
we wreathe thy breasts? Why dost thou grow pale under the
garland we have woven for the adorning of thy brow?

Iridion. See, the unhappy child is swooning.

Masinissa. Nay. She is beginning to live as it behoves
her to live.

Elsinoe. I cast off my father's threshold. My father has
condemned me. My brother has condemned me. Oh, never
more will I return. I go to torment and long mourning.

Iridion's aim is secured. Elsinoe successfully works
on the fears of the childish emperor. She shrouds herself in a haughty mystery that whets his superstition :

she throws over him the spell of her aloof and disdainful beauty till he is wax in her hands. On his side Iridion, having gained through his sister constant access to the emperor, plays the game of feigning that he is Heliogabalus's only faithful adherent. By skilfully manœuvring with the young emperor's arrant cowardice and love of pleasure Iridion's cue is to induce him to consent to the destruction of Rome, and to retire to the East where he will be lapped in security and free to follow his indulgences. And all the while the Greek is carrying on intrigues among the praetorians, the gladiators, the slaves, the barbarians, the rabble of Rome. They are ready. Iridion has only to give the sign and they will follow him.

Heliogabalus is one of the types in the play whom Krasinski has depicted with the most consummate art : a half crazy vicious boy, a whipped cur at the feet of the beautiful Elsinoe, amusing himself like a child with his baubles, dabbling with the degraded mysteries of eastern religions, clinging in terror for his life to the false friend who is betraying him. In him Krasinski concentrates the moral decay of Rome and the pagan world. But Iridion has to contend against yet another element than that of which Heliogabalus is representative, an element on which he reckons for his victory or his failure: the Christians. We have here the pivot on which the whole drama turns. No new life to revivify the Roman world can be born of the pagan Rome of Heliogabalus, nor yet of the one virtuous heathen trio whom Krasinski places against the universal degradation ; Alexander Severus, his mother, and the Stoic Ulpianus, the last a fine example of ancient Roman integrity. But Masinissa, the Mephistopheles of the play, foresees that Rome will not pass away into the lost empires of history, because on her ashes shall rise from the catacombs another Rome. Iridion, therefore, cannot hope for the downfall of Rome unless he gains the Christians to his side. But their faith forbids them to wage war against their persecutors. Consequently Iridion must, Masinissa tells him, undermine their morals, deceive them, bring into their midst a new and fatal discord. This counsel satisfies Iridion's thirst for revenge on Rome, beyond which he does not look: but the truth is that Masinissa, as Satan, is using Iridion as a tool not against Rome, but in the everlasting war between Christ and Satan.

Krasinski's conception of Mephistopheles is neither obvious nor conventional. From this Mephistopheles breathes the majesty of old age, the mystery and the remoteness of the African desert whence he professes to have risen. He takes the lineaments, not of a Miltonic fallen angel, but of an awful and majestic being with infinite aims, who seduces by the very greatness of his objects. His temptations are not addressed to what is base in man, but to what man holds most sacred[1]. His means—such as the sacrifice of Elsinoe's honour, the ruin of Cornelia—are vile: but it is in the name of what Iridion loves beyond all, for the sake of his country, that he is bidden by Masinissa to do these things. The colloquies between the Greek and his evil genius, with the exception of the last scene, give no impression of an ensnared soul battling against temptation. Masinissa scarcely urges. He suggests: and these suggestions have the magnetism of a compelling sovereignty whose word has but to be uttered and it is accepted. Masi-

---

[1] J. Kleiner, *History of the Thought of Zygmunt Krasinski.*

nissa seems more the complement of Iridion's own nature, Iridion's lower self, than an extraneous force[1].

In *Iridion* Krasinski's subject, says Count Tarnowski, is not the individual soul: it is humanity. The characters are not so much men and women as symbols. It follows then that Krasinski's Mephistopheles is scarcely a devil leading a soul to perdition, albeit at the close of the play this is his endeavour. Rather he is the Satan of the universal race, the evil spirit of history, destroying not this or that soul, but turning nations from their highest end, deflecting the spiritual progress of the commonwealth, polluting even the sanctity of patriotism[2]. He is, says Krasinski himself, defending his idea under the concealment of a third person against a critic who opposed it, "the element of all-evil which constantly transforms itself by the very necessity of creation into good; the Satan of all centuries and civilizations, eternally warring, eternally vanquished[3]." This psychological signification of the tempter links the Rome of *Iridion* with the poet's own country[4]. The rebirth of humanity coincided for Krasinski with the redress of his nation's wrongs. Therefore whatever false or misguided principle arose to bar or delay the advance of the world to the desired goal was to the Anonymous Poet the satanic incarnation. Hence his original and daring presentment of Mephistopheles as Masinissa, who ruins the work of Iridion for his country by its ethically false direction.

Again, Masinissa is the embodiment of reason in

---

[1] A. Małecki, quoted by J. Kallenbach, *Zygmunt Krasinski*.
[2] St. Tarnowski, *Zygmunt Krasinski*.
[3] *Letters to Gaszynski*. Kissingen, June 6, 1837.
[4] J. Kallenbach, *Zygmunt Krasinski*.

whom are absent the love and passion that rend Iridion's soul. At this time of Krasinski's life when he was driven into sophistry in order to justify his love for a married woman, his idea of Satan was that of reason opposed to passion. "Do you think pride is a passion?" he writes to Reeve. "No. There is no passion except love, and love is God. Pride, hatred, are daughters of reason... To produce evil of whatever kind passion has not been necessary, but cold, observing, perverted thought[1]." Iridion's heart can be moved by his sister's anguish, can shrink before the thought of wronging Cornelia: but Masinissa remains the everlasting enemy of the heart.

To ensure his success in the catacombs Iridion simulates Christianity, and receives Baptism under the name of Hieronimus. He then sets to work to convince the Christians that they must vindicate Christ by declaring war on those who persecute Him in His members. His fiery words carry away the young men, at the head of whom stands one Simeon of Corinth. The old men seek to restrain what they consider a youth's hotheaded zeal by their appeal to the Divine law of forgiveness. Then Masinissa unfolds to Iridion another stratagem. He shall gain the ear of the Christians through Cornelia, the beautiful maiden whose virginity is consecrated to Christ, the saint and prophetess of the catacombs, who has talked to Iridion of heavenly things.

"Lead her thought from Christ to thee," says Masinissa. "He is far. Thou livest and art near her. Why dost thou waver and doubt? She must be thine, not for vain pleasure, but because our work calls for her destruction."

But for once Iridion recoils. He has kept faith with the furies to whom he has vowed that no stain of pity

---

[1] *Correspondance.* Krasinski to Reeve. Rome, Dec. 20, 1834.

or regret shall ever be seen in him: yet now tears rise
to his eyes.

"Thou knowest not," this again from Masinissa, "that each
of you might be almighty by your own inexorable, enraged
thought; but your enemy foresaw and sowed in your bosoms
a heart—fear, delusion, baseness."

Iridion. Of whom speakest thou? Who made me abject
and unhappy? I know but one murderer of all my hours—
whose name is Rome.

Masinissa. There is another Rome which cannot perish.
Not on seven hills but on millions of stars do her feet rest.

Against her, even after the other Rome has fallen,
Iridion must war for ever. In the meanwhile, before
the victory for which Iridion, only half comprehending
Masinissa's words, is panting, the work in question must
go forward. Iridion remembers "unhappy Hellas." For
her sake, cries he in despair, the son of Amphilochus
must ruin the happiness of an innocent girl, must tear
hope from one who hoped.

The scene shifts to the catacombs. On every side
branch out the long corridors lined by graves, dying
away into darkness. Iridion, at the feet of the bishop
Victor, as a rash but obedient son, insinuates his request:
may not the Christians for the glory of Christ join hands
with the praetorians and overthrow the oppressor?
Victor points to Christ dying on the cross, and bids this
beloved erring member of his flock believe in the force
of spiritual arms, and sin no more: and Iridion, piously
praying aloud for deliverance from temptation, turns to
Cornelia.

Is Iridion's adhesion to Christianity entirely feigned?
He is among the Christians in all the falsity of an in-
trigue, but not from any hatred of Christianity[1]. We
have some faint impression that he is not wholly un-

---

[1] St. Tarnowski, *Zygmunt Krasinski.*

moved by what he learns, chiefly from Cornelia, of the Christian faith. Certain it is that in the last scene when he looks upon the cross he does so as no mere stranger[1].

Krasinski paints few women, but always with that singularly delicate and tender beauty that is so marked in Elsinoe and still more in the exquisite, ethereal figure of Cornelia. By a diabolical ingenuity, by the insinuation of the love that almost without his knowledge had forced its way into his soul, and is in its turn pressed into his deadly purpose, Iridion is exploiting Cornelia as a weapon in his war. He stands, a demon of guile, among the dead in the catacomb alone with the beautiful girl whose eyes are filled with love for the unseen. Certain that he is preparing with the other youths some wild act of bloodshed she entreats him for the sake of his salvation to desist. Iridion hisses into her ear words new to her: words of flattery.

Cornelia. Alas! Art thou the same with whom I knelt in the cemetery of Euphemia? Hieronimus, is this thou? So long I prayed. Such hard penance have I done for so many days and nights.

Iridion. And thou shalt reach heaven. Who could doubt it?

Cornelia. Oh, it was not for myself—not for myself.

Iridion. Then for whom?

Cornelia. One of my brothers.

Iridion. One of thy brothers! Speak truth—tell me his name.

He approaches her, speaking the language of a jealous lover, which she takes for delirium. He drags out from her the admission that this brother was Hieronimus:

but as he once was, not he who gazes so wildly, who stands before me without his senses. *Apage!—*

Iridion. See! I am calm now as before.

[1] *Op. cit.*

Cornelia. Gentle as thou wert once?

Iridion. Humble before thee.

Cornelia. Before the Lord. Promise that thou wilt not join them, that thou wilt not arm for earthly and condemned violence.

The bloodshed and carnage which she holds for crime, Iridion says shall be the triumph of her God. She prays for mercy on him, a sinner, that God will not suffer him to perish before her eyes.

Ah! what say I? Surely, oh, Lord, I have vowed my whole heart to Thee. What gloom is here! For the first time terror of the dead has seized me.

Iridion. Lean on me.

He then tells her his story: how the son of Amphilochus swore to his dying father to know neither love, joy nor pity, but to live in order to destroy.

In revenge must I live and die.

Cornelia. On whom wouldst thou wreak it? Who wronged him, who hath wronged thee?

Iridion. They who have compelled you all to wander whence the living flee after they have laid down the dead. They who have a thousand times reviled thy God. My father preceded Him Who shall conquer—Him Who shall reign as king—Him Whom thou hast doubted.

Cornelia. I!

Iridion. Because thou hast believed that He will leave this earth to be the prey of Rome.

Cornelia. He is lost. And yet the eternal fire of the Cherubim shineth in his eyes.

He hears Victor approaching, and retires into the dark passage. Perturbed and terror-stricken, Cornelia feels her heart beating with a strange, unknown emotion. Never before has she turned her eyes from the cross to a human face, and now it is this face that pierces her memory: "and as a prophet and a saint he stands before me."

Once more she is alone. Iridion enters. She clings

to a sarcophagus with the cry: "Ashes of the saints, defend me in this night!" Iridion tells her to leave him. Not, says she, till he will turn from the sin of his revenge. Delirium is seizing on her. She kneels and prays for him. For one moment his soul revolts against the wrong he is about to do her. "You are my witnesses, bones of the dead, and thou, mother earth, that I would fain have spared her, and only her." She entreats him to kneel with her and pray. Simeon's voice rings through the vault, calling his leader. Iridion seizes Cornelia in his arms. His kisses are on her brow. She swoons in his embrace, crying out that he and she are damned together. Awakening, her disordered brain is given to understand by Iridion that he is Christ, come at last to conquer with earthly weapons. His command that he shall summon her brothers to arms is to her the mandate of Christ: and she disappears, running, her cry " To arms!" re-echoing through the catacombs.

Wild tumult follows. The Christian youths, carried away by Iridion's eloquence, are divided between ardour for his cause and doubt. Then Cornelia enters, crying: "To arms!" The young men, long used to listen to her as to an inspired saint, now take her summons for that of heaven. The catacombs rock, flames break out, in token of hell's victory. Amidst the fire appears Masinissa to gaze on the spectacle of his triumph.

Faith, hope and love! Trinity which wert to last for ever, to-day I have torn Thee asunder in the hearts of the most beloved children of Thy benediction. Henceforth in Thy name they will slay and burn—in Thy name oppress—in Thy name rebel and rage. Thou shalt be crucified alike in their wisdom and their stupidity, in their cold calculation and their frenzy, in the sleepy humility of their prayers and the blasphemies of their pride. In the summits of heaven Thou shalt drink this cup of bitterness till Thou cursest them for ever.

Iridion 155

Iridion's hour is now approaching. Outside the city
the praetorians, led by Alexander Severus, are about
to march against Heliogabalus. Iridion is apparently
negotiating with them on the part of the Emperor. In
reality their movement is serving his plans. When they
attack Rome he will let loose his own forces, and there
will be a general destruction in which it is the Greek's
intention that Alexander, rather than live to save Rome,
shall perish. Iridion had in the past dissembled friendship with Alexander for his own ends. Now Alexander
believes him to have forsaken his party for Heliogabalus: and across the clash of hurrying events and
contending factions there breaks that tender and pathetic
moment when the young Alexander pleads with the
brother of Elsinoe.

"Dismiss him with the silence of contempt," says Ulpianus.

Alexander. I cannot. Leave him alone with me. Friends,
retire. Son of Amphilochus, have the avenging gods stretched
between us some cloud of delusion? I understand thee not.
Affront me not with double meaning words: for thou dost owe
me gratitude for that I trust not my own eyes, albeit they show
me clearly thy change of face.

Iridion. My thanks, Severus. If the fates had created me
a man and had willed to endow my heart with the sweet gift
of a friend, it is thee I would have asked of them.

Alexander. Renounce the tyrant's cause. Speak to me one
word of affection, and I will not doubt thy faith. Iridion, where
is thy sister?

Iridion. Where fate has chained her.

Alexander. Iridion, I call on thee—Iridion, I stay thee.
I have read in her eyes intolerable torture: and wouldst thou
fight in his defence?

" Oh, fresh shoot of youth," murmurs Iridion, pierced to the
heart as he hears accents that have never been his to utter.
"Why are thy days so short? Of thy transports towards
beauty and virtue, there shall remain no trace."

"Why," says Alexander, "dost thou gaze upon me with
such a mournful look? Come what may, stay thou with me.
I will snatch Elsinoe from the tiger's jaws, and Rome shall

once more stand in the springtide of her power, armed in immortal thunderbolts. Why dost thou shudder?"

Iridion takes his hand "for the last time—the last, for we both stand above the grave, and ere a third dawn shall rise one of us will go down to Erebus."

The Greek returns to the imperial palace. Heliogabalus has fallen asleep on a heap of roses and violets. Tormented with the terrors that follow him into his dreams, he shrieks out the names of the two he trusted, Iridion and Elsinoe, who, cursing him, stand and watch. A messenger from the senate comes in with the tidings that Rome has sentenced Heliogabalus to death and is about to raise Alexander to the purple. The shouts of Alexander's followers are heard beyond the palace. Mad with fear, Heliogabalus is prevailed on by Elsinoe and Iridion to give the latter supreme command over the army.

Then follows the farewell between Iridion and Elsinoe. She has done her part. All that remains to her now is to keep guard over Heliogabalus till Iridion returns, victorious, to bear her away from the scene of her shame. She is in her brother's arms, murmuring into his ear her last request.

Let the eyes die beneath which I withered. Let the arms which crawled about my neck fall like two crushed adders. Let the lips which first touched mine perish in ashes.

Iridion. On the same pyre and at the same moment, both he and Severus.

Elsinoe. Not so, not so. Let me be given my last desire. Spare Alexander on the field of battle. He alone with one look calmed my despair. He alone guessed—ah! why hast thou turned thy face away from me?

Iridion. Think not of him. He alone is now tearing Rome from the clasp of my hatred.

Elsinoe. Then once more press thy sister to thy bosom. Feelest thou how this heart throbs? Ere thou returnest it will

have broken, son of Amphilochus. But remember Elsinoe
desired no blood of thee. Let live all, all! Even he, the abomi-
nated, let him live.

Voices outside the palace. Forward, in the name of the
Fortune of Iridion the Greek!

Iridion. Away with untimely mourning when Nemesis
already holds the crown of vengeance for us in each hand. In
that clash of arms, in those cries leaps my life: and must thou
die? Rather be happy and proud. What thy father invoked,
what long centuries have besought of the gods with tears, ap-
proacheth with the swiftness of the thunderbolt.

Voices. Iridion! Iridion!

Iridion. Farewell.

Elsinoe. Go! Be thou happy and great: and if ever thou
shalt sail on the Aegean waters cast a handful of my ashes on
Chiara's shores.

They part, never to see each other more. It is the
night for which Iridion has lived, the night of Rome's
destruction. His barbarians, the slaves he has bribed
by his gifts, his gladiators, his soldiers, are outside
his palace together with Masinissa. Scarcely able to
brook the delay before Rome's funeral pyre shall be
fired, Iridion feverishly awaits the advent of Simeon's
Christians, when the slaughter is to begin.

Iridion. The whole city is in flames. Nay—it was but in
my eyeballs that fires burst forth. Where are they? Where
are the Christians? If they have betrayed me I am lost.

Masinissa. They are finishing their hymns.

A messenger from Simeon here hurries in, summon-
ing Iridion to the catacombs. Victor is keeping back
the Christians.

From a literal point of view the refusal of the
Christians to rally round Iridion could not doom to
failure a leader who had by now nearly every element
in Rome under his control[1]. But *Iridion* is not meant
to be taken literally. It is an allegory, and as such

---

[1] St. Tarnowski, *Zygmunt Krasinski.*

must be read, with on the one hand its various historical
inaccuracies, required by Krasinski for his purpose, such
as the open displayal of the cross in the catacombs, with,
on the other, its strong colouring of historical truth.
Iridion's dependence on the Christians is one of the
ethical foundations upon which the whole of Krasinski's
conception rests.   Whatever the material strength on
Iridion's side he cannot win because hatred is only
destructive, and in the Krasinskian theory love only
can build the edifice.   The work, therefore, of the son
of vengeance must be shattered by the only force in
Rome that is more powerful than his, because this force
only is the force of love.

Iridion rushes to the catacombs.   On the steps of
the altar stands Victor with his priests behind him.   On
one side kneels Simeon, on the other Cornelia.   Further
off are Christians fully armed, but also on their knees.
Stern and immovable, Victor sees the delusions of Satan
equally in Simeon's whole-hearted but filial pleadings
for war and in the frenzy of Cornelia.   Into this scene
of discord bursts Iridion, greeted by Cornelia as Christ,
calling upon the Christians to follow him where :

Caesar and the gods of the city only await the resurrection of
the saints to perish.

Simeon.   Hieronimus, Hieronimus, I stretch my hands forth
to thee, unto our hopes.

Choir.   Ask Victor.

Iridion.   Father!

Victor.   To-day thou hast lost thy Father Who is in heaven.

Cornelia (*to Iridion*).   Forgive him, Lord! He knoweth not
what he doth. To arms! To arms!

Then Victor is suddenly moved to give his flock a
sign that will convince them.   He constrains Cornelia
to kneel before the chalice, he takes holy water, and
begins the exorcism.   For the last time she cries:

To arms!

Victor. Silence, evil spirit, that speakest through her delusion. With the sign of the cross I encompass thee. With the word "Jesus" I command thee.

Cornelia. I hear a hundred wails in my bosom that are not mine.

Iridion. Here, beloved, to my arms!

Cornelia. Oh, earth, sink under me, hide me from his deadly look!

Iridion. Cornelia, thou, thou art mine.

Cornelia. Call her not by that name. She trusted thee. She hath perished for ever. Laughter tears the air. Black spectres circle round thee.

Victor. Apage, Satanas!

Cornelia. Come not thou near me. Where is my God?

Victor (showing her the cross). Here, daughter.

Cornelia. Give it to my lips. (*She kisses the cross.*) Forgive me, forgive me!

Victor. Dost thou abjure the evil spirit?

Cornelia. I abjure him. (*She falls.*) Brothers, he duped her, he duped you all. I die. But listen! listen! I die in the Lord.

She sinks at the feet of Victor with his blessing in her ear. One last cry of Iridion calls her to his arms in vain. "Hieronimus, I pardon thee. Hieronimus, pray thou to Christ": and she speaks to him no more, dying amidst the scent of flowers from paradise.

Not a Christian, except those few from the north who are faithful to the son of Grimhilda, will now join Iridion. He dashes away the cross that he carried upon his armour: then rushes to the war whence as he knows all hope has gone. Soon a slave escapes from the palace, which Alexander's troops have captured, to carry to Iridion the account of the death of Heliogabalus and Elsinoe. Whimpering and singing by turns, Heliogabalus was found by the soldiers fingering the cup of poison that he was afraid to drink: and they despatched him off the stage as ignominiously as he had lived upon it. But Elsinoe, having robed herself in imperial purple and taken a dagger in her hand, sat silent and calm on the throne, listening as the clamour of the conflict swelled ever nearer. Soldiers rushed into her apartment with, at their head, Alexander shouting to them to save her life. The slave who had protected her with his own body falters out to the brother her last words: "Iridion, I will not love thine enemy": and—a victim to the end —she stabbed herself and died.

"Death to Alexander!" is now Iridion's cry. He is seen by his foes, fighting, says Ulpianus, "more like the spirit of incarnate hatred than mortal man." The chorus of the mourning women has not died away around Elsinoe's bier in her father's palace when Ulpianus crosses the threshold, with overtures of peace from the new emperor, Alexander Severus.

Now for the first time Iridion throws off the mask which he has been compelled to wear in the face of Rome, and appears as his true self, the avenger upon the race that has destroyed Greece. He is no longer the feigned favourite of a despicable tyrant, or a cunning intriguer. In this scene he has the grandeur of one who is speaking in the name of a wronged cause to the representative of a nation whose right is might, who—such is Ulpianus's proud boast—has conquered the world by iron and will keep it by iron: and Krasinski strengthens the position by making the spokesman of Rome no effete decadent but the survivor of the best traditions of a bloodthirsty and overbearing race. The question at odds is that of the unending war between the material, represented by Rome, and the beautiful and ideal, represented by artistic Greece: it is that of the struggle between brute force and the idea: but neither of these, reading between Krasinski's lines, was uppermost in

Iridion

his mind. This last colloquy between Roman and Greek is in truth one of Krasinski's great outbursts of nationalism. In the impassioned reproaches of the Greek are those of the Pole, speaking in the person of his Iridion the complaints of another conquered people against another empire in the only language free to him to utter —the language of symbolism.

"Tell him," says Iridion, motioning to his crowd of gladiators and slaves, "who was it that thrust you from the highroad of the human race and forced you to tread the paths of darkness? Who from your cradles stamped on your brows the sign of hunger and thirst? Who would not suffer you to love a woman and to sit in the light of your domestic hearth? Who, herself mortal, based her sweetest hopes in the misery and degradation of mortals? Who hath emptied to its dregs the chalice of the world's woe? Who hath grown drunken in the nectar of tears and blood?"

And the answer of all is: Rome.

"Wouldst thou," disdainfully asks the Roman, "give the sceptre to playing, singing Hellas? Rule is with the power of arms under the protection of unfaltering reason."

To which Iridion:

The martyrs of the nations have heard of your reason. Thou hast spoken truth. Never has Hellas polluted herself with a like reason.

What have you done with the world since the gods of evil gave it to your hands? There stand triumphal arches and the highroads of the aediles. Ye have inscribed the stones of them with the blood and sweat of the dying. Where have thy forbears lulled the grief of the conquered with tender song, with the teaching of wisdom?

Ulpianus. Dost thou refuse the mercy of thy lord?

Iridion. Who is my lord? I have known none on earth. I have had enemies only, a few brothers who served me faithfully, and one godlike moment, short as the clash of swords that are shattered at one stroke. The torch of vengeance flared in this hand. The doomed city lay at my feet. Ah! Nemesis! (*He leans on the statue of Amphilochus.*)

Cursing Rome, he returns to the battle. An unseen

presence hovers about him, at the thought of which his
cheek blanches and his sword trembles in his hand.

Ah, why dost thou pursue me, invisible spirit? Christ—
Christ—what is that name to me? Off! Torment me not,
Cornelia.

His soldiers abandon him for Alexander. He steps
upon his sister's funeral pyre, and summons death.
Masinissa snatches him from the flames: and the two
disappear to human sight.

They are on a mountain near Rome. There lies the
city in the mists of distance, beautiful, superb, eternal.
For what had Iridion sacrificed himself and all those
whom his road had crossed?

Oh, thou whom I loved for thy sorrows, Hellas, Hellas, wert
thou but a shade? Thy enemy stands unmoved as erst, and
displays her marbles to the sun like the white fangs of the tiger.
Wherefore am I here?

He flings himself upon the ground.

Masinissa. Thy calling is not over yet.
Iridion. Torture me not. My father died in thy arms.
My sister expired in the palace of the Caesars. I at thy feet
breathe my last. Is not this enough for thee? The innocent
maiden I sacrificed to thee hath floated in the sky on mournful
wailings. Ah! if her God lived over all other gods—if He were
the one truth of the world!
Masinissa. What wouldst thou do then?
Iridion. Dying with this shattered steel in my hands I would
call upon Him.
Masinissa. Our Father Who art in heaven give long days
to Rome. Forgive them who betrayed me. Save them who
through all time have oppressed my native land.
Iridion. Nay. Our Father Who art in heaven love Hellas
as I loved her. Tell me in this last hour, Masinissa, thou who
hast deceived me,—oh, speak swifter, swifter,—if Christ is the
lord of heaven and earth.

This witness Masinissa bears. It is that of an

immortal enemy to his immortal Enemy. Gaze on the city of
thy hatred. Knowest thou who shall tear it from the hands

of thy brothers when they shall plough Italy into furrows of blood and beds of ashes? The Nazarene! For the second time He shall deify Rome before the nations of the world.

Iridion. Ah! I desired without measure, I laboured without rest to destroy, even as others desire without measure, labour without rest to love. And now to one who dieth thou announcest the immortality of Rome.

Masinissa. Despair not, for the time shall come when the cross shall in vain stretch out its arms to shelter in its bosom those departing from it. Then at all the gates of the city shall be heard complaints and lamentation—then the genius of Rome shall again hide her face, and her weeping shall have no end: for on the Forum shall remain only dust, in the Circus only ruins, on the Capitol only shame. And my war on earth shall be drawing near its end.

Iridion. My heart beats once more. Is that day still far?

Masinissa. I myself can scarce foresee it.

Iridion. Oh, Amphilochus, then thy son was but a dream. (*To Masinissa*) Go! On this rock, gazing in the eyes of Rome, I will die as I have lived in solitude of soul.

The tempter's direct assault on a human soul now opens. He is Satan undisguised. His instruments are still man's higher instincts. He makes no attempt to slay Iridion's newborn, if flickering, faith in Christ. On the contrary he directs that faith itself against God[1]. If Iridion will abjure Christ Masinissa promises him that he shall behold the humiliation of Rome. He shall be plunged into a sleep of ages to awake therefrom on the day: "when on the Forum there shall be only dust, in the Circus only bones, and on the Capitol shame." In exchange he must be Masinissa's eternal prey. Iridion swears to the bond: and as the words leave his lips a cry of grief and despair, uttered by the voice that had once spoken to him of Christian prayer and pardon, wails in the sky above him. He is led by Masinissa to a cavern under a mountain where there is " nor dawn

---

[1] J. Kleiner, *History of the Thought of Zygmunt Krasinski.*

nor stars nor voice nor pain nor dreams." There shall
he sleep till the day of vengeance.

Here ends the dramatic form of the play. Krasinski
tells the final fate of his Thought in an epilogue re-
sembling in style the introduction.

> Oh, my Thought, thou hast lasted out the centuries. Thou
> didst slumber in the day of Alaric and in the day of the great
> Attila. Neither the ring of the imperial crown on the rough
> brow of Charlemagne, nor Rienzi, tribune of the people, woke
> thee. And the consecrated lords of the Vatican passed one
> after the other before thee, as shadows before a shadow. But
> to-day thou shalt arise, oh, my Thought!
>
> The voice which reacheth not heaven but to which the earth
> thundereth back from her hidden depths has cried : "Oh, my
> son !"

and at the call of Masinissa Iridion rises and is led by
him over the Campagna into the Eternal City.

> Thou hast stood in the Roman Campagna. She hath
> nought with which to conceal her shame before thy gaze. The
> aqueducts, running to the city, finding no city have halted.
> The stones that have fallen from them lie there in graveyard
> heaps.
>
> The son of the ages beheld, and rejoiced in the justice of
> his vengeance. Each ruin and the plains, widowed of amphi-
> theatres, and the hills, orphaned of temples, were his recompense.
>
> And by the road of graves his terrible guide led him to the
> gates of Rome.

They traverse the streets of the city, the ruins of
imperial Rome. They reach the Forum, where Iridion
can "recognize nought, call nought by its name in the
hour of his triumph." They behold on the Palatine shapeless remains through which Iridion had last walked as
the Caesar's palace. They reach the Coliseum: and here
their pilgrimage is ended.

> On the silent arena, on the silver sand, amidst arcades
> changed into wild rocks, with ivy on their summits, with great
> fissures in their wombs, thou didst praise the fates for fallen
> Rome.

As he stands where all is silence and decay he hears in fancy the trumpets that shall never ring there again, the cries of combatant and populace, the hymns of Christian martyrs. He sees as he stands gazing on the moonlit ruin, even as Krasinski himself stood there, dreaming the dream of which *Iridion* is the realization, a cross erect on the spot where its followers died.

In thee a strange feeling wakes: not pity for Rome, for her desolation scarce sufficeth for her sins; not terror at thy chosen lot, for thou hast suffered too much to fear: not grief at leaving mother earth, for in thy sleep of ages thou hast forgotten the love of life: but some remembrance of a maiden's face—some sorrow for that cross which of old thou didst disdain. But now it seemeth to thee that thou desirest war with it no more, that it is weary as thou, mournful as erst the fate of Hellas—and holy for evermore.

In the Coliseum begins the last struggle for Iridion's soul. Masinissa, with the fury of the captor about to claim his prey, strives to drag him from the cross where with prayerless lips he stands. Below are the wails of the martyrs whose blood once reddened the arena: on high the wails of the angels. But above them all rings a louder cry. In the light of the moon shines a radiant form, and Iridion, raising his eyes, sees a face he knew, now transfigured for ever, on which he gazes to take his everlasting farewell.

"Immortal Enemy," cries Masinissa, "he is mine because he lived in revenge and he hated Rome." But the arena is silver with the wings of her who is wrestling for Iridion's salvation, whose cry is ever: "Oh, Lord, he is mine because he loved Greece."

This conflict between the pleas of love and hatred can by the very idea of *Iridion* end only in the victory of love. Hatred falls beaten twofold. Because though Iridion had hated Rome he had loved Greece. He had

sinned, not because like Henryk of *The Undivine Comedy*
he had loved too little, but because he had loved much:
because the love of Cornelia, whom he had wronged,
and who, forgiving him all, saved him by her prayers,
must be stronger to bring about its end than the hatred
of a Masinissa.

> Arise, oh, son of Greece! In the mist of dawn the linea-
> ments of thy foe fade ever more darkly away. His voice is
> now only as the murmur of far off waters. By Cornelia's
> testimony, by Cornelia's prayers, thou art saved, because thou
> didst love Greece.

But because for the love of Greece he had hated,
and had fought for her with ignoble means, he can only
work out his promised salvation by expiation. Herein
lies the grandeur of the Polish poet's conception and
the peculiar point of all his work for his country. The
fruit of hatred is death and destruction. Love only is
constructive. Iridion worked in hatred and his work
failed. Now he shall work in love, and his work shall
triumph. In the sentence pronounced upon him by God,
as he still stands in the Coliseum, the Anonymous Poet
abandons so far as might be the allegory under which
he was constrained to tell his Thought, and speaks as
directly as he dared to Poland.

> "Go to the north in the name of Christ. Go and halt not
> till thou standest in the land of graves and crosses. Thou shalt
> know it by the silence of men and the sadness of little children,
> by the burnt huts of the poor and the ruined palaces of the
> exiles. Thou shalt know it by the wailings of My angels, flying
> over it by night.
> "Go and dwell among the brothers that I give thee. There
> is thy second test. For the second time thou shalt see thy love
> transpierced, dying, and thou canst not die: and the sufferings
> of thousands shall be born in thy one heart.
> "Go and trust in My name. Ask not for thy glory, but for
> the welfare of those whom I entrust to thee. Be calm before

the pride and oppression and derision of the unjust. They shall
pass away, but thou and My word shall not pass away.

"And after long martyrdom I will send My dawn upon you.
I will give you what I gave My angels before the ages—happiness—and what I promised on the summit of Golgotha—
freedom."

And the sun rose above the ruins of Rome: and there was
none whom I might tell where were the traces of my Thought
—but I know that it lasts and lives.

Such is *Iridion*, the Thought that the Anonymous
Poet of Poland conceived in his and his nation's anguish.
It represents the spiritual victory of one who at the cost
of his heart's blood tore the truth that would give life
to his people from his own passion and conflict. His
secret sympathies could not but be, as he told Gaszynski
in the letter on the play that we have already quoted,
with the Iridion who craved for vengeance. But, thus
continues this letter which was the answer that Krasinski
desired Gaszynski to give a critic of *Iridion*, worded
for the sake of preserving his anonymity as though
the poet had held a conversation with the unknown
author, "logic, necessity, led the author to that end. What
is, is. It is not our caprices that rule the world, but the
mind of God[1]." Krasinski freely owns that the faults
of execution in *Iridion* are many[2]. The play is in fact
of excessive length. It is at times overladen with ir-
relevant details and side scenes that distract the
attention from the broad lines of a magnificent idea. But
these are mere blemishes. *Iridion* remains one of the
splendid monuments of Polish literature and thought:
an enduring witness to that high spiritual vision by
which the Polish nation has risen above the powers of
evil set loose against her by an oppression which has
striven in vain to destroy her soul. Its author fearlessly

---

[1] *Letters to Gaszynski.* Kissingen, June 6, 1837.   [2] *Ibid.*

laid down a principle for his people at the moment when it was most bitter to hear, hardest to realize. While their country was rent and ravaged by a persecution that knew no mercy, the Anonymous Poet against the cry of his own heart entreated his fellow-Poles to rise, not to revenge or retaliation, but to the more rugged road of love. Krasinski's own language on what he calls the " dream of his youth, the wail of an unheard-of Titanic grief," is its best justification[1]. Let, says he to Gaszynski, let the critic to whom these words were addressed, let whoever reads *Iridion* be free to judge it as they will. One thing alone they must acknowledge: its truth.

And to prove its truth the author might call upon the shades of the dead and the tears of the living. He might ask many a one: "Didst thou not feel thus, didst thou not dream thus?" And many a one would answer: "It is so." Not only many a one, but a whole nation[2].

[1] *Ibid.*   [2] *Ibid.*

CHAPTER VIII

THE DEVIATION: *A SUMMER NIGHT*
AND *THE TEMPTATION*
(1836–1838)

After Krasinski had written *Iridion*, he swerved aside in the development of his master thought. In the years that followed his great drama he could speak to his nation with no certain voice, because he himself was wandering in doubt and darkness, intensified by the influences of pantheism and German philosophies.

"As to pantheism," he wrote to Gaszynski, "I doubt if you will succeed in finding any consolation in it... Pantheism is a reasoned out despair. Pantheism has poisoned much of my faith[1]."

With its theory of the absorption of the individual pantheism could not fail to be a horrible nightmare to Krasinski, under which his clear perceptions were staggered. For if the unit must lose its individuality, what hope was there for a nation that in the eyes of the world was being slowly done to death, but whose resurrection was the belief to which every Polish heart has always clung?

His soul, he told Reeve, was:

equally disgusted with the idea of nothingness, of the want of individuality after death, and, on the other side, with the idea of an activity without pause, an eternal metempsychosis of misery and pains...I cannot get out of this fatal dilemma. My brain will dash itself out one day against it[2].

[1] *Letters to Gaszynski.* Kissingen, June 12, 1836.
[2] *Correspondance.* Krasinski to Reeve. Florence, March 6, 1836.

"He is," he writes to Gaszynski, as usual speaking of himself in the third person where his literary productions were concerned, in reply to his friend's urging him to write upon certain patriotic themes, "at that time of life when everything is dried up and wearied out by doubt.   May God grant him to emerge from those depths with a new and manly faith[1]."

He re-read the gospels—this confidence is to his father—and: "they brought me no comfort, no hope." Some power, he said, had left him: "and that power was faith[2]."

Krasinski was now tasting the whole bitterness which passion had brought upon himself and Joanna Bobrowa.   The love on her side had always been greater than on his.   As, inevitably under the circumstances, his love died down and infinite compassion took its place, he felt himself the more bound to Mme Bobrowa by the fact that it was affection for him that had caused her misery: and against the entreaties, remonstrances or commands as the case might be, of his friends, Danielewicz, with whom he lived, Reeve, and above all his father, he refused to break with her.   It accorded with the inherent nobility of Krasinski's nature that, bitterly as he rued the personal sufferings that the whole affair had caused him, his chief thought throughout was for the woman, and the keenest edge of his anguish the knowledge that her happiness was wrecked.   Tortured by this reflection, by his conscience, by her reproaches, chiefly carried on by correspondence, for they met seldom during these years, engaged in a perpetual conflict with his father on the subject, his nerves were

[1] *Letters to Gaszynski.*   Kissingen, June 6, 1837.
[2] J. Kallenbach, *Zygmunt Krasinski.*

strained to the breaking-point and his eyesight again began to fail. Such was the inner life of the poet, little guessed at in the cosmopolitan salons of Rome and Vienna where he appeared as a youth of peculiarly courteous manner, with an exceptional brilliance and wit in his talk—which characteristics remained always his.

Whatever his own troubles Krasinski never put aside the concerns of his friends. The younger of the two daughters who had been taken from Sołtan died in 1836, when a child of eight years old. To the doubly bereaved father Krasinski wrote:

Your little girl is happier than all of us. She only dreamed she was on earth, and after one night she woke, back in heaven. There is nothing more pure, more blessed than a child's death. In later years to die amidst the temptations of life and its difficulties is a different matter. Certain it is that, dying, she did not regret the unknown world. Perhaps the thought of her far off father came to her as through a dark mist, and then the mist broke, and clearly with an angel's eyes she beheld her earthly father and, having clasped her little hands in his, gave herself to her heavenly Father. And when they bring you flowers in spring, think that you have one fresh in heaven whose fragrance is prayer and song for you. Do not weep over her early grave, but rather say: *manibus date lilia plenis*[1].

Krasinski had already been leaving no stone unturned to obtain the Russian government's restoration of Sołtan's surviving daughter. Through the influence of Wincenty Krasinski he at last succeeded: and in the midst of his mental tortures, hampered by semi-blindness, he, with that touch of womanly tenderness which was so marked in his character, arranged every particular of the girl's long journey, thinking out every little detail for her comfort till she could reach her father.

In the spring of 1836, while he was in Rome,

---

[1] *Letters to Sołtan*. Vienna, Nov. 12, 1836.

Krasinski had met another young Polish poet whose place in the national literature stands by his own, above his own as regards form. Juliusz Słowacki had left Poland during the troubles of 1830. He wandered about Europe and the East, eating his heart out in the loneliness from which a premature death delivered him. There is both in his life and in his early work a strong strain of the fashionable Byronism: yet beneath this ran the undercurrent of that deep love for his country under the influence of which he enriched his nation with magnificent patriotic song. In the opening days of Krasinski's friendship with Słowacki, whom he fondly calls Julek, he saw clearly his defects—his restless egotism, his petty jealousies, the want of spiritual perception which characterized the youthful production of the future mystic and which, observes Dr Kallenbach, the Anonymous Poet was at that moment in no condition himself to strengthen in another. But he likewise saw, and was among the first of his countrymen to call public attention to it, the promise of Słowacki's brilliant art which he whole-heartedly admired. The two youths, both consumed by poetic genius and patriotic fire, were wont to walk together in the garden of the Villa Mills on the Palatine, and hold moonlight conversations among the roses and ruins in that romantic spot.

At this period of Krasinski's life inspiration left him. In his tension of mind and soul he could write but little, and nothing that was worthy of the creator of *Iridion*. His fragment of a drama on Wanda, the heroine of Polish legend, lies in the limbo of the unfinished. To the two prose-poems *A Summer Night* and *The Temptation* we will return. There remains the little collection of prayers which he composed for Joanna

Bobrowa and which was published forty years after the poet's death, in 1899.

At heart a deeply religious woman, Mme Bobrowa's most persistent accuser had been her conscience. Lost and unhappy himself, Krasinski realized that religion could be her only comfort, and so wrote out these prayers. They are more poetical exercises than pious outpourings, though their form is prose. Placed as they are on the lips of a miserable woman, their accents are of grief and desolation. There is something in them that invariably falls short of the true language of spirituality. It is obvious that the writer stood on no certain ground himself, albeit it must be taken into consideration that Krasinski is speaking in the person of another, and had he been speaking in his own might have expressed himself differently[1]. Be that as it may, passages border on the blasphemous. Others are inspired by pantheism. And yet moments occur where, given one degree further, and the poet would be pouring out his soul with the devotion and the fire of a Christian mystic.

For Thou art the first, the only, the highest love: for all the love of hearts on earth are only rivulets, flowing from the sea of Thy brightness: for Thou wilt save me when my days are numbered, and Thou wilt comfort my distressed soul...For Thou wilt not forsake the work of Thy Hands, Thy daughter who here weeps and wails to Thee (*Litany*).

As an illustration of the development of Krasinski's thought, the prayers are not without importance. They put forth the theory of vicarious suffering which was to be the corner-stone of his prophecies for Poland. On the other hand their note of despair has no place in Krasinski's subsequent scheme.

In one direction these years saw a new departure of

---

[1] J. Kallenbach, *Zygmunt Krasinski*.

great significance in the history of the Anonymous Poet. It was now that he began to write verse.

He sent his poems, for the most part written to or about Mme Bobrowa, in letters to either Sołtan or Gaszynski, as experiments, with no intention of ever publishing them: and only after his death did they see the light. Krasinski thought poorly of them. In one he complains that the Creator had denied him the power of expression, and that he felt in his heart heavenly accords which were shattered before they could reach his lips. (*God has refused me.* June, 1836.) Far inferior to the love lyrics he was to write later to another, these early poems express sorrow and remorse, not love. Krasinski was eating Dead sea apples. He realized with an anguish of regret that the powers of his mind, the brilliant gifts of his youth, had been squandered in a love which was from the outset doomed to ruin.

"My heart is broken" is the burden of a poem he sent to Gaszynski, of which we quote some extracts because, to comprehend the fulness of Krasinski's spiritual uprising, we must first go down with him into the abyss of his despair.

All that I loved is far away as God, or fadeth as a cloud. What has the spark of genius wrought for me? It only glimmered in the deep places of my soul. Had I not loved a mortal beauty or laid my lips upon an earthly brow, I might have lit a flame upon the vale of earth with that spark which fell to me from eternity. Too late to-day! The soul is even as the body. Once it is marred, and the marred part thou tearest not away with all thy strength from the whole members, the evil overrunneth all and multiplies. Happy the body, it alone can die.

Ever between two waves the spirit rocks. Her thought in heaven dwells, her heart sinks ever lower into hell. Immortal war she wages with herself, she may not die, and at each moment dies in double woe. All is unbearable; for guilt and sentence in each spark of life commingle. Ah! life seems but a mockery only. Unbroken sleep, peace of the grave, are false, even as happiness is falsehood. Even as the world is great, it is the fallen field. Even as the world is great, it is the rock of shipwreck. With endless toil, with everlasting pain, so all is wrought, so all is ended. (*My heart is broken.* November, 1837.)

These lines are the only acknowledgment we have from Krasinski's pen of his own genius. Not long after he had written it he tells Reeve, in the last letter but one that ever passed between them, that his position with his father and Mme Bobrowa had become intolerable. He met the latter in Kissingen during the summer. Their interviews took place in a cemetery, as the only place safe from observation where they stood among the tombs, rain beating on them unheeded.

"In one word," says Krasinski to Reeve, "she was a woman who had reached the last stage of exaltation, who had thrown off the conventions of the world, considering with a calm eye that society would soon reject her and seeing in this world no one except him who ought never to have brought her to so terrible an extremity. Then there came into his head a thought of despair and love. He resolved to sacrifice himself for her. He wrote to his father that he wished to drive her to divorce her husband, and he would marry his beloved. Then began an atrocious tragedy. The father no longer answered him, he would only write to his friend [Danielewicz]. He threatened his son with his curse. He accused him of driving him into his grave, and declared that this marriage should never take place without entering into war with him, without being separated from him for ever, and neither ever seeing each other again. What could the son do against such terrible threats?[1]"

Krasinski was gradually brought to the point of acknowledging that he must break for ever with Mme Bobrowa. He refused to do it in the drastic manner enjoined by his father. He would only consent to take the step in some natural, inevitable way that would spare her feelings.

[1] *Correspondance.* Letter to Reeve. Vienna, Dec. 29, 1837.

"I loved that woman," he wrote to the General. "That woman has been good to me. I will maintain in regard to her all the forms of friendship, all the precautions of affection: but I will not wound either her pride or her heart[1]."

The time allowed to Krasinski by the Russian passports had now expired, and in the summer of 1838 he was obliged to return to Poland. What that return meant to him he had already told Soltan two years earlier.

If we return *coram in patriam*, I confess it will be for me a plunge into complete darkness, a descent to hell...On that frontier where our ancestors once drew with happy emotions their native air into their lungs, where they knelt to thank God for having granted them to return from distant wanderings, to-day we, when we stand there, must say farewell to the feelings and persons dearest to us. To-day a foreign land is our home. Our own has become worse than foreign, worse than far away, because it is a prison. In that land of ours, except for my father, I have no friend, scarcely anyone known to me[2].

His friends were all in exile.

"My Konstanty, may God guard you," he wrote to Gaszynski on the day when he began the journey which he always believed would end in Siberia. "Remember you are in a foreign country among foreigners, and it is your most sacred duty to maintain the purity of the Polish name. In the nightmare of which life is woven remember always that you have a friend who, far off or near, will always remain the same to you[3]."

On his way through Germany to Poland Krasinski met for the last time as her lover Joanna Bobrowa. He wrote to Soltan:

Oh, Adam, unhappy is he who with the naivety of a child, dreaming of noble deeds, did violence to another's rights, tore a wife from her husband, a mother from her children. I did this, thinking in my madness that there were poetry and spring on that road. Now, now I am deeply abased before myself, and she before the world[4].

---

[1] J. Kallenbach, *Zygmunt Krasinski.*
[2] *Letters to Soltan.*   Kissingen, July 10, 1836.
[3] *Letters to Gaszynski.*   Vienna, May 14, 1838.
[4] St. Tarnowski, *Zygmunt Krasinski.*   J. Kallenbach, *op. cit.*

Perhaps the most tragic feature of Krasinski's relations with his father is the deep mutual love that
survived the father's utter want of comprehension of his
son. Together with the expression of an unusually close
affection that we find in those letters from Zygmunt to
his father to which we have access in Dr Kallenbach's
pages, there is again and again the evidence of the son's
wounded feeling: his guarded defence of himself against
the General's reproach for not returning to the home
that the father's own conduct had rendered intolerable
to his son: his protests against his father's false conception of his character. During the years of Zygmunt's
attachment to Mme Bobrowa Wincenty Krasinski had
occasionally crossed the frontier to spend a few weeks
with his son. These meetings had brought small joy to
either. They were passed in a battle between the father
whose one desire was to see his heir make a brilliant
marriage, and the son who loathed the thought of marriage in itself, and who compassionated Mme Bobrowa
too much to consent to place the barrier of marriage
with another woman between himself and her.

"You cannot imagine," wrote he to Sołtan after he
had joined his father in Poland in the summer of 1838,
"what my daily life at home is: how I feel that I am
killing my father and that I am being killed in my
turn[1]."

The summer which the two spent together at
Opinogóra was one painful struggle between the father
and son. At last the father wrung from Zygmunt his
promise to see and write to Mme Bobrowa no more.
Wincenty Krasinski went to her in person and brought
back her written farewell to the man to whose memory

[1] *Letters to Sołtan.* Danzig, Aug. 12, 1838.

she remained faithful all her life. Tortured by the
thought of her grief, Krasinski in repeated letters begged
the friend who had originally made him acquainted with
the lady to watch over her, and to help her in any and
every way he could. From this closed chapter of his
life he carried a bitter searing of soul. At this time he
was corresponding constantly with the young Pole for
whom he wrote *The Temptation*, and who afterwards
became his brother-in-law by marrying into the Branicki
family: Adam Potocki. Krasinski was now only twenty-
six: but these letters warning a boy of sixteen who had
not yet bartered innocence for passion to shun the same
road that the poet had himself trodden, to strengthen
and beautify his character while it was still as clay for
the moulding, throw strong light on the tragic swiftness
with which Krasinski had laid down his youth:—and
as strong a light on the nobility, the undestroyable
idealism that were the possessions from which Krasinski
never parted. His experience had led him to that mile-
stone where he saw the only beauty of life in stern moral
obligation, life's greatest danger in the indulgence of
dreams beyond the sphere of action. Innocence is the
beautiful gift of Adam's age, but:

You at this moment are not yet standing in the vestibule,
you are still rocked on wings. But remember, so that you shall
not despair when those wings fall from you, that you must end
the journey on foot which you began so lightly, so charmingly,
so sweetly—I repeat on foot—and on their knees even must
each approach the sanctuary of life where the sacrifice is
celebrated, where for the eternal instruction of mankind God
clothed in our very flesh suffers and dies on a cross. This is
the difference between innocence and virtue. Virtue knows all,
understands all, has experienced all, has passed even through
hell, and has risen on the third day. In virtue there is the same
purity as in innocence, and, besides, the knowledge of all, of
good and evil. Your future is that virtue. So know this before

the time, so that virtue shall not reveal itself to you in intolerable burdens[1].

To save this boy on the brink of a precipice Krasinski told him what he would tell no one else.

None can adequately picture to himself how fearfully my soul has been ruined by love, how I deprived myself of the powers inexorably necessary for life, if we call labour, strength and virtue life. For your instruction, for your good, I will tell the frank truth which I should confess to no other. I became stupefied, I became degraded, as the result of exaltations and continual emotions of the soul. You would have the right to be angry with a man who could not understand you and who himself had never suffered as you are now suffering. My heart is perhaps torn more deeply than yours, my soul yearning with a greater despair, but I have behind me the series of the years of my past youth, I know what seeds existed within me ready to be developed, to give out their later fruit, and I can perfectly appreciate why perhaps nothing will come forth from me any more—I know what has killed me, and when it was that I killed myself with all my flaming heart in that suicide[2].

In November Krasinski left Poland and travelled with his father through Italy. His faith in Poland wavered together with his religious faith, both of which were always inseparable in Krasinski's heart. He was at the cross roads, perturbed, restless, unhappy, swept from his spiritual bearings, still seeking endlessly wheresoever he discerned a glimmer of light. When he mentions his nation in his correspondence it is generally in a widely different key from that of his early letters to Reeve, his later letters to his Polish friends. There is a tone of profound discouragement. No hint is given of the calling of a chosen country that remains to succeeding generations as the trumpet call of the Anonymous Poet to his people. At moments he could see nothing

[1] *Letters of Zygmunt Krasinski to Adam Potocki.* Opinogóra, Oct. 5, 1838. *Biblioteka Warszawska*, May, 1905 (Polish).

[2] *Ibid.* Warsaw, Oct. 20, 1838.

but the faults of his nation: utter blankness and desolation for her future. Death in these days seemed to him the only outlet for the Pole from miserable existence.

"Who cannot struggle against the stream," he once said, "and who will not degrade himself with the slime of its turbid waters ought to leave the scene. To live in order to eat and drink of shame, to grow fat on shame...is not worth while[1]."

The moral stress that sapped at the roots of his life reacted upon the artistic worth of Krasinski's work, no less than upon the evolution of his national theory. *A Summer Night* and *The Temptation*, both written in 1837, but published a few years later, fall far short of *Iridion* or *The Undivine Comedy*. Indeed *A Summer Night* seems a distinct return to the immaturity, we might even say the tediousness, of *Agay Han*. It appears at first reading a not very intelligible Byronic sketch in poetic prose of a girl, forced by her father to marry a prince of an alien race. Her lover watches the ceremony in the church; makes his way into the newly wedded wife's apartment and, with all the accompaniments of a romanticism, banal to the present day reader, but affected by the contemporaries of Krasinski's youth, he slays his beloved and himself, while the aged father dies for grief at having sacrificed his daughter's happiness.

This is the literal aspect of *A Summer Night*: but there is something deeper behind it. In whatever straits of pain Krasinski was immersed, his thoughts and fears could not leave his nation. The vagueness and confusion of the style of *A Summer Night*, the scenic effects that bewilder the reader and go far to blot out the main point, are in part attributable to the in-

---

[1] *Letters to Soltan.* Prague, Aug. 5, 1836.

fluence of Jean Paul: but still more are they Krasinski's shield of defence by which he protected both his father and himself from discovery. With the increasing severity of the Russian censors, Krasinski was driven to redouble his precautions. Sołtan was bidden to look for the manuscript of *Iridion* among Krasinski's papers in Rome and to destroy it: and so no autograph of the play exists. Gaszynski, if he mentions *Iridion* in his letters to Krasinski, must write merely a capital I. To his father, probably warned by the latter to do so, the poet wrote, denying the absurd rumour that he was the author of *Iridion*[1]. *A Summer Night* is the history of the marriage of a Polish girl, a lady of the Radziwiłł family and a cousin of Krasinski's own, with a Russian prince. When a boy of sixteen in 1828 Krasinski had been present at this wedding: and even before the events of 1830 had placed a great chasm between the Pole and Russian, such an alliance, entailing, moreover, the passing into Russian hands of the heiress's immense estates, was one that every patriotic Pole would regard with abhorrence. Under the squandering of decorative devices, we had almost said upholstery, the hand of the author of *A Summer Night* was trembling, not only with indignation against the ambitious parents who compelled their daughters to such a lot, but with profound compassion for the victims.

"She": "The Father," or "The Old Man": "The Bridegroom," or "The Youth": "He," meaning the lover: are the designations of the chief movers in the drama. They are shades, not men and women of flesh and blood; symbols who, as often is the case with Krasinski, represent ideas.

[1] J. Kallenbach, *Zygmunt Krasinski.*

"I saw her," the prose-poem begins abruptly, "when they led her in. She walked in terror in white robes with a wreath on her head."

Reading between the lines, and grasping those few clues that penetrate through the mystery in which Krasinski purposely shrouded them, there appears little doubt that his thoughts were painfully reverting to another, if not wholly dissimilar, story than that of a Polish girl, sacrificed to her father's self-seeking : to the tragedy of his own life.

"I grew beneath the shadow of his hand," cries the lover. "It was he who first taught my lips the name of my country, he who first made me know the desire for war."

What other language is this than that of Krasinski's reminiscences of his childhood with his father? When the bride justifies to her lover the marriage she had made, we might be reading one of those confidences to Henry Reeve during the terrible struggle that Krasinski underwent in the year of the Rising.

"Ah, my father came and entreated and implored. Thou knowest how he can command with a harsh voice : but for me he summoned not his orders from the bosom of a judge. He veiled the thunder of his curse with tears, and sighed and complained of his only child that she would thrust him down into his grave."

The autobiographical allusions, or rather hints, in Krasinski's writings are too valuable to pass over in silence. Another personal thread that runs through this allegory refers to his separation from Joanna Bobrowa, typified by the marriage which divides the lover from the bride of the Russian prince. Twice does Krasinski, as Dr Kleiner notices, emphatically repeat : "What the priest shall bind, man will not unloose[1]." There are

---

[1] J. Kleiner, *History of the Thought of Zygmunt Krasinski.*

other expressions that are clearly explainable by this unfortunate love affair. And a touch purely personal, and yet impregnated with the patriotism that is never far to seek in what Krasinski wrote, is to be found in the lover. The youth is a soldier, leading his followers to some great battle—which is of course, in the hidden language that Krasinski was forced to use, war for Poland. With the warlike tradition of his house in his veins, Krasinski had a craving for the battlefield from which his physical weakness alone was enough to debar him; the heroes of his works are always soldiers. In addition, his regret at not having fought for his country when she rose in 1830 was an ever living one. " He fought at Ostrołenka[1] ": are the words by which he would have Słowacki understand the depths of his grief when he saw his dearest friend Danielewicz die[2].

Further, it is worthy of notice that Krasinski places the lover, as he gives his farewell charge to his men before he himself seeks the bride in the castle, among those " three gentle slopes " which had been the poet's country home. He alludes proudly to the inheritance of freedom which was the possession of all who gathered on that soil, till the " southern king " came, bringing bondage with him. The youth promises his people deliverance, but only after long labour on their part. They must " beware of the tempters "; and this is Krasinski's guarded message to the Polish emigration, for even now, when the Anonymous Poet was not at his moral best, desire for his nation's highest good never ceased to devour his soul. " Lift your eyes. Space

---

[1] One of the famous battles of the Rising.

[2] *Letters of Zygmunt Krasinski.* Vol. III. Lwów, 1887. To Słowacki, Munich, March 26, 1842 (Polish).

enough for your souls hath remained in that blue sky."

The Temptation, although it also is a far cry from the great dramas that went before it and the lyrics that were to follow, is more interesting and more poetical than *A Summer Night*. It too shows the influence of Jean Paul and has also a suggestion of Scriptural style. Krasinski wrote it for the young Adam Potocki, who was bound to Petersburg, as a warning from his own experience against the temptations that awaited the Pole at the Russian court. The point of the work was too dangerous to be told openly. It is therefore clothed in another confused allegory, and covered with the same mannerisms as those of *A Summer Night*. Whatever their faults, both these works are the stifled cry of a Polish heart. They are the words of one striving to make his voice heard to those who could understand what lay behind half uttered hints, scarcely articulate murmurs. Yet even so the moral of *The Temptation* was too obvious: and hundreds of young Poles went to a Russian prison for having disseminated the poem.

"Mother slain six times," begins the poet in a transport of love and grief. "Unhappy mother, with but one of thy meads of green, with but one of thy fields of wheat, thou bindest memory, and henceforth thy sons must suffer, wander, love thee."

Krasinski then recounts, as a vision, a day in the life of a Polish youth whose nationality is of course only indicated. He is mounting a fiery horse: one foot on the stirrup, the other still on "the sweet grass of his home," he is about to set out for the court of the "lord of life and death," otherwise Nicholas I. His old mentor, who will appear at his side from time to time, prays that he may serve "only the Mother slain six times," and that he may be spared not pain, for all must suffer, but "the blush of shame and the ignominy of weakness."

For the descriptions in his poem Krasinski drew freely on his memories of Petersburg. *The Temptation* is the only record that he has left of his sufferings during those long sad months in the Russian capital. Under an over elaboration of style and hyperbolical detail the foundation of the work is truth, and a truth known from a harrowing personal experience. We may regret that Krasinski overlaid his recollections with a fanciful colouring instead of telling them with a directness that would have added tenfold to their power : but he could do nothing different. This tragic figure in Polish literature must hide his heart's agony under flowers and fantastic shapes.

"They spoke there in the palace"—Krasinski had done the same—"with a stifled voice, as if they feared the ear of their enemies behind the walls. The old man took the youth by the hand, and led him to the window. Hence could be seen all the city, and the crowds that swarmed past. Mighty city, strangely uniform and white":

wrote Krasinski, remembering the snow-shrouded town at which he had gazed during the tedious winter.

As the youth, disregarding the warning of the older man, looks admiringly at the women who pass by :

amidst the sombrely clad people, men began to ride, before whom the people bowed low. A long thin weapon was at their sides. Great plumes were on their heads. Crying out with a rough voice they went by in their might, and struck the children who had remained in the road...till one on horseback rode up, and all fell with their faces to the earth. That one was the lord of life and death.

The adulation with which the Russian Tsars were surrounded, especially during the reign of Nicholas I, was an attitude so foreign to the nature of the high-spirited and freedom-loving Poles, who called their fellow-citizens brothers and who were the equals of their kings, that it could not fail to arouse a Pole's biting sarcasm. Whenever Krasinski introduces the Tsar, his contempt of the Asiatic servility of the Russian court that he had seen with his own eyes finds free vent.

And again the boy gazes, fascinated, heedless of the words of his companion :

and only when the latter repeated them a second time did he cover his eyes with his hand and utter the name of his murdered Mother, as a remembrance of his childhood.

" Now alone, he is alone in the great city " : and here enters Krasinski's recollection of another boy, weighed down with the grief he could not tell among his country's enemies.

He concealed his unheard-of suffering under the aspect of a tranquil face. On all sides is danger, on all sides torture. There is none in whom he can confide. He must lie even to women and children. He learns lying as a masterpiece of art, and he became the master of artificial looks and of his tears and of his movements till the light, like the rays of day, vanished from his eyes. Oh! God, and his very garments became a lie. He threw off his old garments in which he had galloped over the steppes. He placed upon his head the plumes and girded the thin weapon to his side. The crowd began to make way before him, and his own horse knew him not.

Then in his vision the poet sees him enter a church, once more with the old man. The latter :

looked on his friend with a gaze filled with grief. The youth at first could utter no word, for he had forgotten how to show the depths of his soul with words. Once only he cried aloud. In that cry rang all the truth : the slow destruction of a soul that did not wish to fall.

" Follow me! " says the other, " so that thou mayest recall thy Mother's face." He is led past cemetery after cemetery till to the echo of national song, with banners fluttering and swords flashing under the stars, and mournful voices of spirits above them—a sort of setting in which Krasinski delights—they reach the spot where she who was "slain six times" lies on her bier : and the youth falls on his face weeping, and curses life.

This symbolism of Poland's grave and her resurrection will remain with Krasinski to the end. Though he was far as yet from the clear formulation of his great national mysticism, its germs are here. The spirits complain that God has betrayed them; "because our holy one is dead." The youth's guide bids them "blaspheme not, for your holy one still breathes. She shall rise again." To Krasinski, and to every one of the great patriot-prophets of Poland, the doubt of their country's resurrection was in truth a blasphemy, because it left the action of heaven unjustified, and the destruction of Poland an unredeemed crime.

Krasinski then brings the youth to the crisis, into the gay and splendid show of the imperial court. In the midst of the crowd of servitors, the play of the women's silks of every hue, the violins and incense, he is led to the feet of "the lord of life and death." And that audience, where the Tsar seeks to load the young Pole with his favours, in Krasinski's case in vain, is, allowing for its poetical and purposely disguised phrasing, the actual incident in Krasinski's life when he stood before Nicholas I.

The lord of the castle descended from his throne, and walked slowly, like a god, amidst the people falling to the ground. He went straight to the seat of the youth...marvellously handsome and strong. The youth rose, and boldly looked in his eyes. The lord of life and death spoke with beguiling tones :

" Come, we will go together, and I will show thee the wonders of my castle." And when the youth arose, as one riveted, he dropped a kiss on his brow.

With the bier of his Mother floating before his eyes, the youth went, and his hand shook with the throbbing of his boiling blood on the hard arm of the sovereign, who spoke with his stern voice sounding as thunder to those making way before him, but to his companion strangely sweetly and nobly. He reminded him of the past. He even pronounced the name of the slain Mother without trembling, as though her death weighed not upon his conscience. He appeared not to doubt for a moment that she had now perished from the earth for ever, and he showed the youth another future, great, engraved in the books of destiny. He lured his young desires towards it. He spared not his promises...From his comely face, like the face of Antichrist, the unhappy youth turned his eyes to the earth. Each word of the tempter fell upon his heart like a drop of poison.

He is led through the imperial treasuries: and the thought of Krasinski turns to the riches bought for the Russian crown by the blood and sweat of his fellow-countrymen, toiling in the mines.

And to the youth it appeared that he stood on the brink of mines, stretching out without end...He heard the hissing of subterranean fires...Sometimes too there rang as though a cry of the dying, as though a rattle of chains from the pit: and human figures crept through those streams of light, like black spots on the moon. The figures lifted their hands and, dragging their chains, cried long for one drop of water, for one moment of rest...It seemed to the youth that he had seen certain of their faces somewhere of old on the surface of the earth: but the lightnings veiled their faces, the roar of the melting metals stifled their wails.

Then the beautiful women of the conqueror's race surround him, tempting him by their charms.

For two long hours of that night I saw how, entangled, bewildered, struggling, he ever and anon besought the heavenly Father for strength and virtue, then again in despair rushed through the festal halls and sought a weapon to drive into his breast: but found it nowhere.

Gradually he yields. He consents to betroth himself
to a "maiden of the alien race." He sits by her side at
the banquet. Only when he sees through the glitter of
the feast the urn containing the ashes of his "slain
Mother" all grows dark before him, and his hand,
holding the goblet, trembles.

Ever more terribly wrestled his wandering soul, struggling
to return to its old faiths and hopes: but all that surrounded
him darkened his understanding with a heavy veil.

"The lord of life and death smiled graciously," and
bade him swear service to him and renounce his old
name. He flings him a handful of diamond crosses.
Word by word, the youth, "not hearing his own voice,"
repeats after the herald his abjuration of his country.
Crying "Shame" upon his own head, he rises and
escapes, mocked by all, cursing himself, and falls senseless in the courtyard.

This episode is no mere fancy. Krasinski wrote it
as a direct admonition to young Poles. The Pole who
accepted honours and decorations from the Tsar's hand
could only do so at the price of his nationality. Through
the apparently artificial passage throbs the grief of
a Pole who had seen his own father decorated by the
conqueror of his country.

The wretched boy comes to himself and to a speech-
less despair. Beside him is his mentor, who tells him
that:

"in another time and another place thou mightest have shone
a hero: but under a heavy test thou knewest not how to remain
virtuous. The seen reality overpowered for thee the invisible
but eternal truth. Thou art lost."

Krasinski further developed the scheme implied in
these words, and those that follow. The nation that had
defended Europe by constant war against the Turk and

Tartar was now called to a sterner conflict: that of a conquered people battling for moral life.

"The time for outward war has not yet come," is the mentor's reply to the youth's passionate entreaty for his horse and old weapon, with which he will avenge the wrongs of his country and his own shame.

"Long must last the days of silent sacrifice. Hearest thou? The enemies are pursuing thee. If they capture thee, for the rest of thy life thou wilt be the slave of their will, the participator in their crimes...One only, one only means of salvation hath remained for thee": and he drew forth his dagger.

"Strike!" cried the youth. "I die in the name of my Mother, slain six times."

And the old man kills him.

It will be seen that both *A Summer Night* and *The Temptation* end in an immoral situation. In *A Summer Night* it is the murder of the wife in her bridal chamber at the hand of the lover in whose embrace she dies. This may in part be put down as a piece of the Byronism of the day: but the fact remains. It is more apparent in *The Temptation*, where the murderer thanks God for the crime he has committed, and prays that the blood he has shed may flow before the heavenly throne with that of the martyrs. Count Tarnowski sees in such false positions a proof of the spiritual confusion into which Krasinski had drifted when he wrote these words[1]. At this time the Anonymous Poet, the future apostle of hope, met despair face to face. In both poems death is the only end to the intolerable national conditions[2].

Krasinski's father had done what the youth of the poem had done, and what Krasinski himself had not done. This incurable wound that Krasinski carried in

---

[1] St. Tarnowski, *Zygmunt Krasinski.*

[2] J. Kallenbach, *Zygmunt Krasinski.*

his heart all his days gives its peculiar point to the whole tale of the temptation and the fall. His anguish for once—and for this once only—breaks the bounds of his self-imposed silence: and the epilogue of *The Temptation* is the son's heart-broken lamentation for his father.

Oh, Mother, slain six times, when thou shalt arise from sleep, when once more thou shalt seat thyself upon the fields of corn, amidst green woods from sea to sea, and in the moment of the renewal of thy youth shalt remember the long nightmare of death, the fearful spectres of thy martyrdom, weep not for those who died in thy name on the battlefields of their country or beyond seas. Though vultures and wolves have torn asunder their remains, happy are they. Nor weep for those who died among executioners in deep dungeons. Though a prison torch was their only star, though the harsh word of oppression was their last farewell on earth, happy are they. But cast a tear of pity for the lot of those whose minds thy murderers duped with the glitter of falsehood, because they could not by the command of violence tear their hearts from thee. They, Mother, they suffered more than thy other sons. Their deluded hopes pierced like daggers their bosoms. In the secret of their souls were waged a thousand unknown wars, bloodier than the battles that thunder in the face of the sun to the ring of steel and the roar of cannon. The glittering eyes of thy foes led them over the icy slopes to the depths of the eternal cold: and on each mound they halted and wept for thee—till their hearts were withered for yearning, till their feet and hands wasted away in the bondage of invisible chains: and they became as living corpses, alone amidst a hated people, alone in their own homes, they only alone on the wide earth. My Mother, over their fate, over a sorrow of sorrows, do thou, do thou, utter a soft word of memory.

CHAPTER IX

BEFORE THE DAWN:
THE *THREE THOUGHTS* AND
THE TREATISE OF THE TRINITY
(1839–1842)

In the early part of 1839 Krasinski was in Naples. Each evening he was the guest of a Polish family. In letters to Sołtan he describes at length one of the daughters, Delphina Potocka. She was separated from a husband who had made her miserable, and who had been the cause of the death of her five young children. Beautiful, possessed of high mental gifts, an exquisite singer, she had turned the heads of Flahaut and of an Orleans prince. Chopin worshipped her; and it was her voice that soothed his dying bed.

The first impression that she made upon Krasinski was that of an "unbearable coquette[1]."

"When," he wrote to Sołtan, "I see human beings who need no comforting it seems to me that they have no need of me. Nothing attracts me to them. But it is exactly the reverse when I see on anyone's brow the trace of mourning, stamped by the vicissitudes of life. Then it is my dream that my words or my friendship or a pressure of my hand may perchance wake new life in that bosom...At first we quarrelled terribly, because I would not bow my head before her external *fashion* [the word is in English]. We even quarrelled so much that she said strangely disagreeable things to me and I to her. But when

[1] *Letters to Sołtan.* Naples, Jan. 1, 1839.

she changed her Parisian tone and began to speak sincerely, I changed my tone too, and every evening sadly and mournfully she describes her moral life to me, and I listen and sometimes cheer her[1]."

Such was the opening passage of Krasinski's love for the woman whom he has immortalized as his Beatrice. Whether hers was in reality the nobility with which Krasinski, who always idealized those he loved, invested her is a question difficult to resolve where evidences differ, and seems to us to matter little. The point remains that under the influence either of what she really was, or what Krasinski believed her to be, the Anonymous Poet reached the heights of poetical and national inspiration of which *Dawn* was the first fruit. His love for Delphina was of a far higher and more idealistic nature than had been his for Mme Bobrowa. To the latter he had never given his whole heart. He had, as Count Tarnowski says, been in love rather with the sentiment of love than with the woman herself[2]. But for years, until after his marriage, he as he expressed it lived in and for Delphina. With her he came to associate his hopes for his country, his own resurrection from death and despair.

"May God guard thee, love thee, bless thee," he wrote to her from Rome in the end of the year when he had first learnt to love her. "The power of prayer has again awakened in me for thy sake. Each evening with my whole heart, my whole spirit, I pray for thee[3]."

"In your heart," he wrote the following day, "in your intellect I felt myself once more, I gained life again; in the desire to give you new strength, or to pour new thoughts into your soul, I awoke a threefold power within myself. Through

[1] *Op. cit.*

[2] St. Tarnowski, *Zygmunt Krasinski.*

[3] *Unknown Letters of Zygmunt Krasinski to Delphina Potocka,* published by R. S. Kaminski. *Tygodnik Illustrowany.* 1899 (Polish).

you I became filled with strength and understanding. To-day I am stupid and worth nothing. But love me for the reason that a benefactress loves those on whom she bestows benefits, that an angel guardian loves those he guards[1]."

The series of Krasinski's love poems to Delphina Potocka now begins. How different was the character of his new love and his old may be gauged if merely from the fact that it was only after Delphina's death, and long after his own, that any eye but his and hers saw them[2]. These exquisite lyrics are among the most beautiful of Polish love songs. They carry the impress of two human hearts that had suffered deeply in life. They crown a human woman with the aureole of a patriot's devotion for his country and with the light upon Poland's fate that Krasinski always associated with Delphina Potocka. Their note is that of a high idealism. Delphina is the angel who shines upon the sadness of the poet's soul. Through her he knows the lost spring once more. Through her he learns again what happiness may be. She is the sister, as Krasinski, who had yearned for a sister in his lonely life, repeatedly calls her[3]; the sister saving a lost brother. "Descend into my hell and light my subterranean darkness, even as an angel, with one ray of thine eyes. Be my protection, be my hope and my salvation." *Again I bid farewell to thee* (Naples, 1840). "God only," the poet sings in an early poem, "can count the thorns in the garland of thy brow. I count them not,

---

[1] *Op. cit.*

[2] Except that Krasinski enclosed two or three of the less intimate ones in his letters to Gaszynski.

[3] "I never had a sister, but I think there is no more beautiful relationship on earth than that between brother and sister." *Letters to Adam Potocki. Biblioteka Warszawska*, May, 1905. And to Delphina: "Call me your brother, for I feel myself to be the brother of your soul." *Tygodnik Illustrowany*, 1898.

I only feel them, for I have taken all to the depths of my soul, as though they were my own." *Scarce have I known thee* (Naples, 1839). He had bowed his head, as he once told her, before the multitude of her suffer- ings[1]: and again in one of his letters, when his love for her was creating difficulties between herself and her family, he tells her how his hope had been that in his soul she would have found tranquility, in his love the dream that all her pain had passed away, in his love the land of the ideal where alone she could forget reality[2]. Exaltation, tinged with the dignity of his and her long sorrow, has also its place in the song inspired by his love. One of the finest of these poems casts a challenge to angels and spirits. They are in a happy eternity, but he is better off than they. For they do not know, as he knows, resurrection after the bitterness of death. They do not know, as he knows, the high betrothal of two hearts, threatened with the pain of separation. They do not know, as he knows, what is sorrow shared.

The flower of the white thorn on this sad earth lasts against rains and storms and hurricanes. From pain it grows, from sadness fructified. Spirits and angels! Such a flower you do not know within your skies of blue, for it blooms only in a fount of tears, for in the depths it grows and never on the heights. *To the Spirits* (1840).

On the other hand a little song which Krasinski wrote to Delphina on the eve of a journey to join his father shows a grace and lightness of touch that are entirely uncharacteristic of the Anonymous Poet.

I am stifled with my tears. My whole soul I gave to thee, and to-day I must depart. And I loved thee so. Ah, parting is as death. Yea, as death is parting.

---

[1] *Letters to Delphina Potocka.* Rome, 1839. *Tygodnik Illustrowany,* 1898.

[2] *Ibid.* (undated). *Tygodnik Illustrowany,* 1899.

Yesterday was still so joyous. Lo! To-day may not be borne.
Ever greater grows my sorrow. And I loved thee so. Ah,
parting is as death. Yea, as death is parting.
Where I go is dark and desert, for thou wilt not be with me,
thou my angel, watching o'er me. And I loved thee so. Ah,
parting is as death. Yea, as death is parting.
But, by God! I shall return. Days of grief my will shall
shorten. I will sing joy's song again, new inspired to ecstasy.
Parting is not death. Not as death is parting.

While Krasinski was thus pouring out his heart to
his love, he sent Sołtan a short poem, dated August 9,
1840, which he described as "a sudden explosion of the
soul[1]." After his death it was published, with some
changes and omissions that the author had made, from
a later MS. under the title *To the Muscovites*. It is
remarkable as being perhaps the only one of Krasinski's
poems that speaks the language of a boundless hatred,
and is the strongest comment upon the moral victory
of his *Psalms of the Future*. Its power, its superb
disdain of moral abasement before the enemy, causes
one of Krasinski's Polish biographers to rank it with
the greatest utterances of its kind in persecuted
Poland[2].

I know—for me the hangman's halter, the prison chain[3] are
ready, if before you I do not bow my brow, if humbly crieth
not my stubborn soul: "It is not God Who is my lord, but you."
Leave me in peace. I can find anywhere six feet of earth.
There is my home, narrow, but full of freedom, and better than the
castles where you dwell. There shall I be without you for the
first time in this world. I choose the darkness of the coffin rather
than the sun shared with you. If I could strangle you in one
embrace, thrust you all down into one pit, I would fain remain
in your hell-given conquest, and live on earth—for my dear
Lady's sake.

[1] *Letters to Sołtan.* Karlsbad, Aug. 9, 1840.
[2] St. Tarnowski, *Zygmunt Krasinski.*
[3] In the Sołtan MS. it is first Siberia and then the halter. I follow the
text of the later MS. as given in the Jubilee edition.

Then, his tone suddenly changing, he speaks with a tenderness that in itself explains the passion and bitterness of the preceding lines. He speaks of his Lady, his dying and afflicted country.

And I count the minutes before my beloved shall die, and I with her will go to seek somewhere God. For in life I loved her with such passion, loved her infinitely, loved her ever, everywhere, that my spirit bears her stamp for ever, and where she is there I must also be...Whither goes she there I go with her, where she halteth there I will with her remain. If overthrown beneath the stone of death she may not rise again, then may I neither rise!

So think of me no more, mine enemies! Vain is your labour, for I desire not shame, and fear I do not know. If you would tempt me you must seek temptation—in my grave. And when ye are able to tempt the bodies that are dead, and to degrade hearts that lie beneath the graveyard cross, then, and then only, in my subterranean hovel will ye see degradation on my corpse's face. So I await you, yea, when my heart is broken, not before; for I sucked in with my mother's milk that to hate you is beautiful and holy: and in that hatred lieth all my weal. I would only sell it for the Polish crown, and for nought else, not even for the veil that hides the image of the unknown God.

About the time that Krasinski first met Delphina Potocka he renewed his friendship with a Pole with whom he had played as a child in the nursery under the same French governess—the famous philosopher, August Cieszkowski. Cieszkowski's work, and especially his treatise on the *Our Father*, published in part in 1848 and subsequently after his death, has had an immense vogue among students of philosophy, and largely influenced Polish thought. His conception of the development of the spirit of humanity and of the three epochs of history was so instrumental in shaping the theories in which Krasinski found life that the poet could write to him :

Twice you appeared to me in my life. Once when I was childish wax you impressed yourself upon me: and the second time when I was melted and boiling gold you again impressed yourself upon me and for ever[1].

In 1839, and for three years longer, Krasinski had not yet found his soul. He was still in doubt and transition, though walking towards the light. In this state of mind he wrote in 1839 the *Three Thoughts of Henryk Ligenza*, that were published the following year. Under this collective name are comprised the poem called *The Son of Darkness* and two allegories in poetical prose, *The Dream of Cesara* and *A Legend*. The theme of the first is the human soul, that of the second the destiny of the Polish nation, and the third deals with the future of the Church. These matters—the history of individual and collective man—were so closely connected with each other in the Krasinskian scheme that the continuous thread may be discerned in the three dissimilar works[2]. They are preceded by a short sketch in prose. The imaginary writer and his wife are travelling in Sicily : and the little incidents of their Italian experiences are told with a lightness and humour such as we find in no other of Krasinski's writings.

The travellers stumble across the traces of a Pole, dead of consumption in the island. There is a touch of true pathos when the Polish visitors search for the forgotten grave of a lonely compatriot, and raise a tombstone to tell the passer-by that a Pole lies there. To papers purporting to have been left by this Pole Krasinski gives the title: *Three Thoughts of Henryk Ligenza*.

[1] *Letters to August Cieszkowski.* Munich, Feb. 25, 1842.
[2] St. Tarnowski, *Zygmunt Krasinski*.

Pantheism, Hegelianism, metempsychosis have all influenced the difficult poem, *The Son of Darkness.* Polish critics differ considerably as to its literary merits: we will therefore leave that side of it alone. Upon the value of its matter opinions are also at variance[1]. The theme is highly complicated and obscure, so that as the present study is not a philosophical work perhaps the writer may be excused for dealing with it somewhat cursorily.

The poem sets forth the origin of the human spirit and its journey back to its last end. Some "unknown power" cast it forth from darkness to the earth. "Half slumbering," it wanders and gropes to the dimly discerned light, struggling with Titanic tortures, till it clothes itself "in the garments of humanity," and, becoming man, recognizes its own consciousness. In its beginning it knows God only as the "lord of wrath." It endures suffering, yearning after God, by which it advances to a higher life. Its throes are crowned by the union of the Word with flesh, of God with man, by the victory over evil and the "clay of the heart," which is the triumph of love[2]. Again returns a period of longing, doubt and torment: but "the evil is only a transition, only the highway's dust"; and the son of darkness ascends, the son of light, to the stars.

Step ever further then, oh, son of light! Step to the boundaries of the undiscovered worlds!...What thou didst grasp with thought thou shalt with thy hand attain. What thou didst feel by inspiration with thine eyes shalt thou behold.

There is no death. Before the spirit stretches cycle

---

[1] Compare St. Tarnowski, *op. cit.*, with J. Kleiner, *History of the Thought of Zygmunt Krasinski*, and Prof. Zdziechowski's *Vision of Krasinski.* Cracow, 1912 (Polish).

[2] M. Zdziechowski, *op. cit.* J. Kleiner, *op. cit.*

after cycle of life: and it passes through successive transmigrations till at last more or less pantheistically it is fused in the All Spirit of the Divinity, and henceforth through eternity must "think, love, create a heaven in heaven[1]."

The Dream of Cesara is once more national, though the distinction between what we call Krasinski's national writings and those in which he occupies himself with universal spiritual problems is more apparent than real. Krasinski was led to the great interests of humanity by the desire that they might throw light on the problem of his country. One enigma was the complement of the other.

Neither *The Dream of Cesara* nor the *Legend* is comparable to Krasinski's greater works. They are written in his most highly decorated manner. Related in the style of apocalyptic vision, they convey to the reader's mind a strange sense of things seen in the confusion of a dream. And, in fact, we have the testimony of Mickiewicz who knew it from a friend of Krasinski—Gaszynski, Dr Kleiner conjectures[2]—that *The Dream* and the *Legend* were the poet's actual dreams[3].

A voice [Delphina's] called me by my name, "Cesara! Cesara!" And I went forth I know not where, but that voice will I follow, if needs be even to the end of the world.

[1] Dr Kleiner gives an interpretation of the poem as referring to the history of humanity in general. The allusion to the spirit's conception of God as the "lord of wrath" is explainable by the Judaism that preceded the Incarnation of Christ. The fresh sufferings that befall the spirit of humanity after the time of Christ depict Krasinski's own epoch which he hoped was to be merely the transition to the third and last epoch of humanity. The spirit in the poem ascends to the other world: and here ends the earthly development of the human race. J. Kleiner, *op. cit.*

[2] J. Kleiner, *op. cit.*   [3] Adam Mickiewicz, *Les Slaves.*

The voice leads him to a mighty cathedral. Its elaborate description is modelled on Krasinski's remembrances of Freiburg cathedral where he had wandered, surrounded, it seemed to him, by invisible spirits of those who had died for their faith, and asking himself if they would rise again[1]. Against a mysterious background of moonlight and music Cesara sees the hosts of the nations, and among them the last Poles left on earth, advancing in chains and mourning garb to the tomb.

> And grief encompassed my heart, and tears flowed to my eyes. And the voice cried to me as the wind: "Cesara, Cesara, behold the people who are going from the earth, and will return no more."...I heard the voices of multitudes crying: "Live and be our slaves."

The Poles prefer death. The floor of the cathedral yawns before them and, accompanied by the figure of Christ, they go down to their grave amidst sorrowful music. Over their tomb lies a great stone marked by the inscription written in blood: *The Nation.* No trace of them remains: but a beautiful mourning woman rises before the poet's eyes, the sister, says the voice, of those who have fallen. "Like a dream though ever visible," she, who Count Tarnowski hazards may be the memory of his country, or the love of her or hope for her, floats before him through nights and days, through the mists of his vision, whither he knows not:

> but whither she goes I go, and where she pauses there will I halt, and where she disappears there will I disappear with her.

As they pass on they reach a spirit in the guise of an old man seated on a rock above the mists, playing a harp on which there is only one string left. In this

[1] *Letters to Soltan.* Freiburg, Sept. 20, 1839.

202 The Anonymous Poet of Poland

obscure allegory where, according to Dr Kleiner, it is
not clearness that is aimed at, but the mystery of a
vision, we can only conjecture for whom the different
symbols stand. Count Tarnowski suggests that the
harpist may represent Time or Satan or Brute Force[1].
Whoever he may be, he conjures the poet to "forsake
her who will never live again."

And the figure halted and turned her face upon me. All
the unfulfilled dreams, all the slain hopes of her race, all their
life, all their pride and their death and now their slumber in
the grave, together at one moment were reflected on that face...
And again the spirit sang: "Return and live among the living
peoples. And I will remain here with her and will sing to her
my song without hope on this last string. For the others have
played their music away and are shattered. All together were
once called faith, courage, love. This only one left to-day is
called Nothingness."

He calls to the poet: "Choose." The voice of the
woman calls: "Cesara!"

And I followed her who will never return, to the cemetery
of death. She whom I loved has vanished in whirlwinds of
snow. And I felt all the pains of parting, all the emptiness of
void. I thought that the figure of Christ had deceived them,
descending with them into the grave, for they shall wake no
more, and that she whom I defended had deceived me likewise,
for she had left me among those who were dead for ever.
And I sat on the shores of that sea and besought my soul to
leave me.

"What now?" is the mocking reiteration of the
harper: and it must be remembered that the temptation
to despair of Poland's resurrection was to the mind of
Krasinski and the great Polish patriot mystics as the
direct assault of the Evil One. And again, "either in
the depths of my heart or beyond the clouds," the voice
that had led Cesara calls.

[1] St. Tarnowski, *Zygmunt Krasinski.*

And I started up and cried: "Save me, for I die: and I die because thou didst deceive me."

She answers :

"Cesara, Cesara, wherefore dost thou grieve, because thou hast sacrificed thy life for her who is dead ? Knowest thou not that there is a resurrection ? She who took away thy life shall give it back to thee, for her death was only an illusion."

I beheld the figure, rising as a new-born star from the bounds of the horizon...and around me were men being raised up from the dust, and the vision of Christ flashed white above them in the sky. I closed my eyes, and fell with my face to the earth among those who were rising from the dead.

This is the pith of *The Dream of Cesara*, taken from a crowd of details, some of which appear wholly extraneous to the matter. Although its general impression is that of a bewildered despair, yet it ends on the note of resurrection, and contains Krasinski's favourite moral of the "test of the grave."

The *Legend* opens in the Roman Campagna, in the twilight of the last Christmas Eve that is ever to be. A boat comes across the sea, and lands "the last left of the Polish knighthood," bound for the midnight Mass in St Peter's. The dreamer leads them across the Campagna and through the streets of Rome. The description of the crowds of pilgrims, carrying flaring torches, hastening to St Peter's, where the last Mass on earth is to be sung, the clashing of all the bells of Rome, lights flaming on towers and gates, have the feverish effect of a nightmare and lend credence to the story that Krasinski was writing down what he had dreamed. With the sorrow of death imprinted on their countenances, the Polish knights pass. The citizens of Rome try to withhold them from entering the basilica that seems on fire with light. A cardinal clad in purple appears on the balcony, and bids the Romans "let enter

those who erst redeemed a strange nation from death[1],
and later for that same faith died themselves. Let the
dead enter."

They enter, and kneel at the tomb of St Peter,
swords in hand. The eye and ear are wearied by the
ornate vision of the interior of the church, filled with
countless throngs : how it is dim with "silver smoke"
from the thuribles, how the marble columns flash as
brilliant snows, how the Pope in golden vestments comes
in, surrounded by a glittering retinue, and for the last
time in the history of the world celebrates Mass. The
Cardinal summons all to "pray, for the time is short,
and to-day prayers are needed on earth and in heaven."
There is throughout the premonition of a terrible
approaching cataclysm. At the moment of the Elevation
the form of Christ with bleeding Hands and Feet is
seen raised in the air. The chalice trembles in the
Pontiff's fingers. The Cardinal cries out, " The time
is fulfilled," and, stretching out his hands to St Peter's
tomb, conjures the apostle to "arise and speak." The
figure of Peter half emerges, and as his voice peals
forth: "Woe!" to all it seems as though the piers of
the dome rocked.

"Peter, dost thou know me?" [asks the Cardinal, to which
Peter answers]: "Thy head at the last supper rested on the
Lord's bosom, and thou didst never die upon this earth."

And the Cardinal answered : "And now it is bidden me
to dwell among men and shelter the world in my bosom, as
the Lord sheltered my head in His at the last supper."

Then the mighty building begins to sway to its fall.
The terrified crowds flee. Only the Pope remains. The
Polish knights, commanded by the Cardinal to follow

[1] The Lithuanians who were won to Christianity by the self-sacrifice
of Jadwiga, Queen of Poland.

him outside, refuse to leave the Pope to perish alone. Baring their swords, they surround him where he kneels at the high altar. The dome crashes in, and the basilica, the Vatican and the square are a heap of dust.

It is the dawn. The Cardinal, otherwise St John, seats himself on the ruins as on a throne. His purple garments fall from him, and he is transformed into a white figure, sparkling with soft light, while his face breathes love and peace.

> I approached him, and at the very moment that the sun rose I said : " Lord, is it true that yesterday for the last time Christ was born in that Church which to-day is no more ? "
>
> And he, " Henceforth Christ is no more born nor dies on earth, for henceforth for the ages of the ages He is and will be on earth."
>
> And I, hearing this, cast off all fear, and asked : "Lord, and they, whom I led here yesterday, will they lie for ever beneath these ruins, all dead around the old dead man ? "
>
> And that white holy one answered me : " Fear not for them. Because they rendered him that last service the Lord will reward them—for, in their setting even as in their rising, dead, even as they lived, they are of the Lord. Yea, verily, it will be better for them and for the sons of their sons."
>
> And when I had understood I was glad, and my spirit woke.

We are thus left with the death of Poland and with nothing more beyond a vague promise that is too indefinite to convey any certitude of her resurrection. Count Tarnowski looks upon this work as Krasinski's greatest swerving from his patriotic and religious faith. But the allegory that Tarnowski considers as well nigh a blasphemy against Krasinski's national convictions and openly hostile to his Church, Dr Kleiner is inclined to regard as illustrative of the doctrines of development that at this time began to take hold upon the poet. The old Poland dies with the old Church. Both will

rise again, but in a completely different form in the
new epoch, which is to be the epoch of love[1]. We
shall see how Krasinski modified this theory, which in
the *Legend* is almost too vague to be called a theory,
and, bringing it into far more orthodox lines, worked it
out in *Dawn*. The contradictions to be found in the
Legend are, Count Tarnowski suggests, not to be in-
vestigated too narrowly. After all the *Legend* is not a
treatise. It is a dream with the inconsistencies of a
dream[2].

As regards the three epochs of the Church or of
humanity, we do not know whether Krasinski had
learnt them directly from the writings of Joachim of
Flora, which is improbable, or through Schelling and
Swedenborg, who both refer to them, or through the
medium of Cieszkowski, or again whether he evolved
them out of his own brain[3].

"After the Resurrection," he wrote to Delphina Potocka
who was the constant recipient of his highest philosophical
theories side by side with the outpourings of his love, "Christ
takes not Peter, but John. But Peter is the Roman Church,
the practical militant governing Church, and John, who begins
the gospel from the 'Logos,' signifies the epoch of thought
and of the highest love. This has greatly struck me[4]."

This language, as Dr Kleiner remarks, indicates
that the Anonymous Poet reached his point by a
process of his own, and probably only discovered later
that it was several centuries old[5].

Krasinski was now rapidly advancing in the forma-
tion of his idea. In 1840 he wrote to the friend

[1] St. Tarnowski, *op. cit.* J. Kleiner, *History of the Thought of Zygmunt Krasinski.*
[2] St. Tarnowski, *op. cit.*   [3] J. Kleiner, *op. cit.*
[4] *Letters to Delphina Potocka.* Rome, Dec. 20, 1839. *Tygodnik Illustrowany*, 1899.   [5] J. Kleiner, *op. cit.*

whose life was darkened by the acutest griefs of a father :

> There are certain sufferings of yours about which I never write to you : both because I do not wish to aggravate them, and because it is better not to set on paper what has taken up its abode in the very depths of the heart. But do not therefore think that I do not think of them and that I do not feel them together with you.

Assuring his friend how the latter's afflictions rend his heart, he goes on :

> Oh, Adam, only, only faith in a higher ordering of the world, faith that all the happenings and bitternesses of the earth are discords let loose in the Divine accord, in the accord that as yet has not reached our hearing but must some time reach it, can save us. Therefore we believe that we know only one half of life. I speak incorrectly, we know the whole of life by thought, but we know by our own experience the half of that all-life, and because it is only the half it is evil for us. But we are spirits, not perishable stones. The spirit has its resurrection from pain ; happiness and divine peace are our destiny, for they are our nature. Thence we came, and there shall we return. Let this thought be my wish for you in the year that is now to begin[1].

This conception of the half of life being ours, and not the perfect whole, was one of the foundations upon which Krasinski was now raising the solution of un-explained suffering that gave him the clue to the mystery of Poland's tragic history.

"Where there is pain," he wrote to Słowacki on a Roman Easter Eve, "there is life, there is resurrection." Death was no more death in his eyes. There is no death save moral abasement. "Only where there is abasement shall there be no resurrection[2]."

While Krasinski was thus on the highroad to the vision that brought him hope and joy for his nation he

---

[1] *Letters to Sołtan.* Rome, Dec. 20, 1840.

[2] *Letters of Krasinski.* Vol. III. To Słowacki, Easter Eve, Rome, 1841.

was passing through the crisis in his private life that
he had greatly dreaded. His father was insisting
that his son should marry the lady whom the elder man
desired to secure for his heir. Krasinski, as we have
seen, had always regarded with aversion the thought of
his marriage, and had indeed, as Count Tarnowski
notes, no inducement to look upon marriage as a happy
lot, considering the experience of the two women he
had known best[1]. Still more, his heart was bound up
with Delphina Potocka. Just before his departure from
Rome in the summer of 1841 for Germany, where he
was to meet his father and where he knew that the
question would have to be decided, he addressed a
poem to Delphina, breathing grief and eternal love,
praying God, as he goes forth "into a terrible world
where love is not," to grant him, barren of hope and
happiness himself, to be the sweetener of the sorrows
of her whom God had given him as his sister. Three
months later when he and his father had parted company
he tells Sołtan :

"You cannot imagine what it is, after having spent two
months in continual wrangling, to regain a little freedom at
last." He solemnly charges his friend that he shall allow no
other ear ever to hear these confidences, for if he does: "I cannot pour out to you my breaking heart...My father's despair,
his weakened health, have forced me. I had nothing else with
which to give him strength and life[2]."

He then tells how for that reason he consented to
his father's will. But the negotiations did not result in
anything immediate. Two years passed before Zygmunt's betrothal and marriage. He settled down in
Munich for the winter of 1841 with the friend of his

[1] St. Tarnowski, *Zygmunt Krasinski.*
[2] *Letters to Sołtan.* Munich, Sept. 24, 1841.

heart, Danielewicz. And then the moment came when, after several weeks of close interchange of ideas with this beloved companion, he felt a sudden illumination of vision. An almost rapturous conception of the national theory for which he had sought with such anguish invaded his soul.

"I spent the winter not in Munich, nor in any place in space; but in myself—in the spirit," he told Cieszkowski[1].

And many weeks later he wrote to Gaszynski:

All through January I was possessed by uncommon inspiration. I lived so that the whole of that month was to me one hour, one dream. I have had to pay the fates dearly for that delight of the soul [in the death of Danielewicz]. All day I was at my table, and in the evenings with my dear Konstanty[2].

He embodied his ideas in his *Treatise of the Trinity*, consisting of three sections : (1) *On the trinity in God and the trinity in man :* (2) *On the trinity in time and space :* (3) *On the position of Poland among the Slavonic peoples.* It was never finished. Krasinski enclosed extracts from it in his letters from Munich to Sołtan and his friend and cousin, Stanisław Małachowski. The rest remained among his manuscripts, and was after his death sent by his desire to the priests of the Polish congregation of the Resurrection. He left orders that nothing in his papers that might be against the teaching of the Catholic Church should be published. The Resurrectionists objected to the publication of the treatise by reason of its want of orthodoxy: and, although part of it was given to the public by the poet's grandson in 1903, it was only published as fully as Krasinski left it in the Jubilee edition of 1912[3].

[1] *Letters to Cieszkowski.* Munich, Feb. 25, 1842.
[2] *Letters to Gaszynski.* Basle, April 9, 1842.
[3] It is printed there under the title : *On the position of Poland from the Divine and human standpoint.*

As Krasinski repeated and developed much of the matter of the treatise, and with greater beauty, in *Dawn* and the *Psalms*, we will resist the temptation to do more than summarize its main thesis and quote a few of the more striking or illuminating passages.

In part influenced by his studies in Hegel and Schelling, and still more by Cieszkowski's theories, Krasinski found in the trinity or threefold a solution to his difficulties. The first Person of the Blessed Trinity corresponds to Being. His relation to man is that of Grace inasmuch as He created him. The second Person is that of Thought or Understanding, from whom we receive the consciousness of Being and the knowledge of its conditions. The third Person is that of Love, who unites Being with Thought. " In the image of this Divine Trinity each of us is likewise a trinity each moment...each of us is simultaneously being, thought, life." To the three elements of the Divine Trinity correspond the three elements or epochs in the life of the soul, of the nation, of humanity.

In the beginning is grace, and in the end love. Grace [shown to man in the act of his creation] can only be for those who are not yet. Love can only be for those who are, but who are worthy of it, who have merited it. But the intermediary and the necessary transition from grace to love, from the first being [or existence] to the highest life, is understanding. In relation to us the Divine Understanding signifies the logic of our life, its work, its toil, together with its suffering and its martyrdom, in a word, its merit. And obviously in order to lead those created by grace to the sanctity of heavenly spirits, to eternal life, their merit and gradual progress were absolutely necessary : that is, it was necessary that the Divine Understanding should manifest to and enjoin upon them this indispensable necessity, for otherwise grace would be uncomprehended, and in the end love would likewise be blind, likewise uncomprehended, and therefore would be no love but again only grace. Therefore there would be no change or development from first to last.

Upon this idea of development Krasinski founded his hopes for both his country and humanity. The travail of transition explains to him the riddle of our suffering. This transition is the second stage of our trinity leading to the third, that of love, of the Holy Ghost who as All Love unites the first and second Persons of the Trinity, unites being with thought.

The intermediary in that transition between grace and love, Eden and Heaven, the ages of Jehovah and of the Holy Ghost, between the state of bodily being and the state of the fulness of life and spirituality, had to be the Divine Understanding which, taking flesh and manifested in the human race, woke the soul and understanding of man. Hence Christ is the Saviour...the intermediary, and only passing by Him can we reach redemption...He is...in the highest sense the way, as He said of Himself. By that way only can we attain to the final love : and because as far as we are concerned that way is toil, suffering, merit, therefore Christ had to reflect it, express it, put it into action, as it were throw it into bas-relief by His life and by His death. All the labour and pain of transition is represented in Him...Therefore not by victory but by constant defeats He conquered everywhere...In Him always, in each moment and deed and word of His we see the union of both natures, the continual inflow of one into the other—in a word, we see the transition of which we are speaking, the transition from the flesh to the fulness of the spirit, or from the human nature to the Divine.

The life and death of Christ manifest the road by which man and humanity must pass : and this close likeness of the lot of man and the human race to that of their pattern, Christ, becomes one of Krasinski's master arguments.

Again, from the reciprocal overflowing between the Persons of the Blessed Trinity, Krasinski deduces that of each soul, fashioned in the image of the Blessed Trinity, upon one another. This, too, plays a considerable part in his mystic theories of Poland's apostolate.

In humanity the social state, the sanctification and raising of which is the aim of humanity, is precisely that reciprocal imparting to each other of human spirits. Everywhere and always who gives receives, who loves is multiplied, who pours out of himself or creates something external, is in that very moment created higher himself...To impart self on earth to others is in outward seeming to lose something of self, even to be utterly destroyed—but that is only a delusion. That destruction is itself destroyed, for in truth only by that means does the living spirit grow and immortalize itself...By what it gives out from itself it becomes more powerful.

Showing how Christ wrought out this rule "most sublimely and most perfectly" by His life and death, Krasinski argues that as the plant to become a flower must pass through light, so each man and collective humanity must pass by the law of Christ, "and work it out in themselves to gain salvation. For the individual man salvation is eternal life...For humanity it is the Kingdom of God on earth, that is, the condition of social Christ-likeness."

But as humanity is the collective state of all individual men, each unit composing the aggregate must make himself ripe for this high spiritual calling. "He must fulfil that condition somewhere and somehow." Perhaps by transmigrations, suggests Krasinski (who at that time was inclined to believe in metempsychosis), or perhaps by some state of trial and purgation after human life is over, which state the poet calls purgatory, but which he develops somewhat further than the Catholic doctrines on the subject in which he had been brought up. The state of purgation he looks upon as that of the transition of which he often speaks. Man, deprived of his first condition, that of earthly being or existence, enters the second phase of his trinity, that of thought or mind, impossible to manifest itself by action. This phase of transition, deprived of corporeal existence but where mind and soul remain, leading to the third state or epoch of union by love between being and thought, was to Krasinski the exact counterpart of the then condition of his nation, and this conception cleared his views on her present and future. In that purgatory, writes the poet with his thoughts turned to his country, there is "indescribable yearning, infinite mournfulness," endless searching for what is not yet realized.

But the moment will arrive when the perfect harmony between thought and being will be effected, and that will be the day of the Holy Ghost, Who shall unite them by love. It will be the completion of the trinity both in man's soul and in humanity. Christ left it to "human toil to prove in the whole of nature, in all the departments of life and death, in all the spheres of thought and in every civilization the necessity of Christ's law."

Suffering and struggle are always Krasinski's inexorable conditions. The same law of the torments of transition applies equally to the individual and to the human race. Man is composed in the image of the Trinity: of body; soul, the latter, according to Krasinski, the thought and consciousness of man about himself; and spirit, that is the individuality that binds these two and which is man's personality[1]. These correspond, as we see, to each member of the Divine Trinity. "To reach the spirit it is necessary for the human race to pass through thousandfold and terrible cycles, and equally is it necessary for each individual

[1] See Count Tarnowski's clear summarization of Krasinski's doctrines in his *Zygmunt Krasinski.*

that composes it. Being, or the body, wars in our bosoms with thought or the soul." By this war shall the spirit be born in man. "The All Spirit or the Holy Ghost will manifest Himself to creatures as soon as they themselves reach the reconciliation within themselves of their being with their thought, of the body with the soul." "Action is the sign, the consequence of life. Life manifests itself by deeds." The creation of the world was the highest of deeds. We from afar unite ourselves to God's great deed inasmuch as we act or create perpetually : and when these acts

reach a certain degree of perfection, when there shall be in them harmony of being and thought, then will we attain union with the Holy Spirit...The better and more profoundly we know Him by that deed...of ours the more He will show Himself to us, beautiful, wise, infinite...ever more unattainable, though each moment attained : ever abiding in His relation to us as the ideal, albeit as the reality unfolded about us : as our unceasing desire, as our life that is never ceasing nor possible to end. And this in very truth is eternal love...But it is difficult to write clearly on all that touches the all spirit and the all life, for we, spirits torn asunder and divided into twain, unhappy, suffering, have not reached the ages of life. One torn asunder can only faintly anticipate what are peace, harmony, love, and the creative deed that flows from them. Yes, but it is well to have this anticipation. It is the glimmering spark in us of the all life.

Humanity then toils and progresses to its aim, which aim is the Kingdom of God, or in other words the new Christ-disposition of the universe,

passing into deed and reality ; now not only affecting individual souls, but the whole of humanity, all its laws, statutes, and governments, and thus changing earth into one great living temple of the Holy Ghost.

What then is humanity ? It is the common labour of all human individual spirits, advancing through the ages of the history of this world, so that by their mutual training of self they may reach that rung of time whence they will soar to their eternal life, which is that new epoch when all the universe shall be united in eternal harmony.

If, then, humanity is the common labour of individual spirits travelling to the eternal life, there must be intermediary circles in which is wrought the common labour of individual spirits training humanity in its highest signification, that is, God's kingdom on earth...and from whose organization and harmony is to arise the living and perfect organism which we call God's kingdom and the rule of the Holy Ghost on this earth.

These circles are the individual nations each called to its own working out of one of God's ideas, endowed like man with free will as to whether it will correspond to the Divine grace of its calling. If unfaithful to this vocation, it shall lose its entity for ever, and be swallowed up by other nations.

We only call a nation that collection of living spirits which has comprehended the aim to which it tends, that is, humanity in its highest signification, and has consecrated itself to this by historical deeds, or has so acted as to hasten its apparition and fulfilment.

From this follows the duty of the individual to sacrifice himself for the nation and therefore for humanity, because "the Christ-likeness of the collective spirit is not attained otherwise than by the Christ-likeness of individual spirits." With Krasinski the indispensable condition of the resurrection of Poland will always be the moral worth of the individual Pole.

When the individual spirits give up their body and life for the nation, for humanity, by that very act they gain them back, for the nation is exalted and the day of God's kingdom approaches, consequently the solution of the history of the human race.

"Hence results the sanctity and the inviolability of nationality." A nation's first beginning, her rise from her myths into the light of history, "in which God's

special grace worked under the form of the national
instinct and inspiration," constitutes the first stage of
the trinity in a nation's life, that of being. When after
centuries of labour she gains a clear knowledge of her
vocation and beholds "the secret of her own being,"
she has reached the second stage of her trinity, that of
thought. Then succeeds her long battle between "the
two elements, the body and soul of the nation," that is
to lead her to the third stage, when she shall be a
medium of God's kingdom on earth. "Then only in
that third epoch the immortal spirit of the nation shall
shine in its fulness...having fused body and soul"—
Krasinski's definition of the soul will be remembered—
"in one love and one life."

Krasinski then works out his idea of the trinity in
history : the ancient world, the classical age, corresponding to the first stage of the body or being : the
Christian era to the second of thought and of the soul.

"But before these two worlds finish out the struggle with
each other," writes the Pole, wearied by the evil days in which
his lot had been cast, "unite and flow together into the one
world of the spirit, how many ages must pass ? How many
transformations, tribulations, tempests, must befall ? How
much blood shall be shed by the body, how much despair by
the soul ?...[Our age] being a transition, bears all its signs,
all the marks of disunion, disruption, of the war between being
and thought, between the body and soul of the world."

The idea of nationality, slowly growing through
history, is opposed to the rule of the ancient world
which was of government only, the rule of the body
preceding the rule of the soul.

But we are reaching the ages when such a division of soul
from body shall be no more possible, and the first principle of
public law shall be the dissolution of all governments that are
not founded on nationality.

This is the age of nationalities. The nations "are reaching the consciousness of the inviolability and independence of their life." But as only after Christ's life and death did the individual spirit reach the full knowledge of its life and immortality and of its road to heaven, so now the collective spirit of humanity necessitates its pattern to point it out its road and to prove to it that destruction is impossible.

But such a truth, descending for the first time into the world, can only be proved by death and rebirth. Before we can begin to live lastingly without death, first we must rise from death, to show all who are mortal and our brothers that they are in very truth immortal.

"The necessity of the like examples is the eternal law of history," where:

nothing is brought about flimsily or easily. All is done little by little, with difficulty, laboriously, and beyond measure gravely and sternly. No abstract thought, no idea unjustified by execution, no theory taken by itself can direct the fate of the world. It must first take flesh, become a living example, a doctrine with a beating heart.

There must be in our days some one member of the human commonwealth to be the living proof of the sanctity of nationality and the disseminator of the truths upon which history is built. It can only speak through the power of martyrdom and death by which alone immortality and resurrection can be proved, which have been preceded by a past of glorious deed.

So here we have the poet's own country, now, he says, in the second stage of her trinity.

That will be in some wise the state of Purgatory for the soul of a great nation. Ground down on all sides by a fearful slavery, wounded by daily injustice, suffering and wandering, she, by indescribable pain and an equally infinite ideal strength of faith and hope, prepares for herself a new body for the day of resurrection...No one without deliberation and strong resolution, without a thousand hesitations, researches, painful deceptions, collapses of the powers of thought and transforming uprisings will reach the self-inebriation of its own Christ-likeness, awakened in us by the manifestation of the Son of God. The collective spirit of a nation must pass through precisely the same cycle as individuals if she is to rise from the dead and stand in the band of living creative nations.

The conviction of the identity of the morality of the individual with that of the universal law is always one of Krasinski's fundamental tenets, of which we shall have more to say in another place.

Then with a touch of ecstasy Krasinski sets forth the mission of his nation to lead us by her death to the realization of God's kingdom on earth. But we will not linger upon these fine passages for we shall meet them as sublime poetry in *Dawn*, whither Krasinski had now nearly won his way.

In the third part of the *Treatise* the poet points to the Slavonic race in contradistinction to the Roman and Germanic families as that which will introduce the future element of life into the world. Poland, says he, will be the leader of that race. For in Russia an Asiatic conception of government stamped out liberty, and thus the element of love and life and progress perished. It is curious to note that one of the arguments Krasinski uses in his case against Russia is the denial by the Russian state religion of the equal procession of the Holy Ghost from the two first Persons of the Blessed Trinity. This, as is obvious from the whole tenor of *The Treatise of the Trinity*, proves to Krasinski the rule of all-power in the Russian nation, the deification of power, and hence the loss of the spirit and of progress. But at the moment that he turns fondly to the contrasting image of his own nation, the manuscript breaks off abruptly, never to be resumed.

CHAPTER X

DAWN

(1843)

On the 9th of April, 1842, Krasinski wrote from Basle to Gaszynski:
"Where shall I begin and where must I end, oh, my Konstanty? At that very name "—it had also been Danielewicz's—" my heart is broken. Only two weeks ago there were three of us, united of old together from our childhood. Now there are only two, you and I¹."

In February under the shock of a terrible family tragedy, to which indeed one who knew him well ascribes his death², Danielewicz had fallen sick of typhus. For weeks Krasinski watched by his bedside in an agony where there was small room for hope: and on Easter Sunday Danielewicz died in the poet's arms, the only one of his friends who did not outlive him.

" He was," writes Krasinski to their mutual school-fellow, "my guardian angel, my strength, the intellect of my intellect : and he loved me so, he loved me so that if all had forsaken me I would not have complained if only he had remained³."

Krasinski only tarried in the city that had become hateful to him long enough to lay his friend's remains

---

¹ *Letters to Gaszynski*. Basle, April 9, 1842.
² See Stanisław Koźmian's Introduction to *Letters of Zygmunt Krasinski to Stanisław Koźmian*.
³ *Letters to Gaszynski, ibid.*

in the grave and to write the epitaph that he placed above them: " To him who was pierced with a bullet at Ostrołenka," who: "eleven years later died on foreign soil...to the companion of all his youth, to his friend who was more than a brother, this stone is placed in his despair by Zygmunt Krasinski " : and he ends it by Job's cry of grief : " My days have been swifter than a post, they have fled away and have not seen good." Then sick in mind and body he wandered slowly and sadly into Switzerland, detained on his journey by a physical break-down. "I seek for forgetfulness in the mountains," he told Cieszkowski, " but on all sides of me and behind me and before me goes his beloved form[1]." In June he was at Freiburg, where was also Delphina Potocka. Three years before he had been there with her and Danielewicz; and here he now wrote those beautiful lines, commemorating a dead friend and a living love, that remain to us as the poem: *Fryburg*.

Three were we once. We did not know beneath the shadows of these towers, crowned by the rainbows of these coloured windows, that three years were to pass and we should be alone, and he a memory only to our hearts.

After recalling the days the three had spent together, when Delphina had sung to Danielewicz's piano, Krasinski recounts in language almost identical with that which he had written at the time to his friends the scenes of Danielewicz's deathbed. He kneels before the corpse whose face, he says in the poem as he said in his letters, "was beautiful so that it seemed to me like Christ's own face: and I cried out in certitude, ' He is Thine, Lord God.' "

[1] *Letters to Cieszkowski.* Lucerne, April 30, 1842.

Then did I weep—not for him, but myself; for overwhelmed by egotistic grief I saw around me the desert of my life. Only thy image [Delphina's] rose from far, the figure of the second angel of my fate. No other voice now calls to me, nor other tenderness can move my soul. Whether the flowers bloom or the world fall to dust to me it is the same—the same for evermore, because the spirit of my soul is far from me, he who should uphold me 'midst the billows and with me raise from the grave's darkness the shade of our dead Mother. Now are there ever fewer spirits to defend our Mother. All thither go—by that same road: beyond the world, beyond Poland, to the unseeing grave; and we who here remain can fight no more. High hearts have broken. Every mind, be it but free, strong or great, bids us farewell. All that is godlike doth forsake us here.

With his characteristic exaltation of his friends over himself the poet next confesses that without Danielewicz he is nought: that it was the dead man who was his strength and who gave him comprehension of life and courage for action[1].

And now he in one grave, my country in another: and on those graves I, driven by madness, with thee alone, oh, sister, have remained, only with thee!

Oh, angel woman, thou art still with me. Thou hast not yet departed.

She cannot be by his side in the hour when he will fight and die for Poland, but till its advent:

Thou art my salvation, the only rainbow in the darkened skies, the last song of my love art thou! Oh, let me hear thy voice and touch thy hand![2] That hand perchance shall me

---

[1] Despite Krasinski's eulogy of the friend who had been his protector when his other young fellow-Poles had turned against him, Danielewicz's influence over Krasinski had not, according to Koźmian, been salutary. Danielewicz was strongly affected by pantheism and German philosophy, and had been driven by his troubles into a profound pessimism and loss of faith. At the instance, however, of a Pole, Cezary Plater, then in Munich, Zygmunt summoned a priest to the deathbed of his friend: and it was after having seen the latter die with the last sacraments of his Church that Krasinski returned to the practice of his religion. Koźmian, *op. cit.*

[2] Krasinski found spiritual and national inspiration in Delphina's beautiful voice. He once wrote to her that from the moment he heard

from ruin defend. Thy voice perchance can, with a poet's breath, people and ring within this lonely heart. Come, weep with me above the stones of graves, and from our tears shall grow sad and great roses, dark, like blood congealed from sadness. One of their garlands shall we cast on Poland's grave, the second shall our offering be to him. From heaven he then will send us strength that we shall live and die in faith, oh, sister mine, in faith that she, that Holy One who sleeps in bonds, shall in the end cast off her chains.

That faith Krasinski had by now gained. This year—1842—was to him one of bitter bereavement and of dreary forebodings at the prospect of his marriage. But private sorrow affected not at all his hope for Poland and for the human race in the light of which he was now walking always more surely. The two strands of personal pessimism and national optimism run side by side in Krasinski's life. In this July of 1842 when he was with his father at Kissingen, yearning for his lost friend and too ill to be able to write more than a few words:

In spite of continual physical sufferings, a succession of new and unaccustomed thoughts continually stands before the eyes of my soul...Everything is unfolding itself before me always more broadly and more clearly, at the same time logically and beautiful and holy...When I look into the future I feel faith, love and hope, not as I did of old, because of old grief for the past hid and darkened everything to me. To-day the sun has now risen in my spirit, but many days will still pass before that same sun is shed on the world. As an individual I suffer and shall suffer, but as a link of the great chain I see a splendour of light in the further course of succeeding links, and I bless the Lord[1].

And in October when to the same friend he confides

her sing a certain song there was scarcely a minute in which he did not hear within his soul her high, pure notes ringing to heaven. And again he tells her, when in Rome, that his craving to hear her sing again was almost madness. *Unknown Letters from Zygmunt Krasinski to Delphina Potocka. Tygodnik Illustrowany*, 1899.

[1] *Letters to Sottan.* Kissingen, July 14, 1842.

that since the death of Danielewicz "a thousand troubles and anxieties have come upon me, and the future is also *amaritudinis plena* "—an allusion to his approaching marriage—he adds in the same breath: "The resurrection is near, at least by the spirit and in the spirit[1]." Writing to Cieszkowski—in November, 1842—that he was tempted to suicide between "grief for the past and detestation of the future," he makes haste to add that he is speaking of the individual past and future, not of the universal[2].

Out of all these new-born hopes Krasinski was now writing *Dawn*. After he left his father he stayed a couple of weeks at Nice in the company of Delphina Potocka, Gaszynski and Małachowski. Krasinski had been drawn to this latter faithful friend, not by any intellectual gifts on the other's side, but by the sterling qualities of soul that attracted the esteem and trust of all his fellow-Poles, and by their mutual love of their country[3]. When Krasinski went to Nice *Dawn* was in great part written. Other stanzas were composed there as, always intensely sensitive to music, Krasinski listened to the exquisite voice of the woman who had inspired the poem; and others again came to him as he rode along the shores of the Mediterranean. From Nice, accompanied by the devoted Małachowski who chose to give him the support of his presence in those difficult moments of his life, Krasinski went on to Rome for the winter that preceded his marriage. Gaszynski consented to put his name to *Dawn* in order to avert all suspicion of the authorship, for being in exile he

[1] *Letters to Sołtan.* Genoa, Oct. 3, 1842.
[2] *Letters to Cieszkowski.* Nov. 25, 1842.
[3] See Preface, *Letters of Zygmunt Krasinski to Stanisław Małachowski.*

was beyond reach of the Russian penalties: and in
1843 the poem was published that marks the term of
the Anonymous Poet's seven years' spiritual wandering.

To that most noble paean of victory over suffering
and evil which lives as *Dawn* Krasinski places as
mottoes two prophecies of Christ's reign on earth
before which darkness was to flee—the lines from
the fourth eclogue of Virgil referring to the prophecy
of the Cumaean Sibyl: *Ultima Cumaei venit jam
carminis aetas: magnus ab integro saeclorum nascitur
ordo;* and the adaptation of a verse from Exodus that
the Catholic Church sings in her office for Christmas
Eve: *Hodie scietis quia veniet Dominus et salvabit nos
et mane videbitis gloriam ejus.*

The poem is preceded by a prose introduction
justifying Krasinski's convictions by the logic of historical fact. Krasinski was a poet, a mystic, and he
may even be called a dreamer: but every theory of his,
every vision, must be confirmed by logical consequence
before he would accept it or hand it on to others. His
heart refused to take to itself the conclusions for which
it yearned unless his mind were first satisfied by proof.
So now the obscurity of his former works is to be found
no more. *Dawn* is mystical: but even in its highest
flights it is clear as crystal.

In marked contrast even to the pages of its immediate
predecessor *The Treatise of the Trinity* is the tone of
tranquil certainty that runs through the preface of the
poem.

In the days of Caesar, preceding the great day of Christ,
the ancient world had reached the final consequences of its
history...Wherever you might look there was in the world of
the spirit ruin, licence, disruption—and from those signs it

was easy to recognize that this world was nigh to the day of judgment and to its metamorphosis.

And not only does that mental condition without faith and of vain longings and grief bear witness to this. Another sign steps forth. In the material field all grows and centralizes. Rome ever conquers. Then arose Julius Caesar.

And the Jews thought of him that he was their Messias, and for a moment the world thought he was its God. But you know that he was only the precursor of its God. In the field of historical deed he was as the angel to whom it was ordained to move the impediments from before the feet of the approaching God. He led the world to material unity without which no word of life could be dispersed abroad. He changed the known world of that time into one great, broad highway.

And a few years later who began to tread that highroad, to announce that the new life was already sent down from on high, and that the dead shall not die, and that the God, unknown in Athens, had shown Himself in Jerusalem? Was it not Peter? Was it not St John?...The material unity of government ...was the condition, the necessary medium, of progress for Christianity...

Discite historiam exemplo moniti! Two thousand years have passed, and those same signs are spread abroad upon the waves of time. The last throes of the Roman Republic were reflected in the terrible, epileptic convulsions of the French Revolution. Finally, the days of Caesar were remoulded into the days of Napoleon.

Krasinski, fondled as an infant by the soldiers fighting for Bonaparte, had been brought up by his father in a passionate admiration for Napoleon which, not uncommon even in this country in a generation nearer his age than ours, with the Poles reached something like a religious veneration. To Mickiewicz Napoleon stood for a superhuman figure, imbued with the spirit of Christ, called to the task of redeeming the political world till he forfeited it by personal failing. In Krasinski's case Napoleonism dispelled the shadows that lay before his vision, and led him to the rising of his orient.

G.   15

And the Christian Caesar, higher by a whole past epoch than his predecessor, filled with the knowledge of himself, and with the aim for the sake of which the Spirit of God that directs history had sent him here below, said, as he died on the rock of exile, " The beginning of the new era will be reckoned from me." In that word is contained the truth both of his and of the whole past. But before that truth is developed and fulfilled, before the world shall pass from the Napoleonic standpoint to another, to a more entire and more sanctified transformation, it must first be worn out as the ancient world was worn out...From the time of the Gracchi the pagan world did not rest till it heard the promise of Christ: from the time of Luther the new world has had no rest...and shall not rest till it reaches, not now the hearing, but the understanding and the fulfilment of the promise of Christ.

There is decadence of religion everywhere, goes on Krasinski; an anarchy of thought. All forms of belief have passed over the human race, all crying for the spark of life that shall renew their youth.

That anarchy is so fearful that it necessarily tends to crisis—that desire so great, and up to now vain, that it necessarily calls for the help of the Father Who is in heaven. When was that help ever refused ? When did God ever forsake history when history raised its hands to Him, and in the language of all the peoples of the earth cried out: " Lord, show Thyself to us "?

Endless desire brings with it eternal yearning and endless grief. As the individual, so the human race sinks into melancholy. From collective man shall also often flow the bloody sweat of agony on the Mount of Olives of history. Were it otherwise there would be no spirit of humanity training itself by its own will. Where would the merit be with which it merits in this time? What is that merit if not its life in history, if not that course of labour divided into the moments of death and of the resurrection of the dead from death? And how can it die if it does not doubt? And how can it rise again if it does not believe? Not to die you must be God. To die you must be man. When the spirit of God unites itself with the nature of man, the divine life breaks asunder the human grave—Christ died and rose again from the dead.

And to the epoch, begun in His word, the same must befall before it can by deed be adequate to the whole purport

of that word. Our fathers stood on that declivity which leads
to the grave. Fate carried us further, and laid us deeper—
we are in the grave. I err, we are already beyond the grave.

You all know, my brothers, that we were born in the womb
of death: and from the cradle your eyes have been used to
look on the livid stains of death, widespread on the body of
the European world. Hence the eternal grief that gnaws your
hearts: hence the incertitude that has become your life...But
every end contains in itself the successive beginning. The day
of death only precedes the hour of awakening. Therefore consider attentively, and the signs of death shall of a sudden be
transformed for you into the signs of resurrection...

Christ showed to men the idea of humanity. Before Him
save for the Hebrews there were no nations, for the aim was
unknown to which the nations are advancing, to which they
gravitate like the planets to the sun. He promised that some
day there shall be in the world one only fold and one shepherd.
He bade those praying to the Father repeat each day these
words: "Thy Kingdom come": and with that sigh for two
thousand years we are all imploring God for the sight of the
ideal of humanity on earth.

Somewhat on the lines of what he had already said
in *The Treatise of the Trinity* Krasinski speaks of the
deed, the merit, by which we "become what we shall
remain in the sight of God," and by which we work
out our personality. It is only given to us on this earth
and amidst humanity.

The humanity in the midst of which we gain our eternal
future life must itself be a great and holy harmony in the
Divine thought...Humanity on this earth and the immortality
of each individual beyond the grave are two equal circles,
serving each other reciprocally, not to be parted either in
heart or understanding. Each is the collateral of the other, its
condition, its fulfilment, and both blend into a third and higher,
the power of the very God.

Humanity "is the entirety and the unity of all the
powers of the spirit of man, expressed visibly on this
earth by the concord and love of its members, that is,
of 'nationalities.'" As the members of the human body
are the outward parts of the personality that rules

them, so are the nations the members of one universal humanity.

The realization of Christ's word beyond religious spheres could not be effected before Christianity had prepared the ground by penetrating each individual soul. But now that the individual has accepted this word it is time that its realization shall reach further and, acting upon collective humanity, idealize and Christianize the governments of the world.

The world is near, not to a great change, for nothing can be changed of Christ's words, but to the great transfiguration of them, the deeper understanding of them, the higher admiration of them. Already in these expressions: " Render to God what is God's and to Caesar what is Caesar's," is comprised the whole future movement of mankind. For because all is "God's," the state of that momentary division between what belongs to Caesar and what belongs to God must ever lessen, and what was yesterday considered as owing to Caesar, to-day must be counted as belonging to God until the government of Caesar shall be nought and God's kingdom all.

Governments are a human creation...Only nationalities are the Divine creation.

Hence we see these governments, neither animated by nationality, nor comprehending its sanctity, proceeding to such violations of the moral law as the partition of Poland. That injury deliberately committed against an unoffending nation was, says Krasinski, more than a political crime. It was an outrage upon the Christ-idea that, till it is righted, stands in the way of the grand ideal of the Christianization of policy and earthly government.

In that nationality, in whose wronging the greatest violence was done against humanity, there must break forth most strongly, there must shine forth most clearly, the idea of humanity.

Our death was necessary, necessary shall be our resurrection, so that the word of the Son of man, the eternal word of life, shall flow through the social circumference of the world. By the very fact of our nationality, martyred on the cross of history, will be manifested to the conscience of the human spirit that the sphere of policy must be transformed into the sphere of religion...The Lord shall be present in the whole political sphere where hitherto He was not...and the instrument of His providence to this end shall be none other than the Polish nation.

One of the two—either the sanctified future of humanity shall be forfeited, or the life of Poland shall be the condition of its fulfilment. The only word, the word of Christ, shall either give forth no further fruits, or the violence committed against that sacred word shall last no longer. Such is the truth, but no more a truth of a worldly order, only of God. Therefore I call it a religion.

Let the conscience of each Pole be convinced of this truth. Let him grasp with his mind what hitherto he has only felt with his heart.

These are the principles that led Krasinski to his song of triumph. They explain the rapturous idealization of his nation that we find in *Dawn* and in all the work that followed it. What language on the lips of the poet-mystic could be too exalted to sing of her whose sufferings and death were to prepare the way for the spiritual re-birth of the world, whose resurrection, by being the first step towards the universal victory over political wrong, shall bring humanity to its transformation? Henceforth, "holy Poland," "my holy one," are the tender and devout titles by which Krasinski will call the mystic mistress of his heart, the adored country who is the symbol of his faith.

But *Dawn* is not only a great national outpouring. It is one of the most exquisite love poems in literature. It is dedicated to Delphina Potocka, whose name likewise stands above the second pianoforte concerto and one of the best known valses of the greatest of Polish musicians. Etherealized as Krasinski's Beatrice, linked with him in one common grief for their nation, she is in the poem no mere beloved woman, but well-nigh a mystic part of his nationalism.

And yet again no heart could have conceived such an apotheosis of pain and hope, of victory over the powers of darkness, that had not itself first passed through the sorrows of death. We know, if only from its opening stanzas, that *Dawn* commemorates Krasinski's spiritual fall and resurrection : and throughout the poem we might be reading, even in those passages that apparently speak only to Poland, the language of impassioned guidance to a tempest-tossed soul. Much as the mysticism of Sion in the Hebrew prophecies applies to a personal need, a personal experience, so, not only *Dawn,* but the *Psalms of the Future* and *Resurrecturis,* appeal with extraordinary appositeness to every heart. We have seen that the Anonymous Poet directed his principles of political morality entirely by those of individual morality. In the same manner the national spirituality and the spirituality of the unit is with him identical.

In the beautiful lines of his soul's autobiography that open *Dawn,* Krasinski tells us how he was driven by his enemies from his country to wander on alien soil, hearing from afar the satanic cries of those who had forged the chains of Poland.

At first I trusted that the God of pitying love, proud to the proud, to the faithful full of faith ; at first I trusted after days but few He would send avenging angels from above, and burst that grave which stands before the world. But the days passed by, and passed away the years. In vain dawn struggled with the blinded strength of night. No sun arose above the sainted tomb, and ever more abased did this earth of ours become. Then sank my soul into that chaos of doubt where all light is changed into eternal night, where the highest works of courage like mouldering corpses rot, where the victories of ages in heaped up ruins lie. And from all the cycle of those lived out days one inscription standeth: There is no hope here.

Ah, I dwelt, dwelt long in that abyss, driven by wild rage and despair that knew no shore. And death to me would then have been but my second death. Like Dante, during life, I passed through hell. But to aid me also a lady hastened down, at whose very look the evil spirits fear. Me too an angel from the precipice redeemed : and I too had a Beatrice of my own.

Oh, beautiful as she, from this world of gloom thou didst not wing thy way, leaving me alone, and ascend to heaven to dwell there, heavenly, without pain. Oh, beautiful as she, thou wert more Christian far! For there where sorrow groweth, there where tears are birth, there thou with thy brother remainedst on this earth. Together walked we wearing one self-same crown of thorns. Blood from my hands with blood empurpled thine. And the same empoisoned draught of one hellish spring we did drink together, oh, Beatrice of mine!

And yet, and yet my groaning and thy sighs, mingled, flowing in each other, they passed away to song. From two sorrows linked in bridal of the soul, one only voice was raised —and oh, that voice was joy. Ah, joyousness of faith, ah, mighty strength of hope, that into my heart returned from thy look! Thus when clouds of darkness in the heavens, filled with tears, gather to each other for aerial obsequies, from their weeping by a roll of thunder sudden light is riven: and the mist becomes the golden house of God.

And so this song, oh, sister, I open with thy name. Oh, be linked with me for ever by the ring of one memory and one love. Here we shall die, but the song that dieth not shall return some day, true to me and thee, like an angel guardian to watch us sleeping in our graves. And perchance the moment cometh when, in the time of all the souls, we shall rise, but no more in fleshly prison, rise once more united by the chain of its harmony, and in the memory of human hearts shall live, as a soul redeemed with a soul redeemed, pure and shining forth and sanctified.

The scene of the series of lyrics that make up *Dawn* is the lake of Como, on whose shores Krasinski had spent some time in 1840, and where he had probably begun his poem.

Albeit Krasinski often rises to heights of impersonal

rapture he seldom speaks the language of pure joy. He
had indeed small reason in his life to do so. But in the
first lyric of *Dawn* high hopes for his country, love for
a woman, the beauty that surrounded him, all make up
one harmony of rejoicing in God, nature, man. He
and his Beatrice are in a boat upon the lake. The
snow-tipped mountains rise, peak upon peak, into the
Italian skies. Vines and roses cling about their slopes.

"There is one beauty, there is one God," is the
poet's cry. A few stars tremble in the skies. The
moon is rising over the Alps. On the boat stands
Beatrice, her hands on her harp. Her face, inspired,
shines as an angel's. Against the translucency of the
waves and the blue background of the sky, her figure,
silver in a web of moonlight, seems rapt to heaven.

> Thou with me and we alone.
> On the path with light all laden
> Ever onward floats my boat.
> Oh, the angels cannot feel
> What I feel now in this hour.
> Sister mine, to me it seemeth
> That our holy one ariseth
> At this moment from the coffin.
>
> Ever further we are guided
> By the moon across the waters.
> Let us float, float thus unending
> To peace—to light—to blue—to distance.
> Waves are mirrors, mountains phantoms.
> Heaven and earth are but one land.
> What is real is slowly changing
> To the world of the ideal,
> To a dream of silver, crystal.
> Let me dream, oh, let me dream.

But the shadow of sorrow soon steals back into
Krasinski's song. A son's bereavement of his mother
again breaks forth. He bids Beatrice be steadfast, for :

We raise our eyes on high, and when we see this nature,

in it, beyond it we feel—God. In the changing sufferings of
this life, clasping each other by the hand, in that suffering and
beyond it we feel—God.

> We are the children of a mother slain,
> We who never have beheld
> How the light in mother's eyes
> Shines as an angel's on her child.
> Pray with me, oh, sister mine,
> Pray, kneel in humility.
> Gaze on high with piercing boldness
> As the orphaned child may gaze.
> Look upon that harp unending,
> Where the moon, the stars, the suns,
> Cling as keys all motionless.
> From its depths and highest summits
> Strings of light and strings of azure
> Quiver, stretched to space unmeasured.
> O'er those strings the spirit wanders,
> On those strings the spirit playeth,
> In that song alone it resteth :
> That song—earth's harmony and peace.

One name is missing from this great harmony of
the universe, one ray absent from the symphony of
light. Beatrice must pray that God shall restore that
lost name of Poland.

As God is in heaven so will He necessarily give us our
second body. For we have fulfilled the test of the grave. Our
right is resurrection. To-day or to-morrow Thou wilt give it,
Lord! Oh, Thou wilt give it for Thy justice' sake; not because
Thou owest it to us, but to Thyself.

> When I spoke thus thou wert kneeling,
> Wailing with thy harp's stringed wailing;
> For thou leanedst thy snow-white forehead
> On the strings the moon made shiver
> All around in streams of gold.
> And thus kneeling thou wert sighing.
> Pray, oh, sister, with thy sighing.
> God knows well that in this day
> Sighing is thy country's name.

The poet then proceeds to his favourite theory, the
only one by which he could explain his nation's fate,

that Poland is the victim for the world's political
redemption, and that love and self-sacrifice are the
condition of life.

> Think you then that she who loveth,
> And that dieth she shall perish?
> To your eyes, to eyes dust laden,
> Not to self, nor to all life.
> Who dies in sacrificing self,
> Floweth into lives of others,
> Dwells in human hearts in secret:
> With each day, each little moment,
> Groweth living in that grave,
> Even as God Who is in heaven,
> Gives to all and gives herself,
> Yet her strength is not diminished[1].
> Long invisible remaining,
> Ever heard in depths of hearts,
> She with fire must burn their stains,
> Melt with tears the soul's hard boulders:
> By the grave's toils, by its sorrows,
> By the harmonious song of death,
> She, although herself dismembered,
> Shall join all peoples in one love.
> Ah, in vain you dream your dream,
> Mortals who would take away
> Life from that which is immortal.
> You have wounded but the body.
> Know you not that love and death
> In the spirit world are one?
> He on earth is everlasting
> Who with death gives birth to life:
> He who with his life gives death
> When he dies shall rise no more.

Krasinski inherited the strong idealism of the Polish
race. He had no more mercy for the materialist and
the Pharisee than he had for the tyrant and executioner.
To these the above passage is addressed : and now he

---

[1] This idea Krasinski had developed fully in *The Treatise of the Trinity*,
arguing from the fact that as God in giving out of Himself in His creation
of the finite detracts nothing from His all Being, so in our far off way what
we give of ourselves we rather gain than lose.

pours upon them, standing as they do in the way of humanity's moral progress, all the invectives of a generous wrath. Again he turns to Beatrice. He bids her no longer weep. Before the moon sets he will show her a miracle that is "above oppression, above pain." And so begin the three visions of *Dawn*.

"Knowest thou"—he speaks to Beatrice—"the love which eternally lures the soul to the land of memory? Does the cry of the angel of home call thee by night, and bid thine eyes gaze on the living faces of those long since dead?

"Knowest thou that dumb, winter steppe where in their graves the spirits of our fathers sleep?"

It is lit by no stars, only by the ghost-like face of the moon. There is nothing but the white, desolate steppe, with the graves that alone stand out black from the snow. They seem to wander—the poet and Beatrice —in the endless night of a dream.

> 'Neath the steppe is mournful murmuring.
> All the graveyard trembles, living.
> From the graves blow prayers and wailings.
> Somewhere swords are rattling hollow.
> Clash of armour stern I hear,
> As if our fathers, to this moment
> Life remembering, craving glory,
> Now within their tombs are turning,
> On their sides, for they are dreaming
> In death's sleep of Poland's sorrow.

> Lo, each grave is opened widely,
> Giving thee the dead again.
> Pallid army of our fathers,
> Kings of old, and lords of council,
> Warriors and soldiers' leaders,
> Gather closely all around thee.
> The cemetery of ice and gravestones
> To Diet, army, Poland changeth.

The "spark of the spirit," the old splendour of the Polish senator, the courage and contempt of slavery of an ancient race, still shine on those dead faces through the corruption of the grave.

I beheld them. I wept sorely
In that white land of my dreams.
I beheld them, and before them
Even as falls a corpse I fell.
At their feet I bowed my forehead,
And to them I stretched my hands.
There with tears, cries, my heart's passion,
Asked I them of Poland's death,
I, born after Poland's death.

Wherefore life in life's short moment
Did they squander with such pride,
That nothing to their sons remaineth
Nor of power nor of possession ;
In the stead of mother country
But a torn dismembered corpse?

Scarce I spoke: and lo ! their armour
Rattled with a hollow music.
From all breasts a cry was uttered,
All those eyes that once were dead
From beneath their helms as torches
Flamed upon me. All together
Their right hands were stretched on high,
Veiling with their cloud the moonlight.
Here, before, behind, beside me,
Stand they in a mighty crowd.
Hear I on all sides their breathing,
And their scornful laughter hear,
Till they tore my heart asunder
With their scorn : even heart of steel
Must have broken.

He implores the spirits to take their anger from him, to tell their son, as only they can, "the holy truth." He is answered by the poet's favourite national hero, the Grand Hetman Czarniecki, the Polish champion who drove the Swedish conqueror out of Poland in the seventeenth century, and who won equal renown against the Russians and Cossacks. He tells the poet that he grew not from ease or pleasure, but from pain. "God lays down His promises to those whom He makes suffer. God's grace drove us into these pathless ways.

For to my country He gave rather to die than live ignobly." If Krasinski's ancestors had, following in "the steps of the world," supported "that edifice which stands about Poland," that is, the lust for annexation and disregard of political morality on the part of Poland's neighbours to which she owes her dismemberment, Poland would now be "not a nation but only a shop. Eternally from all sides fate was driving us across the open fields of history to a higher lot, to that Poland which *shall be*." Krasinski always italicizes this phrase. "We walked thither in the ways of old. To-day you are walking thither by the ways of youth. From our blood and from our faults, before this age shall pass away, shall rise the one people of the peoples. Bless the faults then of your fathers."

In this passage, perplexing to those who have not followed the trend of Polish history, Krasinski is drawing upon the historical mysticism which is also very marked in the writings of Mickiewicz. The constitution of Poland, anarchical and subversive of order as most English writers are fond of terming it, was founded on spiritual political principles that were almost un-recognized in the other European states. The duty of every citizen to take his share in the government of his nation was the origin of the necessary unanimity of vote that led to the *liberum veto* with its disastrous results. To the legislator of the hour it was inconceivable that a citizen of the Polish Republic should use his right of protest for any reason except the benefit of his country. The cause of the internal disorders of Poland, when not fomented by foreign intriguers, is to seek in the love of liberty carried by the Pole of the past to excess. In obedience to her high conception of the obligations of political morality to her faith in the good will of the states that sur rounded her, her disbelief in the possibility of such a violation of moral law as the partition of a living country, Poland neglected her military defences so that when the hour of her end sounded she had practically no armies to defend her against Russia, Austria and Prussia combined[1]. Wars of conquest, assassination of the sovereign, never entered into Poland's scheme. All this throws light on Krasinski's exaltation of his country. And yet love never blinded his eyes to her failings. Had it done so he could not have been the great national teacher that he was.

The Hetman has spoken and sinks back into the tomb. The steppe shakes; the sky dissolves; all pass into the unsounded abysses of the poet's soul. But the voice of the dead with the message it uttered still trembles in the listener's ear.

The two dreamers are again upon the lake. Mists shroud the mountains. The moon has sunk within them. But:

> 'Tis no wind that there is whispering.
> Someone softly weepeth, sigheth.
> O'er the shores a wail is spreading.
> On the night wind through the heavens
> Thousand wailings run towards us.
> All the bank, the crags and mountains,
> Are resounding, one deep prayer.

"Mighty God!" cries the poet. "Can this be?" for he sees once more the spirits of his fathers.

---

[1] See among others Adam Mickiewicz, *Les Slaves*. E. Starczewski, *L'Europe et la Pologne*. Paris, 1913. In consideration of the profound ignorance concerning Poland in our country it is necessary to point out that modern Polish policy, while retaining its high ideals, has become the most practical of activities.

Beyond the waters, there before us,
As light dreams, light multitudes
On the rocks and crags are floating.
As will-o'-the-wisps, as wavering flamelets,
Now they rise, and now they fall.
Strike, oh, sister, strike thy strings.
Let the song more surely lure them.
Play in all thy music's thunder,
Play them: *Poland hath not perished* [1].
With harp and voice, weep, pray, and madden!
The song our nation sings shall surely
Draw them here from far off distance.
Is it miracle or mirage?
Sparkles in thy hands the music.
All the harp is glimmering, burning.
Each note from the strings unwinding
Shakes the air in fiery flaming.
Above the waves the song is burning.
To the ghosts it runs, it driveth,
Flaming ever and ever ringing.

In the original this passage is written in short nervous lines, imitating the voice of the harp, and quivering with the beautiful shades of harmonies and echoes to which the Polish language, with its peculiarly rich onomatopoeia, lends itself in a manner that is impossible to reproduce in English. I have only been able to attempt to render its sense, not its sounds.

It is interesting to notice the connection here of light and music of which we have heard much in these latter days. We meet it also in Mickiewicz's *Improvization* in the Third Part of *The Ancestors* [2]. He, we know, took it from Saint-Martin.

"To the flashing of those sounds" the phantoms advance across the waves.

---

[1] *Poland hath not perished* was the war-song of the Polish legions fighting under Napoleon, and has ever since remained one of the most beloved and soul-stirring of Polish national songs.

[2] See my translation in *Adam Mickiewicz, the National Poet of Poland.*

There the horsetails, there the standards,
Fluttering snow white plumes and crowns[1],
There the Catholic cross uplifted,
Shields and coats of arms and ensigns,
And a host of swords and helms.
Seest thou that face angelic?
As a star upon the darkness
On high, on high, she floats, she rises,
Wanes, and glimmers, quivers, flames.
Lo! her veil of blue and crimson
Shines about her as a rainbow.
Set with pearls and set with flowers
Flashes forth her crown of diamonds.
Welcome, welcome! She, the Queen,
Long a widow of her people,
To-day returneth to her kingdom
Which in Polish Czenstochowa
Erst our fathers gave to her,
And those fathers o'er these billows
Lo, she leadeth[2].
                 Play no longer.
To the waves of such a rainbow
Harp of ours can sound no more,
Cannot lure the spirits here.
'Tis God's light that now has touched them.
Gold the lake around them shimmers,
Flasheth dawn upon their helmets.
In war array of ancient Poland,
Now all golden, all divine,
Sweep they into far off spaces,
As again to battle hastening.

With drawn swords and eyes upraised to their star-crowned queen they follow her into unknown regions.

[1] The horsetails were the insignia in ancient Poland of the Grand Hetman. The Polish hussars wore white plumes attached to their shoulders that were an efficacious means of terrifying the enemy's horse in a charge.

[2] After Czenstochowa in 1655 had been the scene of an almost miraculous repulse of the Swedish invaders of Poland John Casimir solemnly placed Poland under the protection of the Blessed Virgin, proclaiming her as Queen of Poland, which title the Poles retain in their prayers and hymns to the present hour. The imagery of Krasinski's vision is taken from the ancient painting of the Madonna at Czenstochowa, whither for centuries Polish pilgrims have resorted.

In ecstasy the poet cries aloud that she who once crushed
the serpent's head is descending to vanquish him for
the second time, as the herald of the new day when
the reign of justice shall begin in the world, and the
Polish nation conquer. His hymn is now turned to the
heavenly Queen of Poland.

> Lo! the hour of mercy striketh!
> With thee, by thee, the eternal
> Thought that liveth in the heavens
> Now begins to live on earth.
> Float thou, float thou, God's own lily,
> Over lands and over oceans,
> Over caverns deep of hell.

The old enemy shall cower at her feet, and her
Polish soldiers transfix him with their swords.

> Then, oh, then and for all ages
> God shall wipe away our tears.

The celestial army hastens ever further over the
water, to the east, the dawn. The snows redden in the
rays of morning. The spirits are seen no more. "They
have gone with the light—and with hope."

> The night has passed, but from its shadows
> Faith remaineth in our bosoms,
> And that faith fate cannot alter ;
> Ours, oh, ours is all the future.

Therefore: "all is mine and all is fair," cries he
whose hope was drawn only from inward vision, when
every outward circumstance pointed against its fulfilment.

> Mine the earth, the plains of heaven.
> With the voice of life shall I
> Make these rocks to ring again ;
> For God's word is in my heart.
> Miracles are here and marvels.
> Lo, my Poland—*Poland shall be* !

G. 16

And he breaks into a song of thanksgiving, praising "God, the spirits, man and thee," praising the living and the dead, praising the universal world.

The third and culminating vision follows. Thought has left earth and is where the poet knows not nor can repeat : neither below nor on high, neither in the waters nor in the clouds, but in some depthless space, in the translucence of eternal light, in an ocean beyond time. There the exiles behold their Poland in the triumph which she has won by her suffering. Krasinski never goes further in the mystic exaltation of his country than in this scene. She is as a mighty archangel, whose look is lightning. She carries the purple garland of memory, but all her sorrows are now past. "Beyond her, high and far, in time and space, on backgrounds of flaming light, on backgrounds of shadow, rise as mists in flame, in the vapours of rainbows, the god-like phantoms of that world which *shall be*"—again Krasinski emphasizes the words that were his hope. The verdure of new-born life, the roses of spring, are round their brows. They cast their crowns with a hymn of joy, while below them "trembles in space a sea of sapphire light," at the feet of her whom they hail as queen. Each wreath bursts forth into rainbow hues. The rain of falling flowers is one great flashing dawn, and the figure of Poland is caught in a cloud of light and glory. The voice of the Eternal Father speaks from heaven : " As I gave My Son to the world so now I give to it thee, oh, Poland": the idea being the theory we have seen in *The Treatise of the Trinity*, and which was Krasinski's firmly held tenet, that as Christ redeemed mankind by His death, so He appointed that one victim nation should save the political universe also by death.

And I saw the all universe
As one thought that is in flame.
Oh! I saw the all present form
Of God's glory without end,
Winds of comets, rings of planets,
Streams of stars o'er streams of stars,
Still more suns above the suns.
And across the seas of light
Flowed one harmony of life,
Song all thundering, all united,
Of the heavens, of the Son,
To the heavenly God the Father.
Athwart the all world unto God
Went the road of earthly nations:
And my Poland as their leader
Thither soared!

    Whose eye
Can overtake her to those heights?
Who shall touch with earthly forehead
Even the feet of the Creator?
Who shall soar with the archangel
Where humanity takes flesh?
Now my heart faints in my bosom.
Vision fades, my thought is failing.
Oh, so madly I entreated,
Oh, so long I prayed to God
For that one, that only moment—
And I saw!

    In that hour
Oh, remember that we were
On the highest height of souls—
There whence flows the source of life.
At the source of life we drank.
With our very eyes we grasped
What is still without a name.
Sister mine, we in that moment
Lived in our eternity.

They return to reality, but a changed reality : one that is still labour and sadness, but to which a high calling has given dignity, hope, purpose.

Throw off sadness, throw off terror.
Well I know what toil remaineth

On the road; what pain, what sorrow.
Trust thee to the poet's vision.
The dawn of victory now shines.

In our native land immortal,
On that soil so dearly loved,
On our soil, that soil of ours,
Shall arise a race renewed,
Never yet by man beheld.

And that new world all rejoicing
As a church shall flower to God.
The Polish land, the Polish Eden,
The desert of an age-long sadness,
Is desolate no more nor mourning.
Nor behind me nor before me
Is there darkness any more.
All is light and all is justice.
Clear is now our hallowed past,
Clear our purgatorial anguish.

Never shall thy spirit perish,
Poland mine, who art transfigured.
O'er earth's whirlwinds thou hast entered
To the land of the idea.
What the eye alone beholdeth
It shall pass into the ocean,
It shall fade away in chaos:
But the idea shall never die.

And so Krasinski's country, standing to him for that deathless ideal:

Art to me no more mere country;
Thou art now my faith, my law.
Who betrays thee, who thee wrongeth,
Lieth he against his God:

because Poland is the depositary of God's thought, and her resurrection the pledge of the future epoch of humanity.

God Eternal of our fathers!
Thou, Who high and far away,
Ever clearer through the ages
Descendest to us, and, dawn-like, strewest
From the eternal gates Thy sparks

O'er time's waves until time flameth!
Now, again, Thy dawn is dawning
Which Thou in Thy love dost grant us.
In the graves the bones shall tremble,
Sighing in a hymn to Thee.

For our souls' and bodies' suffering,
For our hundred years of torment,
We do give Thee thanks, oh, Lord!
We are poor, and weak and feeble,
But from this martyrdom of ours
Has begun Thy reign on earth.

All warring elements shall be united in love. No
longer is the earth's cry of pain the sound that runs
through space, but in its stead a song of melody and
joy. The powerful shall oppress the weak never again.
Christ shall rule the world as He rules over heaven.
And so this song of a nation's resurrection closes in a
rapture of rejoicing that we cannot but believe hymns
likewise the deliverance of the poet's own soul from the
dark and desolate places in which he had long
wandered. The terrible past is but a dream.

Long the power of that dream.
We believed it. We believed
In eternal pain and toil.
It was but the sanctuary's entrance;
But one step upon the stairway.
It was but the night of merit.

Human heart, where now thy shame?
Look into thyself, oh, gaze!
Where of old was bitter weeping,
Rage and cries and lamentation,
Lo, to-day of heaven's high mercy
Is the second house of God.

"Thus," sings the poet in the epilogue, "two exiles dreamed
in the dawning of a better dawn. What they felt in their hearts
they cast into these words. But the word alone is the empty
half of the masterpieces of life. The only prayer worthy of
the Creator begins with a hymn, but knows no parting of the
thoughts with deeds. What it sings with its voice slowly it

puts into form till it creates round about it the world of the real, equal in beauty to the world of the ideal. Never, oh, never shall I string more my harp. Other the roads that are open to us now. Perish, my songs! Arise, my deeds!

"But thou, oh, loveliness I loved, the only sister of my life, watch over me, be with me till I die as one small part in the masterpiece of toils, till I die one verse in the hymn of sacrifice."

Dawn appeared at the moment in the history of Poland when she was the victim of an oppression that sought to stamp out every vestige of her nationality; when lethargy, despair, moral atrophy seemed all that were left to her. In *Dawn* there came to her a call to hope, a promise of resurrection, a cry of passionate love for the country which within her boundaries it was forbidden to so much as name. *Dawn* gave the Poles a motive for which to strive. It proved to them that death was but the necessary condition of life. It pointed to a future which should take away the sting from an intolerable present. The poem could only be smuggled at their own risk by colporteurs into the country for which it was written, read in secret under pain of imprisonment and Siberia, and consigned to the flames or to some safe hiding-place directly the reader had finished it. Those who lived at the time have told us how they saw men and women weeping tears of emotion as they read[1]. Henceforth the unknown poet was enshrined in the hearts of his people as their teacher and their consoler[2].

---

[1] St. Tarnowski, *Zygmunt Krasinski.*   [2] *Op. cit.*

CHAPTER XI

THE *PSALMS OF THE FUTURE*: THE *PSALMS OF FAITH, OF HOPE,* AND *OF LOVE*

(1843–1847)

Krasinski's marriage with Elżbieta Branicka took place in July, 1843, at Dresden. The portraits that remain of this lady, as well as the accounts given by those who knew her, testify to a beauty that was almost flawless. Her face with its tranquil and noble dignity, of the type known to us as Early Victorian at its best, is often repeated in the pictures of Ary Scheffer, the warm friend and admirer of herself and her husband, who was wont to say that he had never seen any other woman who so much realized his ideal of loveliness. Her character, firm, but of a singular sweetness, was in keeping with her appearance. Her intellectual gifts were many. Yet Krasinski married her with death in his soul, with no pretence of love. That love was all given to his Beatrice, from whom his marriage meant parting.

"My mind is shattered," he wrote to Delphina before his marriage, after which he was to live in his father's palace in Poland, "and drags itself to thy feet, beseeching for pity. All with thee, all by thee, all for thee. Peace, strength, greatness, all are attainable for me, all possible, but not without thee. Think of my life. For fate, Siberia: for surroundings, a hated house: for occupation, slavery: for hope, death[1]."

[1] *Letters to Delphina Potocka. Tygodnik Illustrowany,* 1898.

To Cieszkowski, in whom he confided so unreservedly that he called him his confessor, and from whom he
appears to have received a good many home truths in
reply, he wrote in the March after his betrothal:

Do not tell me that my subjectiveness is increasing. My
subjectiveness is now in Eternity...I have transported it there
where the sorrowful find rest, where the oppressed breathe
once more, and I have united it on those heights with the
spirit which, of all the women I have known, is perhaps the
highest on the earth in our days—the spirit to whose upraising
I contributed a little. The thought that I saved that soul, that
I am ever saving it, and that together with her I will wake
some day to the consciousness of past days, at the end of the
age-long labour of humanity, is the most precious pearl given
me by my fate. Beyond her all the rest is loathing and
suffering. To you I am interpreting the most hidden secrets
of my heart, and I of you expect that you will utter nothing
in the least formal on a feeling so strong, so holy that it can
even on this earth, and that in the nineteenth century, cast upon
their knees two beings, and for one moment open before them
the universal kingdom of God[1].

While all was thus dark around him, and when no
external circumstance justified hope for Poland, the
grief and despondency of his beloved Gaszynski, whom
he remembered as a youth full of life and spirit in the
days of their boyhood in Warsaw, wrung from him
these words in which he begged him to take comfort:

Believe, in spite of all visible events, that a better hour is
now near, a second spring in our lives, a restored youth. Poland
will give us back, will give us back what we have lost for her,
joy, fire, the heart's health[2].

His honeymoon was not over when again to Cieszkowski, who it appears counselled him to stamp out
his love for Delphina, he wrote from Poland:

You think that it is possible to overcome the heart, that it
is possible to cast love into oblivion...I am a man in a false

[1] *Letters to Cieszkowski.* Aix-en-Provence, March 25, 1843.
[2] *Letters to Gaszynski.* Grenoble, June 1, 1843.

position, a man who a hundred times a day curses the moment
when he did for his father what even the heavenly Father has
no right to exact…Solitude has become my only relief, my
only comfort.

"If God permits," he adds at the end of the letter, "and if
my very soul does not become utterly corroded, I shall finish
in the winter the first part of the *Undivine*"—the new drama
Krasinski was writing as an introduction to *The Undivine
Comedy*. "But inspiration is difficult…where outside the house
is oppression and ignominy, and inside the house despair[1]."

Long ago Krasinski's imaginative genius had in
Henryk of *The Undivine Comedy* prefigured his own
character as a husband. For the first part of his married
life coldness and indifference, the punctilious politeness
of duty, devotion to the ideal woman of his heart, were
the only return he made to his wife's forbearing love.
She had married him with the knowledge of his affection for another woman: but, drawn to him by sympathy
for the tragedy of his life and by admiration for his
genius and lofty patriotism, she was, Count Tarnowski
surmises, too young and inexperienced at the age of
twenty-three to realize the strength of his passion and
the position that she was bringing upon herself[2]. She,
meanwhile, bore all in uncomplaining silence, concealing
her grief, and setting herself to the task of winning her
husband's heart by her unalterable patience and readi-
ness to meet his wishes. The first two years of their
marriage were spent in Poland in the house of Wincenty
Krasinski who, fondly attached to his daughter-in-law,
viewed with the strongest disapproval his son's attitude
towards her. The situation, says Count Tarnowski,
was disagreeable to both husband and wife; "disagreeable also," he adds drily, "to those who would wish to

---

[1] *Letters to Cieszkowski*. Wierzenica, Aug. 14, 1843.
[2] St. Tarnowski, *Zygmunt Krasinski*.

see Krasinski free from all reproach and who cannot
justify his conduct[1]." While not attempting to palliate
Krasinski's failings, still it is only fair to take into
account that he had been morally forced into marriage
by his father against his every instinct, and that his
peculiar temperament and highly-strung genius were
galled to the utmost by bonds for which he had an
innate repulsion. The strain of embittered domestic
relations, the reproaches of conscience that with Krasinski were always insistent, increased his grief. From
time to time he still unveiled his heart in passionate
and despairing lyrics to Delphina Potocka.

"Pray thou for me," so runs the poem that he wrote
to her the year after his marriage, which in an early
manuscript he called *Last Lines*:

when too early I die for the sins of my fathers and for my own
sin. Pray thou for me, that even in my grave grief eternal for
thee shall not torment me as hell. Pray thou for me that
before God in heaven after ages of ages I shall meet thee once
more, and there at least rest together with thee, for all to me
here is mourning and toil. Pray thou for me. In vain have I
lived, because that thy heart is now turning from me. Pray
thou for me. I faithfully loved thee: even as measureless
measure is without measure I loved thee. Pray thou for me,
for unhappy am I; straight is my heart, but crooked my lot.
Pray thou for me, and speak no reproach, for thou only art
my sister on earth. Pray thou for me, for no other soul's
prayer can now move my heart, but can only redouble the gall
of my grief. Pray thou for me. To thee I still cling, and on
this earth save thee I have nought, and besides thee of nought
beyond this world do I dream. Only I dream that with my
sad soul thine to the immortal shall flow one with mine. Then
pray thou for me, for thy brother am I.

[1] *Op. cit.* Dr Kallenbach's monograph at present takes us no further
than the year 1838. We have no access to the family papers, and must
rely almost exclusively upon Count Tarnowski, related by marriage with
the Branicki family.

Yet in these years, while in his domestic relations Krasinski fell far short of his higher self, his work for his nation was reaching ever further to its noblest realization. The discord between the ideal and reality of the poet's surroundings could not shake his faith in the truth of that ideal. In Warsaw he saw before his eyes on all sides the terrorism of Russian Poland: a generation brought up as a conquered people.

"The youth," he wrote to Sołtan, "are in the most lamentable condition. They are taught historical lies and blasphemies, they are oppressed in every way, they are flogged for the lightest offence, for the want of a button or for a white handkerchief round their necks instead of the prescribed black one ; for the possession of any trifling book they are sent to prison: in a word, those who are beginning life are far more unhappy than those who are ending it. Decaying age is the golden age on these plains. Hence there is among our youth an unheard-of sadness full of unrest, and even of reproaches against fate, or of irreligion. Their hearts are becoming accustomed to complain even of God, for nobody teaches them who God is, and in the name of religion and of the government they continually experience indescribable torments. So the present generation is growing up sad and godless, with confused ideas, soured and embittered in the flower of their years, but at the same time full of hatred and courage, but not our courage of old which never calculated and was pure self-sacrifice. Their courage is the energy of slaves, not of free and highborn men. They do not mind the means if only the end is acquired. This is the necessary result of a soul darkened... by unhappiness and pain like slaves. And such a soul does not know that it is never possible to reach by evil means a great, holy, durable end...It is obvious that such a systematic moral slaying of youth is a powerful means for the sapping away of our strength. It is a hellish invention for the ruin, not only of the present but of the future. To murder the child in its mother's womb, that is its object.

"But, Adam," he goes on, "do not be saddened overmuch on reading this picture which I have drawn here. This picture, these details, are our martyrdom, are our test, but they are not the end, not the final truth. It is necessary to pass through this. Did not Christ in spite of His divinity experience the

final doubt? Did He not pass through the bitterness of all
bitternesses? And so that He might rise again He had of
necessity not only to pass through death, but in the moment
of death itself to experience the most cruel of moral sufferings
...That last cry of His to the Father was at once the highest
degree of pain and merit, and therefore of sacrifice. Not
otherwise could He have emptied the chalice to its last drop,
and it was necessary to drink that last drop so that nothing
should remain. Then only shall death be changed into life,
pain into joy, defeat into victory : *non est saltus in natura*!
We, only looking at facts with the eyes of the body, might
often doubt; but we know that even doubt is only the highest
pain, and no proof, no truth, but on the contrary...a sign that
the hour of rebirth is near...It has rejoiced my soul that I
have been able to bring you some comfort, however transitory
—the one which you tell me is lying in your drawer [*Dawn*].
That idea is my faith, my hope, my love. Without it I should
breathe my last, with it I live. And do not think that our life
has passed and that we have not beheld the Divine Justice,
albeit we are glimpsing at its beginning. All for which I weep
here are our last tears...Without such a faith, without such an
idea, there is no life, and with it even death itself does not
cease to be life. Then how should we not believe?

"We must be sad because we are human beings, because
the flesh is weak, but at the same time we shall often rejoice,
because the spirit is willing though the flesh is weak, and God's
Spirit is within us and in ours and in our cause, which by no
accident of chance has befallen at the end of one of the epochs
of humanity and at the beginning of another. Our corpse is
the bridge of transition for humanity. When it shall reach the
other shore we shall rise living. And let us eternally know
and feel that where there is hellish injustice, there the Divine
Justice must manifest itself; where men have not known how
to love, there God shall love. Otherwise the *universum* would
break. One God and one law and one truth! I enclose for
you here a Psalm written in that faith, in that hope, in that
love [the *Psalm of Hope*][1]."

This letter speaks for itself as to the nature of the
Anonymous Poet's apostolate. It was for this generation of young Poles, exposed to the fearful perils which

[1] *Letters to Sołtan.* May 12, 17, 1844.

he here describes, that Krasinski wrote *Dawn* and was now writing the *Psalms of the Future*.

It is noticeable that, with the exception perhaps of his short lyrics, Krasinski never wrote for the pure artistic joy of creation. He wrote for the sake of his country, and only when she had need of his words. Thus it was that, although he had declared his intention in the epilogue to *Dawn* never to write again, but to devote himself exclusively to action, he found himself confronted with a great national crisis when the only way in which he could warn his nation was by his song: and thus rose the *Psalms of the Future*.

The *Psalms of the Future* were, as Dr Kleiner points out to us, a complete departure from the method of Krasinski's former work[1]. *The Undivine Comedy* and *Iridion* were appeals to his fellow-countrymen under allegorical or veiled forms. *Dawn* is a rapture of spiritualized patriotism where lights of a heavenly mystic country play as in the poetry of the Hebrew prophets. The *Psalms* are the concrete and practical development of Krasinski's system, in which he employs the instrument of poetic form because it was the one most adapted to compel hearing and conviction upon those to whom they were spoken. With the culmination of his idea, says again Dr Kleiner, Krasinski's language and meaning become simplified: and the same interpreter of the Anonymous Poet lays emphasis on the somewhat curious fact that of the three great Polish mystic poets, Krasinski, in contrast to Mickiewicz and Słowacki, was the only one who brought the national mysticism down to a lucidity that any mind could grasp[2].

[1] J. Kleiner, *History of the Thought of Zygmunt Krasinski.*
[2] *Ibid.*

The first three *Psalms*, and more especially the first in point of time though placed as the third in the series, the *Psalm of Love*, differ also from the previous writings of Krasinski inasmuch as they are directed to meet a given occasion. During Krasinski's comparatively long stay in the Kingdom of Poland after his marriage he was closely watching the political and moral conditions under which the youth of his nation were growing up, and which were goading a certain party among them into a revolution, not of a merely national, but of a socialistic and even a Jacobin nature. A young Pole, whose name Krasinski's friend, from whom we have these particulars, does not give, and who was already dead when they were written, came to Krasinski with the secret that a new rising was being prepared, which the lower classes were to be induced to join by the promise of equality of lands and rights, and of a popular government when the movement should have succeeded[1]. The youth begged Krasinski to throw in his adherence with the party. Krasinski refused ; and this was not merely because he was imbued with aristocratic tendencies and because, his sympathies being with his own order, he had small belief in the ruling capabilities of the populace. His clear political acumen was not at fault. He saw that the time in Poland was not at that moment ripe for any democratic propaganda. The conditions in an oppressed country were too abnormal for a class agitation to be productive of anything except anarchy. Krasinski was parted by only two generations from the French Revolution : and when he heard that the Polish democratic

---

[1] St. Małachowski, *Short Sketch of the Life and Writings of Zygmunt Krasinski.* See St. Tarnowski, *Zygmunt Krasinski.*

leaders were prepared to have recourse to terrorism if necessary he foresaw consequences far beyond what the promoters of the rising had in view. In 1844 a Polish exile, Henryk Kamienski, brought out a work entitled: *Life-giving Truths for the Polish Nation by Filaret Prawdoski*—the latter word being derived from the Polish for truth, *Prawda*. On a different line to Krasinski's he too called Poland to the leadership of nations; but one that was to be acquired by a rising of every class in the land. This movement was to link itself to a great social revolution. The revolution should be bloodless if possible, but were bloodshed and violence to be indispensable they must be employed. "We will serve the revolution without regard as to whether it shall be compelled to unfurl the white or the red flag[1]." The redness of Kamienski's views obscured much that was noble in his outlook and alienated numbers of Poles who otherwise would have rallied to his side[2]. In such language sown broadcast among a people persecuted and deprived of all stable landmarks Krasinski saw the gravest peril to Poland.

Appalled then by the danger that was approaching his country, the Anonymous Poet sent forth an impassioned entreaty to his countrymen in the only form that could reach them. He wrote his *Psalm of Love*. But in order that its lessons should more deeply penetrate to the hearts of his compatriots he wrote the *Psalm of Faith* and the *Psalm of Hope* as its introduction, and as the recapitulation of the theories on which the point of his warning depended[3]. They were all three

[1] *Life-giving Truths for the Polish Nation*, by Filaret Prawdoski, Brussels, 1844 (Polish).

[2] J. Kleiner, *History of the Thought of Zygmunt Krasinski*.

[3] St. Tarnowski, *Zygmunt Krasinski*.

published simultaneously in 1845 under the pseudonym Spiridion Prawdzicki, the name Spiridion taken from George Sand's *Spiridion*, which treats of Krasinski's favourite ideas on the new epoch, and the second name chosen as a challenge to that of Kamienski.

In the *Psalm of Faith* Krasinski enunciates his act of faith in the personality of God, in the life of the soul, in the life of his nation and of the human race. Appreciations of style are matters which a foreign writer would do well to leave to native critics: and so we point to the emphasis that Count Tarnowski lays upon the perfect harmony that in the *Psalm of Faith* reigns between word and matter, the clearness and conciseness, often lacking in Krasinski's work, with which a simple diction treats of sublime things[1]. The opening of the Psalm, the fine description of the soul's pilgrimage to its highest good, is significant of the far road on which Krasinski had travelled since, in doubt and distress, he sang a similar theme in *The Son of Darkness.*

My soul[2] and my body are only two wings with which the meshes of time and of space are cut by my spirit in its flight to the heights. Worn out by time and by a thousand trials they must fall—but the spirit dies not, though men call this death. It casts off the wings that are withered and taketh on fresh, and folded in these wakes to life once again: and this do we call the hour of its birth. And my spirit takes to itself un-wearied wings, and with them soars once again—but now to a higher land. Thus ever higher it mounts to the Lord.

Behind it are twilight gulfs of the past. Before it wide plains of the all measureless. Before it the universe—time, endless space, storeys of milky ways and days of thousand years. And further, higher, o'er them and beyond them He Who is all and Who embraceth all, Creator Spirit of the stars,

---

[1] *Op. cit.*

[2] Krasinski here uses the word "soul" not in its ordinary significance but rather as meaning the mind.

of angels and of man, the end and the beginning of heaven
and of earth, He Who for ever higher, further is, not to be
reached, flaming o'er all, rest and together quickening strength,
light of the Most High Spirit-Sun of spirits.

To Him do I ever travel. Thither I first must go through
the toils of hell, through purgatorial trial, till I begin to put
me on body and soul more radiant and ascend to the other
world: to the world that from the ages is called the globe of
heaven; and there no longer need I swoons of death or waking
from the grave to ascend more high. For there is life eternal,
life that ceaseth not. The grave and cradle must be here
below upon this earth wherein the spirit's light is only dawn:
but for the angels death shall never be. The future and the
past with piercing eyes they see and know.

The desire of the spirit that has reached this angelic
life is God: "desire without measure that grows with
each minute, love without bounds, that is life without
end."

He is the centre of creation bound with one chain, He,
Being, Mind and Life, Father, Son and Holy Ghost. And all
of us and everywhere we are fashioned in His image and, by
degrees to ever higher possession ascending, we must immortal
live, with Him together live, born of His bosom, live in His
eternity. And even as He created us, so we must still create,
and from within us draw out worlds to weave to Him, as He
did weave for us, vesture of visible things; and in as far as
we can who are poor, we must with the lowliness of angels
give back to Thee what Thou didst give us of Thy mercy,
Lord, and yet be able never, never, to give back aught to
Thee, and thus eternally live in Thee by eternal love.

Thus for the reciprocal relation of God with man. In
the light of the Krasinskian theory on the application
of individual mysticism to that of nationality and the
human race, it is but one step to the conclusion of the
Psalm of Faith. For: "the history of mankind is the
school of the soul." The human race is advancing to
the day of judgment and to the transfiguration of
humanity.

The stairs that lead us to that day are the nations conceived in Thy grace. In each of them lives some deep thought that is the breath sent down upon them from Thy breast, and from that time is for the nation its predestined calling. And beyond all others some are chosen to combat for Thy beauty on this earth and, for long years, carrying the cross with its bleeding trail, to win by conflict man's higher thought of Thee, a greater love and greater brotherhood in barter for the murderer's knife planted within their breast.

Such a one, oh, God, is Thy Polish nation. Though the world giveth her such pain that she might despair of hope, may she stand steadfast through unheard-of suffering, for, of a truth, she is Thy chaplain on this earth if she is not ashamed of the crown of thorns, if she will understand that Thou lovest without measure those sons whom Thou dost crown with thorns : for the thorn imbrued in blood is the everlasting flower, with which Thou shalt renew the youth of all humanity.

Christ ever dwelleth in thee, oh, humanity. In thy breast He lives, He is of thy lot a guest. His blood is thine, His body is thy body. To thee it shall befall what did befall to Him. All thy vicissitudes He carried in his flesh. To thee He manifested all thy hopes. Whence art thou born? From a pure virgin womb, because from God's own thought in godly likeness. Whither dost thou go? To thy Father's city. By what road must thou pass? Through pain and toil. And when Christ on the summit of Mount Thabor was wrapt around with the eternal dawn, seest thou not what that sign to thee foretelleth? Before thy earthly lot shall be in full accomplished, thou too, oh, human race, shalt be transfigured. Thou shalt leave at the foot of the dark mountains all that deceives and all that is of sorrow: and thou shalt take spiritual knowledge with thee, and the eternal, unending love of hearts. And in the strength of these two hallowed powers like Christ shalt thou ascend to globes of light. All sin shall from thy brow be wiped away ; as lightly moving wings thy members be. Thy hands shalt thou stretch forth to the white air, and in it thou shalt poise—as air thyself.

The following Psalm, the *Psalm of Hope*, plays on a different note to that of the four other Psalms. It is a cry of triumphant gladness. In his *Life-giving Truths* Kamienski had called upon a new poet of hope to appear. "Arise, singer of the future! We await thee with undeceived hope, for thou must show thyself, for the life-giving strength of Poland shall bring thee forth[1]." Elegies and lamentations were according to him to be no more heard. Krasinski took up the challenge, and he begins and ends his *Psalm of Hope* with the words:

Long enough, long enough, has the grief of poets rung upon the strings. Now is it time to strike on a second string, on the steel of deed.

For once sorrow is absent from this one of Krasinski's poems. He sees close at hand the advent of the Paraclete that shall restore a corrupted world and right all wrong.

I say unto you He is not far, He, the Comforter promised ages since. Nor thrones nor crowns shall be the first to see Thee in the heavens. But the innocent martyr shall, oh, Spirit, see Thee. Nor schemes of merchants nor the executioner's hand can prevail against the truth. Oh, come quicker, spring of the world! Oh, come quicker, God the Spirit! Surely, like Christ caught to heaven, we shall ascend to the paradise of love. Surely we are rising ever higher through the ages to the final resurrection. From the spring unto the spring, ever to the spring, the heavenly flower which is our soul is growing, we all are ever growing unto Thee.

Then shall the eternal Gospel, reiterates the poet, reign over the earth when, after long suffering, it reaches its rest.

Farewell, earth, with pain and anguish! A new Jerusalem glitters on the vale of the old earth. Long the road, the toil was heavy, flowed a sea of blood and tears, but the angelic age draws near.

Poland, Poland, thy grave was only the cradle of the new dawn, only one little moment in the eternity where was conceived the divine day.

Let us praise the Lord Who comes. Cast ye palms and cast ye psalms—flowers below and songs on high. Oh, cast

---

[1] H. Kamienski, *Life-giving Truths for the Polish Nation.*

songs and cast ye flowers! Lo, He comes! The Lord is
coming, sad no more as in past ages, freed from thorns and
nails and wounds, now transfigured—from heaven's high summit, from beyond the starry walls of the all-world, as the
horizon of all-blue, flows He to us—flows the Lord.

Oh, drink ye with your souls that heavenly blue, and all
shall grow forth as its blue around you. Though they torture
you and tempt you, in my hope you shall believe. Fear ye not
because to-day vileness ruleth everywhere. From your faith
shall be your will, from your will shall be your deed.

And the *Psalm* ends with the same summons to
the "steel of deed," with which Krasinski began it.

It will be noticed in this Psalm, and even more
in those which succeed it, that whatever the great future
Krasinski promises to his country he never fails
to insist that it can only be realized under the condition
of individual and national purity. When his countrymen accept his belief in Poland's resurrection and high
calling, then let them put their will to the task of its
fulfilment, and from that will shall arise the saving
deed. Hence only the most superficial reader of the
Anonymous Poet could characterize his teaching as
passive, or as too mystical to be taken as more than
a beautiful dream. It has all the exactions of spiritual
combat. The goal shines on the far horizon, radiant
and alluring: but it is practical action of the most inexorable nature that shall attain it. Having thus laid
his foundations Krasinski reaches his *Psalm of Love.*

The *Psalm of Love* occupies a place peculiar to
itself in the work of Krasinski : not only because it is
one of the greatest of his poems, but by reason of the
tragic circumstances that inspired it and the even
greater tragedy of its failure. Count Tarnowski likens
it to the patriotic outbursts of the splendid orators of

Greece and Rome pleading for their nation in a great national peril, and pleading in vain[1]. Although the Psalm is among the most episodical of Krasinski's poems it is as strong a universal message as anything he ever wrote. To the watchword of terrorism flung forth by a brother-Pole the Anonymous Poet opposes the watchword of love[2]. The *Psalm of Love* is a plea to spurn evil means for a right end, to abjure the weapons of a criminal violence, to remember that love is the one saving force.

With the horror in his mind of what the projected revolution would in its train bring upon his nation, Krasinski entreats his countrymen to shun a fratricidal slaughter. Let their weapons be turned against a common enemy. The guillotine and plunder are the resource of the spirit in its infancy, rage the language of children. These things are the liberty, not of man, but of the brute beast.

It is time for the scales to fall from our eyes, time to take to ourselves the toil of angels, time to cast off all stain and by that very deed to destroy slavery. Destruction is not deed. The only godlike truth, productive of deed, is transfiguration through love.

Returning to the point at issue Krasinski points to the

Polish people with the Polish nobles, as two choirs and but one song. From that marriage but one spirit, the mighty Polish nation, one will, one deed. Oh! salvation is only there.

The poet, who saw with horror before his mental vision the white robe of his nation polluted by un-

---

[1] St. Tarnowski, *Zygmunt Krasinski.*

[2] J. Kleiner, *History of the Thought of Zygmunt Krasinski.*

worthy deeds on the part of her sons, then bids them
know that :

> Who shall first lift his hand to shake the snow from off that
> vesture, who changeth pain to crime, who forges fetters into
> the assassin's knife and not into the sword, cursed is he.
>
> When geniuses descend into this world they lead their
> cause by another road. No men by murder and the rack have
> been dictator for the ages. Rather they live in peril, rather
> they perish in the end themselves : but their victory lasts for
> ever. Each bloody name in history was borne by a worthless
> soul. Only the weak soul chooses butchery, whether his name
> be Robespierre or Marius.

Krasinski then utters an eloquent apologia for his
own order. Who, he asks, immolated themselves in
continual sacrifice on the altars of their country ? Who,
with Poland in their hearts and sword in hand, fell in
battle, or were carried away to Siberia ? And who, he
asks, could you find without fault ? "Only He Who
was God and man in one. But from the sinner another
man shall soar through suffering, changed as the
phoenix." He points to sea and land, to the Spanish
sierras where the Polish legions won immortal glory
—Krasinski's father had there headed their most
famous charge—to the fields of France, where the
soldier-nobles of Poland "have sown the seed of future
Poland, the godlike grain—their own blood. And of
that blood you are the sons."

The high ideal of those appointed to lead their
fellow-men is :

> to shed forth the spirit on millions, to give forth bread to
> every body, thoughts from heaven to every soul, to thrust none
> down into the depths, but by the uplifting of others to advance
> to ever higher spheres…Say, oh, white-winged unstained eagle,
> whence is the swarm of the black thoughts [that will slay the
> pure ideal of Poland]? They grow where there are chains.
> Ah! bondage distilleth poison. Nought is Siberia, nought

the knout, but the corrupted spirit of a nation, that only is the pain of pains.

Eternally the usurper stands before all eyes, the tempter already in that he standeth there to say that God is not. He dissolves conscience by the load of pain. He teaches little children to believe in murder as in glory. Maidens shall take daggers in their hands like roses. The sister shall say: "Brother, take them, for butchery is our salvation." Our country shall be not heaven, but hell.

"Oh, my holy one," cries the devout lover of Poland in an anguish of foreboding, "abjure these delusions! They are the nightmares of an evil moment. Thou shalt not rid thee of thy ancient faith that he only shall cut through his bonds who is anointed with the sign of virtue, that to be a Pole upon this earth is to live nobly and to God."

But the powers of evil are thronging close on every side.

Oh, my Poland! Holy Poland! Thou standest on the threshold of thy victory. This is the last term of thy pain. Let it be only manifest that thou art the eternal foe of evil. Then shall the bonds of death be shattered, and thou shalt be caught up to heaven, because even until death thou wert with God.

When the last moment brings death's crisis into life, then is the terrible battle. Sobs of despair, wailings of lament, are moaned by dying lips—oh, my God! In the strength of thy suffering overcome that moment, conquer that pain. And thou shalt rise again, and thou shalt rise the queen of the Slavonian plains.

Let men gaze into thy face with love as though upon the spring. Be thou the mistress who straightens the crooked ways of the world, the herald of all love. Efface all sin. Dry all tears. Rule the world of souls, disdain the rule of flesh. From sheep-like men nations do thou create.

But again all this is conditional; and the refrain of the closing stanzas of the poem must needs be the cry of warning: "Cast away your murderous weapons!" When the harvest is ripe and the word thunders forth, then and only then: "forward in the name of God. Take your swords, your flails, your scythes," cries the poet with the vision of Kościuszko's peasant bands before his eyes. The holy rising of class, fighting side by side for the liberation of their country, shall break down prison and fortress, and then of a surety: "God will not turn away His face."

Thus ends the *Psalm of Love*, which lives in Polish history as a noble piece of pleading, justified too late by the catastrophe that it had striven to avert.

Krasinski spent the winter and spring of 1846 with his wife and infant son in a villa at Nice. Delphina Potocka was also at Nice in her own villa. Krasinski, as we learn from his correspondence with his friends, was already suffering acutely from the goad of his conscience in this false position, when the blow of 1846 fell upon him. The February of that year saw the terrible uprising of the Galician peasantry. A general insurrection had been projected through all Poland. We have seen that one party of young Poles intended to work it on social lines, and in particular to arm the peasants. The Austrian government, having discovered what was going forward, seized the opportunity to carry into effect what its policy in Galicia had been stealthily aiming at: the enfeebling of Poland by deliberately setting one class against another. It sent its agents among the ignorant Polish peasants, and succeeded in persuading a certain number of them that the Polish landowners were their deadly enemies who must be exterminated. Deluded by these secret propagandists, bribed by the Austrian government that paid so much on the head of every Polish noble, maddened by the drink with which the same government incited them to the deed, the peasants, in two provinces, for the Austrian machinations were not wholly successful, attacked the manor houses. Scenes of appalling horror followed, in which thousands of Polish nobles were butchered.

This triumph of the Metternichian policy is one of the most painful pages in modern Polish history.

"Are there words," wrote Krasinski to Małachowski, "in any human tongue with which to express the suffering of this moment?...This world and its each day bears for us the name of hell[1]." Krasinski had interpreted the fate of the nation by the promise of a great spiritual leadership only to be gained by purity and sacrifice; hence the Galician massacres were the visible triumph of the powers of darkness thrusting an adored country into the pit of infamy from the only road that could save her. It seemed as though the catastrophe that had befallen his nation was to cost Krasinski his life. For the next two years he lived in a condition of such physical collapse that those who watched over him were in constant expectation of his death. He never recovered the effect of this national disaster. At the age of thirty-four he became prematurely aged. From 1846 to the year of his death, 1859, his was uninterrupted bodily suffering.

But to him who before the massacres had written:

We shall sink into chaos, our bodies may die in tortures as our souls have died even before them : but our Idea is all powerful like God, for like God it is truth and love, and shall be victorious over our corpses[2]:

to him it was impossible to fall into despair more than momentary. However great the anguish that had invaded his soul the hope which he had won at the cost of pangs of travail did not die. His Idea was to be proved by the test of fire.

---

[1] *Letters to Małachowski.* Nice, March 16, 18, 1846.
[2] *Ibid.* Nice, Jan. 9, 1846.

"I go as a madman since I read in all the papers what has happened": were his first words to Gaszynski after the news had reached Nice.

About myself I know that I shall die, but I know also that the idea shall conquer. It conquers by defeats. That which has to conquer for all ages must suffer before the day of triumph, must be formed by pain, be trained by martyrdom[1].

And later to Małachowski:

See if the lot of Christ is not repeated to the last letter under the figure of the history of the nation. Fearful that moment, that "Father, why hast Thou forsaken me?" We to-day are in that like position...He only felt Himself forsaken in the last moment of death. And those who are to rise again from the dead must pass through this. But before the Resurrection morning how many hearts shall break. Mine first of all[2].

"I am sinking under the burden of life"—to Gaszynski—"where all is like to death with this one difference that there is not the rest of death[3]." "I am exiled from my hopes," he says in one dark moment, when the very faith by which he had lived seemed rent from him. "I am wandering and fugitive. Where should I go?" he adds, in reference to his plans for the immediate future. "Nothing lures me anywhere. The world is to me a desert where here and there lie scattered the dead bodies of the Galician nobles[4]." So run the letters of one borne down under the extremity of mental agony; but even now he can still tell Gaszynski that: "all is lost except faith, but with faith all can be regained."

What cast any stain upon the moral integrity of his nation was far more hideous in Krasinski's eyes

---

[1] *Letters to Gaszynski.* Nice, March 1, 1846.
[2] *Letters to Małachowski.* Nice, March 30, 1846.
[3] *Letters to Gaszynski.* Nice, May 5, 1846.
[4] *Ibid.* Nice, May 7, 1846.

than all exterior persecution. When in the autumn of the year Austria, in flagrant violation of the Treaty of Vienna, annexed Cracow, the last remaining vestige of Poland's independence, great as was Krasinski's patriotic indignation, he wrote the following words on the subject to his friends, the philosopher, Bronisław Trentowski, and Stanisław Koźmian:

When we last embraced each other there was still a span of Polish earth as though independent on the map of Europe. To-day you will find none. This is the beginning of the end, this is the crisis. The last evil must indeed be the last. I am profoundly convinced that if we do not with our own hands give the finishing stroke to ourselves to the glorification of our enemies, our political resurrection from the dead shall begin from the day of Cracow's death. There was never a nation in such sublime circumstances, in such favourable conditions, who was so near, from the cross on which she hangs, to the heaven whither she must ascend. No human history has till now presented, at any period of the development of history, such a concurrence of events facilitating the transition from death to life and triumph[1].

That last span of earth torn from us, that fourth partition, has more than anything else advanced our cause. Every wound inflicted on something holy and good becomes a far deeper wound, by the reflection of the Divine Justice that rules history, on him who inflicted it. Earlier or later—the question is only what hour—from this crime that has been effected absolutely shall come forth our resurrection, or rather the external circumstance which will permit us to emerge from the grave, for our true resurrection is not outside us but within us[2].

The recipient of the second passage, Stanisław Koźmian, had been Krasinski's friend in boyhood. The Rising of 1830 parted them till the year 1843 when, to the joy of both, they met in Rome, and renewed a

---

[1] *Letters*, Vol. III. To Bronisław Trentowski. Aix-en-Provence, Dec. 16, 1846.

[2] *Letters from Zygmunt Krasinski to Stanisław Koźmian.* Nice, Dec. 18, 1846.

friendship only closed by Krasinski's death. After Krasinski had left this world Koźmian published Zygmunt's
letters that he bequeathed to his descendants as the
most precious of legacies : and in the touching notes
which he added to them he tells us how he ranked the
Anonymous Poet "highest among men," and that the
memory of him "will strengthen and support me to the
last of my days[1]."

Borne down as Krasinski was by his heavy sadness
in the fresh national tragedy, his spirit struggled, against
mental distress and physical incapacity, to give his
nation help. In October, 1846, he wrote to Delphina
Potocka:

"I tried if that penalty of speechlessness would not leave
me. I sat for four hours, but all was astray, till at times despair
seized me that such a state of sterility could befall a man's
soul. Oh, my Dialy, pray for me to God. I feel nothing
egotistic in that desire, but I feel that such a sketch "—the
poem he was attempting to write—" is needed : for Poland "
—he calls her by a veiled name—" is driven by all the winds.
She implores, she implores for counsel[2]."

Early in the following year he tells Trentowski:

I have lost all certitude and mental balance. I am not
certain even for one moment of my thoughts or expressions or
of rhythm or any sound...That state is a cursed one. I have
been struggling with it for this year past, and if you could only
know how madly, how bitterly, at times how passionately, and
more often with what despair. The voice of a luring, compelling destiny rings constantly by day and night in my ears.
I would fain follow it, and some infernal power keeps me back.
Now only God knows if I can find again my lost powers and
if I shall ever again be able to clothe in shape the thought and
feeling, to put into words the longing and love, vainly seething
in my heart, into external sound—to create something. I
would wish only once more, and this when there is such urgent

---

[1] *Op. cit.* Introduction.
[2] Jubilee edition. Vol. VI, p. 369.

need, to tear from my heart the Idea of all my life, and then let my heart break[1].

The result of this labour of soul and body was *Resurrecturis*, spiritually speaking perhaps Krasinski's most sublime poem. Although written at this time, it was not published, probably because it did not satisfy the poet, and he intended to rewrite it. Only in 1851 did it appear, as it first stood, with a few trifling alterations. It therefore belongs to the closing chapter of Krasinski's work for his people, and will find its place there. But two other poems that Krasinski had begun in former years were now finished and published in Paris in 1847: *To-Day* and *The Last*.

[1] *Letters*, Vol. III. To Trentowski. Nice, Jan. 2, 1847.

CHAPTER XII

TO-DAY, THE LAST, AND THE LAST
PSALMS OF THE FUTURE
(1847–1848)

As a whole *To-Day* falls below the level of Krasinski's great national work. The first speech of the dying man and the demon's monologue are ranked very high by Count Tarnowski, and it is said that Mickiewicz, penetrating Krasinski's disguise, gave enthusiastic praise to one of its passages[1]. But after the opening the poem drags. All that is noblest in its sentiments Krasinski had said before and with greater force : he was at the moment too spent to speak with the accents of a *Psalm of Love* or a *Psalm of Good Will*.

A Pole—Krasinski himself—lies dying. Around his bed stand his friends, each holding national opinions which are at variance with his, and from whom, in the sadness and weariness of the life that is ebbing away, he turns, praying to be left in peace. Two stanzas where the dying man's wandering fancy returns to his Polish plains contain a poetic and exquisite touch of nature, foreign to Krasinski's usual style, and more akin to the work of other poets of his nation.

---

[1] St. Tarnowski, *Zygmunt Krasinski.*

Oh, come ye, then, come through the hamlets of home, through the green of the meads and the billows of corn. There in each ear of corn murmurs the nation's grief. There does the lily of the field for vengeance cry. In that wide space save for the whispers of the forests nothing shall you hear; and in the forests there are graves of green and stones, and in each grave a martyr sleeping lies, and o'er him pine trees sing the hymn of death.

Then he prays that he may not die with his despair for his nation unrelieved. Where is the angel who had promised him succour in his last hour? This refers to Delphina Potocka, Krasinski having written this part of the poem in the years of his love for her before his marriage. He sees instead his "Satan," come to tell him that his country is destined to purchase the life of the world by her everlasting death, which is of course in direct opposition to the Krasinskian ideal of death leading to new life. Let the dying man bow to reason and necessity. But still he refuses to be overcome by the specious temptation. He answers—and here Krasinski is influenced by the theory on which much of his hope for Poland depended—that the tempter is:

only the half of universal life. From thy lips flows the word of eternal death because thou knowest blind force, not what is will. The desire of many hearts can descend as angels to the grave, and an angelic strength pour into bones and dust. God cast the seed of miracle into the will of man. Eternal humility in tears and blood—before God. Undying strife in tears and blood—before the foe. This is our fate, our faith, our conscience.

And, still calling upon her whom he loved to fulfil her promise, he sinks into what the bystanders believe is death.

It is now the turn of his friends to speak. They do so, some ten of them, one after the other. For the most part each of them urges a special line of policy, which Krasinski held to be injurious to his country: an exclusive aristocracy, democracy, communism, Panslavism, and so on, which they reproach their dead friend for not having supported. In the speech of one there are words so descriptive of Krasinski himself that they sufficiently prove whom the dying man represents.

"See," says he, pointing to the face upon the bed; "on those features grief for his nation has blotted out all else: that grief which for a hundred years tears every heart in Poland. Blessed that grief which is the proof of immortality: that purgatorial, provident and shielding grief which, as religion, unites us who are torn apart."

The fame of the dead man must be not that he was an aristocrat, democrat or any of the rest, but: "if you would mark him out by any sign, call him a Pole, for he loved Poland. In this love he lived and in it died." Such might well be Krasinski's epitaph.

At this moment the dying Pole regains consciousness. He hears the "voice of my angel, the voice of my spring, eternally remembered, eternally beloved."

" O, let them also see thee," he prays, for then they will understand their errors and how they must conquer in the war for Poland. Though he should spend an eternity of joy with his angel it would not be joy if she, refusing to appear to them, leaves them in their mental wandering and "my Poland sad." She hears his prayer. The watchers fall upon their knees, and as her voice repeats the phrase: " Poland shall be in the name of the Lord," they one by one confess that they have sinned and erred.

One tells in all Krasinski's fervid imagery—this was the passage by which Mickiewicz recognized the identity of the author of the poem—of the horror of the Galician massacres, and at the voice from above: "his heart breaks, his thought is shattered." Another, as he said, had urged upon his nation to fling away her diadem of thorns and yield herself to the embraces of the false lover who will be her destroyer. His long speech is the refutation of Wielopolski's famous *Lettre d'un Gentilhomme Polonais au Prince de Metternich*, in which the Pole, whose name twenty years later was to be the object of violent national passions, advocated a Polish reconciliation with Russia on lines which no Polish independent would accept. " Forgive me, forgive," the speaker concludes, weeping. "See how I sob, and how I love my Poland. Through pain I lost my reason." A fourth says he lost not reason, but heart, through the same suffering. So each tells his sin against his nation. The heavenly voice promises forgiveness on the condition of their individual virtue. " The Almighty Himself cannot lay the dawn of ages in an impure heart."

"Alas!" reply the dying man's friends in chorus. "Our errors rose from our despair. By law we were bidden to live by crimes, by law bidden to be spies, by law bidden to betray son, father, brother. Even in God's temples the name of Poland was as a foul word. Only was it free to utter that name aloud —from the scaffold."

" Repay her," the voice answers, " for her cross by your good deeds," and to that the chorus : " There is one road by which we must go to Poland as to God, by that which never was defiled."

All that is now left for the dying Pole is to urge his brothers to be of good heart, for the day so often prophesied by the Anonymous Poet shall be theirs.

I shall not be with you when on that day your hearts resound with hymns, when, as the Jewish prophets sang, the rainbow-hued clouds descend on you from high. Oh, be pure, be holy, and what I have foretold shall be fulfilled for you by a just God.

So he dies : and the last words of the poem are spirit voices, his and the angel's, repeating from unseen worlds : " Poland shall be in the name of the Lord."

The second poem which Krasinski brought out now —*The Last*—is of all his poetic work the most in line with other European verse. It was begun years before, perhaps even as early as the time when the poet, almost a boy, visited with Mickiewicz the dungeon of Chillon which gave him the idea of the poem. Told in narrative form, in style equal to the best in that particular type[1], *The Last* is the story of a Polish poet who has languished for twenty years in a Siberian dungeon. If here and there in the beginning faintly reminiscent of Byron's *Prisoner of Chillon*, as indeed it was almost bound to be, Krasinski soon carries his poem up to those higher planes where at the period of life when he completed it he dwelt familiarly. Moreover, *The Last* is impregnated with that terrible tragedy of real fact which must of necessity be found in the work of any Pole of Krasinski's day, when telling the all too well-known tale of exile and of prison. The captive of *The Last* has in fact been identified with two different Poles whose long martyrdom is conspicuous even in the *via dolorosa* of Poland's national records: Roman Sanguszko, deported to Siberia and personally condemned by Nicholas I to make the journey on foot, and Łukasinski, whose prison was his living tomb. But Count Tarnowski adduces the internal evidence of the poem as proof that its spokesman is intended for no other than Krasinski him-

---

[1] St. Tarnowski, *Zygmunt Krasinski.*

self. The poet's foreboding that he would end his days
in Siberia amounted almost to obsession.

The prisoner tells his story. He has rotted for years
in his underground cell, chained by a hook to the wall.
Days, months, years dragged on, and all his hopes died.
He struggled against the death of his soul, against despair, against the dying out of reason. In the cells above
his where light and air penetrated were confined those
whose crimes in the eyes of the Tsar were less than his.
They had murdered a mother, a father, a brother. He
was a Pole who had loved his country and sung of her
to his countrymen.

To no one I confided my last thought. To my beloved
ones I did not bid farewell. At night—without a trace, in
silence and in secret, the prison cart hurled me away; and only
the stars of Poland may remember those first and hidden, those
my journeys after death.

The Tsar condemned him to his fate :

And I went on foot to beyond the world, into this ice, I, son
of the Republic of Poland and of freedom, among the fettered
droves of criminals.

He was driven into the far north at the end of the
knout.

Would to God I had died in the beginning of my martyrdom. But we die not when death is our salvation. Thou shalt
die in the day of joy, thou shalt perish in the day of victory.
But when thou livest in pain thou art immune.

And in a transport of suffering he cries :

Ah, where are my native flowering plains? Where are my
fields of corn, the marshes of my meadows? Where are the
woods of pines, murmuring' o'erhead like a strange, secret
prayer? Where is the people that calls Mary Queen?

At this sudden awakening of memory that he believed had been crushed out by captivity he, for the
first time for many a year, weeps. Thought is not dead

18—2

after all. He remembers his past visions of the advent of the Paraclete to renovate humanity and of the great mission of his country. Who knows but that transfiguration may have already taken place in the world to which he has perished? He feels his chains no longer The prison walls fade. The spring green of the Polish meads stretches before his eyes, and he sees a multitude of Poles with the national banners of crimson and white. Horsemen in his hallucination detach themselves from the others, and gallop to the north across the Russian steppes towards the prisons of Siberia. One moment more, and he will be delivered: "and Poland shall enter in my prison to give me back what I have lost for her—my life[1]."

Krasinski's poem was to have ended here with the release of the prisoner whose history he in the first instance entitled, not *The Last*, but *The Delivered*. All this part was written prior to the year 1846 while Krasinski was under the dominion of such hopes as inspired *Dawn*. Then occurred the catastrophe of the Galician massacres. In his grief of mind Krasinski changed the end of the poem into tragedy, while at the same time the fear of Siberia under which he had written *The Delivered* left him, and yielded to a longing for death as his only deliverance. The existence of the Polish prisoner is unknown to the rescuers. They are told that there are no Poles in the fortress. Within sight of the walls they turn back, and he, "the last," is left behind, the only Pole to whom the prison doors are not opened. Transports of rage shake his soul. Blasphemies stream from his lips. Then he chances to pronounce the name of Poland.

[1] See the identical expression in the letter to Gaszynski of June 1, 1843.

Poland! Poland! It is true she has arisen. Lord! is it true? To-day all Poland no more awaiteth death in chains as I? Forgive me, Lord, for Poland did I love. She liveth on the earth and Thou in heaven. And therefore do I die, blessing Thy name for ever, everywhere, before and in the grave. With Thine and Poland's name upon these lips which in a few moments shall be stone, I die. Holy Thy will! Holy my long bondage, holy the terrors of my lonely death, since now no longer torn asunder is the sweet soil of my sires.

And, hearing heavenly Hosannas, death delivers him.

In both *To-Day* and *The Last* there runs the strain of a conspicuous weariness. But this is apparent no longer in the poems that followed them in 1848, the concluding *Psalms of the Future*. The fact that in all these poems, and in marked measure in the *Psalms*, the Anonymous Poet could rise above the horror of what 1846 had brought upon his nation, and still speak to her in words of hope, was the greatest victory that even he had ever won. He won it through and for the love of Poland. The Galician massacres however left their deep traces on his national idea. Dr Kleiner notes that the theory of the dependence of Poland's resurrection on each Pole's personal purity of heart and deed, which Krasinski had already indicated in various of his works, now became paramount.

While the motive of the *Psalm of Grief* was Krasinski's wish to console and fortify his nation in the affliction in which she was then plunged, its immediate cause was the attack made by Słowacki against the tenets of the *Psalm of Love*. Słowacki circulated in manuscript a fine poem of which the form was partly modelled on that of Krasinski's *Psalm of Love*, in which he mercilessly derided, with more than one personal thrust at the Anonymous Poet, the latter's forebodings. Against the knowledge or desire of its author who, after strained relations with Krasinski on account of a personal matter, had renewed his friendship with him, this poem was published in 1848[1]. In a few words of introduction to his fourth Psalm Krasinski stated his intention of answering his brother-poet's poem, the style of which he praises unreservedly; and he then opens his *Psalm of Grief.*

Słowacki had thrust in Krasinski's teeth the taunt : "Thou wert afraid, son of a noble." "Did terror speak from me," replies Krasinski, without passion, " when I foresaw that we were going forward into darkness, not to dawn ?" Yes, his accuser spoke truth. He trembled indeed, but at the sight of evil menacing his country, when he sees murder and ignominy ready to descend upon her.

"Let the Lord judge between my fear, thy courage. Would to God thou hadst truly prophesied," continues the poet to whose warnings the truth had been given in blood. "Would to God I had been the liar, thou the inspired prophet, and that no stain rested on our country's plains!"

In Krasinski's self-vindication against the man who had once been his friend, whose work Krasinski had publicly praised when Słowacki had had the chagrin of seeing it passed over in silence, once only a bitter retort passes his lips. Had Krasinski been proved in the wrong, "we should both have walked in gladness, thou with thy own glory, I with the redemption of Poland."

---

[1] Słowacki had fallen in love with Mme Bobrowa who, still devoted to Krasinski, did not reciprocate his affection, and had spoken of her in some disparaging terms when writing to Krasinski. The latter resented these for the lady's sake, and a coldness ensued between the two poets.

Beyond this single stab at Słowacki's egotism Krasinski's whole answer breathes a dignity and a
nobility that would not descend to the acrimonies of
personal strife. His concern was not with individual
considerations, but with the substance of Słowacki's
theories. Słowacki had urged progress with no regard
to the means by which it should be secured: "the
triumph of the soul," says Dr Kleiner, "albeit in the
midst of blood and ruins[1]." This was of course a doctrine
directly opposed to that which Krasinski held was life.

After the personal preliminaries which poetically
are great, the style of the poem deteriorates far below
the standard of the two Psalms between which it stands.
The nobility of the *Psalm of Grief* lies not in its form
but in its matter. Krasinski was now developing nothing
further. He was recapitulating what he had already
taught. The *Psalm of Grief* is the plea that he had
often uttered for the works of the Spirit against those
of human baseness. Eternal is the strife between the
beast and the idea: blood, violence, destruction are the
inheritance of every century.

Who shall redeem us? Who draw out harmony from the
battle of place and years? He in Whose depths is the height
of life, in Whom flesh and spirit move at one—the Holy Ghost.
Beneath His rule the earth shall weep no more in blood. In
the morning He waketh to hope the people that slumber. He
shall hasten to make the dark of the deep pools silver till the
morn waxeth into the broader day.

With an increasing want of poetical fire Krasinski
goes on to tell of the general judgment on the ages:
how, with the avenging angels sweeping down like
hurricanes upon them, they stand trembling on the
brink of the pit of damnation till clinging heart to

[1] J. Kleiner, *History of the Thought of Zygmunt Krasinski.*

heart they are redeemed, because while they were sundered they were as hell, and when they become brothers
they are saved.   In the third part Krasinski points once
more to the ideals that alone can bring salvation to
man, a nation, the human race : purity, the love that
accepts toil, the courage that does not shrink from
suffering.

> Be unpolluted in the midst of vileness.   In the midst of
> outrage hold fast thy love.   Let thy heart be strong as steel,
> and thine eyes weep over every alien grief—and so reach God
> by the one chain of deed, by a pure and sincere soul.
> And I gaze 'midst the whirlwind at the death shroud of the
> skies, and I hear amidst the clouds the choir of those risen
> from the dead.   Ah! a voice I know! But the blood shed by
> vengeance shall not touch the cause of Poland.

She shall shun all evil if she would both live and
banish eternal death from the nations.   "Thus shall be
the resurrection": and so the *Psalm of Grief* closes on
the note of hope.

We now reach the poem that brings the epoch of
the national mysticism which rose out of the sorrows of
the Polish Rising to its magnificent close—the *Psalm
of Good Will*.   Here, with the full powers not only of
his poetical genius but of a great heart and soul,
Krasinski spoke the last and grandest word of his
nation's prophetic and mystic nationalism.   Under every
aspect this Psalm is the supreme masterpiece of the
Anonymous Poet of Poland.   The exultation of *Dawn*
is absent.   Nor is there any abandonment of grief.
With the dignity of one who, after long battling with
the tempest had gained the goal, Krasinski turns to his
people with his farewell message.   The deep and sorrowful accents of the Psalm roll on like the tones of a
great organ till they die away in the Anonymous Poet's

last prayer for Poland that hers may be not earthly glory, as the world knows it, but good will.

The peculiar correspondence of Krasinski's national mysticism with that of the unit is perhaps more apparent in the *Psalm of Good Will* than in any other of Krasinski's directly patriotic work. The conditions of moral resurrection, the struggle against temptation, the all conquering power of the will, as Krasinski sings of them in relation to a country, not only read as a page of a soul's experience; but in at least one line Krasinski distinctly argues that, as of the man, so of a nation.

"Thou hast given us all that Thou couldst give, oh, Lord." Each stanza of the Psalm begins with these words until the scene of the final temptation, and each closes with the petition: " Now that Thy judgment has thundered in heaven on the two thousand years that have passed, grant us, oh, Lord, in the midst of this judgment to raise ourselves to life by holy deeds." In both of these refrains is contained the epitome of the whole moral idea of the *Psalm of Good Will.* Every gift has been bestowed upon the nation ; her salvation, as with the individual soul, depends upon her response to the vocation with which she has been endowed and called to carry out. Now let her answer the Divine summons by deed.

"Thou hast given us all that Thou couldst give, oh, Lord ": rule for a thousand years, a history of love unstained by the lust of conquest[1]. "When we descended from the life of the Capitol [*i.e.* the heights of power[2]] into the pit of our dismemberment, Thou didst keep us who were dead living upon the field of

---

[1] See Chapter X, pp. 237, 238.

[2] Note to Jubilee edition. Vol. V, p. 73.

war. We were not, and behold, we were": as soldiers
in the Polish legions on the battle-fields of Europe.

Thou hast given us all that Thou couldst give, oh, Lord:
the purest life and therefore worthy of the cross, and the cross
itself, but such a cross as brings us to Thy stars. Earth Thou
didst take from us and heaven send down, and on all sides
Thy heart doth shelter us. But our free will Thou hadst to
leave to us. Without ourselves Thyself canst not redeem us;
for so hast Thou ennobled man and every nation that Thy
design, on high suspended, awaits till by their choice men
and a nation go upon their destined roads. Forever is Thy
Spirit the spouse of freedom only.

An eternal idealist, Krasinski has, his own countrymen are the first to acknowledge, transfigured the history
of Poland. If however his language may be called that
of a lover, not of sober fact, is, pertinently asks Count
Tarnowski, the conclusion of Krasinski's whole teaching
and of the life which was one long labour to attain it,
erroneous because his premisses were at fault[1]? Does
not this glorification in itself lead directly to the rigorous
truth of his summons to the battle that can, and it alone,
make a nation worthy of her heroic destiny[2]? This is
not the place to enter into an argument as to whether
the reminder of past failings or the appeal to live up
to a sublime ideal, whether it had in reality ever been
reached or no, were the more profitable spiritual spur.
Krasinski chose the latter.

Thou hast given us all that Thou couldst give, oh, Lord:
the example of Thy unhappy Jerusalem in whom Thy love
dwelt so long.

The conception of a certain analogy between the
lot of Poland and of Sion is not uncommon in Polish
mysticism: but Krasinski viewed it on a curiously

[1] St. Tarnowski, *Zygmunt Krasinski.*

[2] *Op. cit.* See also J. Kleiner, *History of the Thought of Zygmunt Krasinski.*

different line to that of Mickiewicz or Goszczynski.
The resemblance was to him a sinister one¹. Jerusalem
had fallen for ever. Krasinski's idea is that Poland
must take warning for should her sins be like to those
of the Hebrew race—the disdain of the cross and of
the law of love—by which Jerusalem "lost her queen-
ship and is now a widow," the fate of his nation shall
be like Sion's.

Thou hast given us all that Thou couldst give, oh, Lord:
in the example of the foul deeds of wrong of our oppressors,
for which the weeping of our children curses them, for which
they stand by the shame of their own hearts ashamed before
Thee. Not by the death of others, but by their own, all crimes
finish without fruit upon this earth.

Then for the first time in the *Psalm of Good Will*
the note of a mortal anguish sounds. The moment is
here of the conflict for life or death that beats around
the poet's country, defeat in which means not only her
ruin but the retrogression of all humanity. Krasinski
represents it with the strange imagery peculiar to him
in which perhaps it were not wholly fanciful for the
English reader to discern some resemblance to the
painted clouds and mists and waves of Watts, illuminated
by the celestial vision of a devout son of the most
Catholic of lands.

Thou hast given us all that Thou couldst give, oh, Lord.
We are above the abyss upon the narrow pass. Our wings are
growing to the resurrection, our lips are parted for the cry of
joy. Towards us from the blue, as from Thy bosom, golden
shafts of dawn as though Thine arms are hastening from the
heavens to the earth, to take from our foreheads the load of
agelong sorrows. All is ready. The east is all aflame. The
angels gaze. And there on yonder side is the dark beneath
the unbottomed sinking of the shore. And the abyss is rising
surging, growing, sweeping on us—eternal death where Thou
art not, which from all time engulfs the proud and evil, and

¹ J. Kleiner, *op. cit.*

is itself pride, strife, and passion, and is that murder old as
is the world, the seething sea of blasphemies and lies. And it
has risen foaming where half above the grave, yet half within
the grave, we stand in this first span of our rebirth. If we cast
one backward glance upon it, if we move one only step towards
it, then the light of dawn shall grow pale upon our temples, the
Son shall shed no tear for us, and never shall the Spirit
comfort us.

Have mercy, Lord, defend us, be with us! In vain! Here
must we stand alone[1]. In this transfiguration of our final fate
none of Thy angels to our aid shall hasten. Thou hast given
us all that Thou couldst give, oh, Lord!

But remember, remember that we are Thy servants of old,
[and that] since the nation first showed herself from the mists
of time millions of Polish souls have gone forth from Polish
bodies with her [Mary's] name upon their lips in death. Let
her to-day remember them with given back remembrance.
Girt with the mighty cloud of all those dead, let her upon Thy
skies pray Thee that nor devils from hell shall bind our feet,
bent to the heights—no, nor yet abject men.

Look on her, Lord, as, with that host of souls that round
about her throng in heavenly wreath, slowly she rises on un-
measured space to Thee. Towards her all the stars have
turned in prayer: and all the powers eddying in space are
stilled. Higher and still more high she rises, borne by those
pale shades. She floats into the azure beyond the clouds of
Milky Ways, beyond the sun, higher and still more high.
Look on her, Lord! Amidst the throngs of seraphs lo! she
kneeleth at Thy throne. And on her brow flashes the Polish
crown, her mantle strews forth rays of which the skies around
her there are made, and all the spaces wait while she prays
very softly. Beyond her, stand the phantoms of our fathers,
weeping; and in her hands of snow two chalices she holds.
She gives to Thee Thine own blood in the right, and in the
left, held lower, the blood of these her subjects on a thousand
crosses crucified, shed by the sword of their three executioners.
And with the first, divine and upraised chalice, for mercy on the
second she imploreth Thee, oh, Lord. With its loud laughter
roareth the abyss. We hear the thunder of its subterranean
waves. It rolls in ever eddying rings of snaky deeps. With
tempest, mists and foam it blinds our eyes to slay our life into
the murderers', liars' death. Oh, vain one, it seeth not what is

---

[1] Because Heaven had done its part in giving all that was requisite,
and it now remained to the tempted to correspond with Divine grace.

being wrought on high. Oh, vain one, it seeth not that its storms are nought when such a heart for us is wrung.

Then—and we are tempted to believe that Krasinski could have written this passage only on his knees—the poet, who had taught his nation the secret of death and suffering, pours out the heart that had carried the sorrows of his people since his ruined boyhood into the prayer which sweeps in unbroken majesty to the end of the last *Psalm of the Future.*

Oh, Lord, Lord, then not for hope—as a flower is it strewn: then not for the destruction of our foes—their destruction dawns on to-morrow's clouds : not for the weapon of rule— from the tempests it shall fall to us: not for any help—Thou hast already opened the field of events before us: but amidst the terrible convulsion of these events we beseech Thee only for a pure will within us, oh, Father, Son and Holy Ghost.

Oh, Thou most dear, hidden but visible beyond the veils of the transparent worlds; Thou present everywhere, immortal, holy, Who dwelling in each motion alike of hearts and stars shatterest to nought rebellion of the stars even as Thou shatterest the wanderings of the heart—Father, Son and Holy Ghost; Thou Who commandedst the being of man that, poor in strength and puny in his birth, he should to an angel grow by might of sacrifice, and to our Polish nation didst ordain that she should lead the nations into love and peace ; Thou Who in the tumult of the world's confusion piercest to the sod children of wrath and savest the upright—because that they are upright—from their torment; we beseech Thee, Father, Son and Holy Ghost, we, suspended between Thy kingdom and the pit, we beseech Thee with our foreheads sunk to earth, with our temples bathed in the breathing of Thy spring, surrounded with the wheels of shattered times and perishing rules, Father, Son and Holy Ghost! we beseech Thee create within us a pure heart, make new our thoughts within us, root out from our souls the tares of sacrilegious falsehood, and give us the gift, eternal among Thy gifts—give us good will.

CHAPTER XIII

THE *UNFINISHED POEM*

From 1847 to 1852 Krasinski's life was passed mainly in Rome, Germany and Warsaw. When in the late forties Europe was threatened on all sides by the revolutionary movement, Krasinski was divided between apprehension of such scenes as he had foretold long ago in *The Undivine Comedy* and the hope that Pius IX would inaugurate a new political and spiritual era. Through all this storm of unrest in which he dreaded to behold his country either a prey to communism, or to the engulfing power of a Panslavism in which the Polish nation must perish, Krasinski remained firm to the principles he had already laid down. Poland should be saved if she continued faithful to her soul. He addressed memorials in French to Montalembert, Lamartine, Pius IX, all expressing his unwearying love of his country and the political ideals that we have already examined in his writings. In his letter to the Pope he appealed to the Holy See to champion the cause of Poland before all Christendom. Late one night in the April of 1848 while the revolutionary forces were gathering about Rome, he walked with Pius IX in the Quirinal garden, then defended by soldiers and guards, and begged him to declare for United Italy.

On the occasion of the outbreak of the revolution in Vienna in 1848, Krasinski sent Trentowski one of the best of his purely episodical lyrics, called in the early editions *Windobona*, written on an October night: "in ignorance of what had become of Vienna," so the author adds to the poem. No Pole can forget the fact that Vienna, which owed its deliverance from the Turks to Sobieski and a Polish army, repaid Poland by dismembering her. Describing the tumult in the streets of Vienna as the writer of *The Undivine Comedy* could well do—the whistle of bombs, the crashing of alarm bells, houses laid in ruins, the shrieks among the flames of women and children—Krasinski ends each verse with the cry of avenging irony: "Vienna, to-day there is no Sobieski here."

To take one stanza:

And the night is denser, and morning is not near. Vienna has grown pale, has cried aloud and fallen on her knees: gazeth from old habit with eyes of terror to the quarter whence came Polish mercy, to the Kahlenberg[1]. But in the whirlwinds only hears repeated: "Vienna, to-day there is no Sobieski here."

Since the spring of 1846 Krasinski's affections had gradually turned to his wife. He never ceased to be Delphina Potocka's friend, assisting a lonely and unprotected woman through harassing cares: but, as time goes on, Elisa Krasinska plays an ever larger and more intimate part in her husband's correspondence with his friends till at last she is the "Incomparabile Donna," as Krasinski styles her; the object of those poems of love and passionate regret in which he seeks the pardon of her whose youth he in an agony of repentance confessed that he had ruined, and who now had gained his whole heart[2]. He became, too, a devoted father to his children. To them, in absence, he wrote letters of fond affection

[1] The heights whence Sobieski led the Poles to the relief of Vienna.
[2] "I spoilt, I consumed, I poisoned Elisa's youth." *Letters to Cieszkowski.* Baden, June 1, 1855.

after the early Victorian pattern, filled with moral precepts somewhat above childish comprehension, carefully
calling the attention of his little correspondents to any
mistake in spelling or grammar on their part. One
daughter died in infancy two years before Krasinski's
own death. The three others survived him, but none
of them lived to old age, and with the premature death
of Count Adam Krasinski the male line of the poet died
out in 1912. As both a father and a Pole the thought
of the future of his children in those troubled times often
filled Krasinski's heart with foreboding. Telling his
friends how he and his wife when their eldest son was
at the point of death watched by what seemed the child's
dying bed :

When these terrible days came upon us, when we saw that
beloved and strangely lovely little head sinking into the depths
of eternal sleep, when all hope failed in our hearts, we looked
upon each other in the silence of despair and with one and the
same thought in our hearts, and at last that thought burst from
our lips: "Perhaps if he had lived it would have befallen him
to rot in the prisons or to wander exiled in Siberia—perhaps
the knout would have torn that fair little body. To-day he will
breathe forth his soul—and he will never perish like Sieroczyn-
ski[1] under 7000 strokes because he loved Poland." With this
consolation, with this, in the second half of the nineteenth
century, do Polish parents save themselves from despair when
their loveliest, purest child dies. And I shed still more bitter
tears, and said to myself: "Oh, unhappy race, to whom the
death of their children must seem their salvation[2]."

Towards the end of his life we can picture Krasinski
in a happy domestic circle. Besides the company of a
wife linked to him by the strongest mutual affection and
of cherished children, he was surrounded by those who

[1] Who was flogged to death in Siberia under circumstances of indescribable brutality.
[2] *Letters to St. Koźmian.* Heidelberg, April 22, 1851. *Letters to
Cieszkowski.* Heidelberg, April 21, 1851.

The Unfinished Poem

loved and admired him. Gaszynski was often a permanent member of the family, acting as amanuensis in the poet's recurrent attacks of blindness. The relations of Krasinski's wife and his own devoted friends were constantly coming and going. To all of these Krasinski was as a beloved brother, taking upon himself all their troubles and their affairs as his personal concern. Of further intimate details of his private life we have none, beyond those few that Koźmian relates in his introduction to his share of Krasinski's letters. Strangely few personal anecdotes remain of the Anonymous Poet of Poland.

After Krasinski had published his *Undivine Comedy* he formed the plan of writing a trilogy, that play being its second part. The subject should be the progress of humanity and—in the first part—his poetical autobiography. In the first part Henryk as a youth must know the "eternal Divine truth and the contemporary truth of the earth." He must pass, led by another Virgil, through the hell of our own days. "The journey to hell," said Krasinski with bitter irony, "is not so far as in the time of the ancient Ghibelline. You can find hell now by remaining on the surface of the earth[1]." This second Virgil, Aligier, is Krasinski's tribute to his friendship with Danielewicz; but when he first started upon the work his intention was the immortalization of Delphina Potocka. "If I die early," he wrote to her, "remember that desire of mine that thou shouldest never die on earth, that thou shouldest be remembered for ever. Thou hast given me happiness: oh, would that I could give thee immortality[2]."

[1] *Letters to Gaszynski.* Naples, Jan. 10, 1839.
[2] *Sketch of the Undivine Comedy*, written for Delphina Potocka, March 20, 1840. Jubilee ed., Vol. V, p. 351 *et seq.*

G. 19

As a matter of fact Krasinski's scheme underwent many modifications with the passage of time, and not Delphina, but Danielewicz, is the leading influence of the work as we know it. The third part of the trilogy was to treat of the transformation of humanity after the cataclysm in the second part, *The Undivine Comedy*. Here Henryk reappears. Saved by angels as he had leapt to his doom, he has learned in the solitudes of the deserts from his own heart and from his guardian spirit, Delphina. He who had fought for the past returns to unite past and future, to transform "the poetry of his youth into reality. He will raise and ennoble all men. All become equal, but on the heights, not below[1]."

From 1838 to 1848 the poet worked intermittently at this drama. The failing health of his last ten years on earth put an end to its accomplishment. With the exception of a single episode, the *Dream*, that was published separately in 1852 with the initials J.S. (Słowacki's), and which had been begun in 1838 and completed, it is believed, in 1843, though some time later additions were made, all the rest stayed in manuscript during Krasinski's lifetime. The year after his death what was found of it among his papers was made public, under the title of the *Unfinished Poem*, albeit it is written in prose. In the Jubilee edition it is called *The Undivine Comedy*, Part I, which name Krasinski himself gave to it. I follow Dr Kleiner, and to avoid confusion retain the earlier name.

The third part of the trilogy was never begun, and how far the remaining *Unfinished Poem* stands as Krasinski intended it to stand is utterly uncertain.

In this *Unfinished Poem* Krasinski is profound, he is

---

[1] *Op. cit.*

idealistic, as always; but, save for passages of the *Dream*, he is not poetical. The *Unfinished* is not only disappointing as a work of art. It is dull. Its value lies in the fact that it is the completion of Krasinski's national, religious and sociological theories, in which he shows us sidelights of his personal life. The autobiographical element, inasmuch as the youth is guided by a beloved friend, and becomes deeply enamoured of an unhappy woman, though the latter episode is not worked out, is stronger in this play than anywhere else in Krasinski's works.

The introduction shows us Henryk hunting chamois in the mountains above Venice : a youthful Henryk full of the clean and fresh joy of life. The difference between him and the man he has become in *The Undivine Comedy*, for Krasinski gives us none of the intervening process, is startling and infinitely tragic. The younger Henryk is not depicted with the extraordinary genius of the Henryk of *The Undivine Comedy*. There seems to us a hint of overdoing in the exuberant youth; a too insistent note on his ardour and vitality. His almost childish eagerness is both irritating and unconvincing. But no doubt Krasinski wished to emphasize the gulf between the boy and his later self. In the mountains with him is the friend and mentor, Aligier (Danielewicz). When Henryk runs off in chase of a chamois Aligier, looking after him, trembles at his ignorance of life.

He may become all or nothing: the chosen of heaven, or the victim of hell. Ceaselessly, itself not knowing it, his soul struggles to Thy heaven. The seed of all beauty, Thy spark, burns in its depths...and he has not yet seen that Thou art not only high above him, not only deep below him, but alike dwellest within himself. And I am sorrowful to death, for the time of his innocence is passing away, for soon his heart shall be torn by the war of good and evil, the only, dread mother of virtue.

The prayer of the Pole for the Polish boy goes on:

I do not pray that Thou shouldest take him from the toils of life. Thy Will be done. Scourge him with the hail of griefs, humiliate him among men. Let them lay fetters on his hands, let his body endure the extremity of martyrdom. Only spare him the shame of abasement, only deliver him from the eternal night of the spirit.

As the two leave the mountains the youth asks Aligier if he remembers their first meeting: and then Krasinski gives in a poetized form the scene that had burnt itself like fire into his memory, when he had been insulted in the University at Warsaw.

Oh, I see that ancient building in whose halls a thousand of my comrades sit. I see that stone stairway on which thou didst appear to me. I passed among them all with pride upon my brow. They pressed around me, ever closer. Oh, God! for the first time hell was born at that moment in the heart of a child. I caught at the iron railings. Perchance I would have fallen underneath their feet, but thou didst show thyself. I still feel the pressure of thy hand, I still hear thy voice: "They are unjust. Be thou more than just. Forgive them in thy soul and love them in thy deeds."

Aligier. And from that day we were inseparable.
Henryk. And will be until death.

Krasinski finishes this apotheosis of his friend, dead when the words were written, by Aligier's presentiment that death is soon to divide the two. "But my spirit shall not die in thee, though my form shall depart. Thought passeth on wings from heart to heart." And he bids Henryk as the lover of beauty to be careful that his soul shall be, above all, beautiful. "Give thy brothers that happiness. Be a masterpiece among them."

Aligier then leads Henryk through mysterious mists suddenly rolling about them to a cemetery where he tells him he must sleep. The face of the guide has

become Dante's : the youth sleeps, and we reach the
Dream, told in the poetical prose that Krasinski in his
earlier days affected.

It seemed to the youth that the figure of Dante turned to
him and said: "Where are eternal Love and Reason and Will,
thence have I been sent to show thee the hell of the days that
are now : so cast off all fear, and whither I go come thou."

They pass through the inferno of all the miseries
and crimes of the world. They meet first on the descent
into hell armies of men driven like cattle to take the
lives of their fellow-men, for no love of country, but for
the greed of tyrants. Then comes the terrible picture,
only too real to the Pole, of the man dealing out gold
giving his instructions, to the spies and delators. They
shall worm themselves into the home, flattering the
magnate, pitying the poor, sympathizing with the sad.
Where the weak are oppressed they shall defend the
weak :

"and all their complaints and hopes, like hidden treasure, shall
be opened to you. If any one be silent and filled with gloom,
begin ye to express despair, and your cry shall awake his
voice. If you meet youths, trembling with impatience for
action, bind them by fearful oaths. Give them hidden weapons
to carry beneath their garments. Love children and play with
them. Often on the lips of infants are heard the family's
secrets." [The final triumph of the spy is when a poor wretch
dying of starvation is haled to a table of food and, before he
may touch it, is told to swear before the crucifix that he will
reveal everything he sees and hears, whether it be his own
brother and sister he betrays. He struggles to resist. Then
hunger is too strong for him, and he swears. The cry of an
angel is heard.] That cry pierced the heart of the youth
through and through, and it seemed to him that he must bow
down his head for his unendurable grief.

The vision proceeds on these lines. The youth is
guided through the varying scenes of what is pitiable

and ignoble. He sees the world as a great money
market, whose god is mammon and where there is no
other God. He sees the oppression of labourers, the
horrors of unbridled revolution, the degradation of
women, and the like. In the light of what the young
Henryk has gazed on at the moment when his nature
was most liable to take fire at such a sight, we understand the strength of Pankracy's appeal, in the duel
between him and Henryk, to what had once been near
to the latter's heart. The same moral of *The Undivine
Comedy* is here too. Dante reproaches the godless
hordes with the words : " Look in my dead eyes. Shall
not your hearts burst for shame ? Know you not what
is the liberty of the spirit ? You only know what is the
comfort of the body."

Where the women tell of their wrongs the Beatrice
of Dante appears, faint and shadowy, merged into
another woman, a sad woman, unhappily married,
who reproaches the onlooker with the words: "I loved
him, and he left me." This is Delphina Potocka's
entrance into the drama, and these words must have
been penned in the light of the poet's marriage.

When that episode is over, a great multitude passes
before the eyes of the youth, all hastening in one
direction, mothers abandoning their infants, all hurrying
not to be left behind. To Henryk's wondering question:
" Master, is this the hour of the last judgment?" comes
the answer that it is only the hour of the money market
and of the bargains. It is a pandemonium of the lust
for wealth, in which Krasinski read a true picture of
the world in which he lived, where the weak go down
before the strong, where there is no mercy, but one
insensate cry for gold, purchased by crime. This is

the modern hell, and, cries Dante, "the hell of the men of old pained me not as this."

After hell follows purgatory.

> "There is no death," [says the guide to the youth]. "God never, nowhere, conceived it, for Himself everywhere and ever liveth. Only by our degradation of self can we inflict upon ourselves eternal death. But who shall live again must transfigure himself. Each transfiguration bears the aspect of death. This is the test of the grave."

Here, then, is Krasinski's purgatory, the "test of the grave," the epoch of transition, the hour of a nation's seeming death in which she but awaits, in penal fires, the summons to her resurrection. The forest of gibbet trees, upon each of which hangs on his mother-soil a martyr for Poland in the moonlight, till all space seems dying with them, while a weeping woman stands by each, is a fine descriptive scene. Tears blot out the boy's vision, but his guide exhorts him : "Turn not away. To conquer pain we must steep ourselves in the knowledge of pain." The martyrs are summoned by their tyrants to renounce their country and their God, and they shall be given every earthly good. None answer, the women are silent, their children all cry No. Then, told in Krasinski's favourite imagery, two Milky Ways run together in the sky and form one mighty cross. From the wounds of the Figure thereon crimson moons flash out and rainbows that break into myriad stars till the martyrs on their crosses pass into its radiance. "Too late, too late," groans the youth. His nation is slain. But the guide answers :

> "This is the purgatory of our present days, for all flesh on these plains is tortured, but over the soul of this nation the Most Dear and Hidden One Himself watcheth. Weep not for them, but for those in the grey world, for there is hell, and

here is pain only. I have told thee that from pain the soul
riseth from the dead. Only from self-degradation shall there
be no resurrection."

"Oh, Master, Master," [cries Henryk with outstretched
hands]. "Show me heaven—that third estate—on earth."
"Hitherto on your earth," [is the reply], "there have been only
hell and purgatory, but the spirit of the Lord hath dwelt in
your hearts. Awake it by faith to life. Lift it by the wing of
a holy will on high, bring it forth externally. Cast it wide
from horizon to horizon, above you, before you, around you by
the deed of love."

These last passages of the *Dream* were added by
Krasinski, as might indeed be gathered from their moral
resemblance to the *Psalms of the Future*, after the rest
had been written.

The *Unfinished* then returns to its dramatic form.
Having learnt the sorrows of humanity and of his
nation and beheld their remedy, Henryk is plunged
into the Venetian carnival. His cicerone is a prince-
banker, the type of the man of money, whose incapacity
to understand any dream or aspiration is in glaring
contrast to the character of the young man beside him.
"I felt like that when I was eighteen," is his would-be
sympathetic answer to the youth whom he means to
please. Henryk is too true a lover of beauty for the
Italian sky not to claim his gaze rather than the
masqueraders; too much of a patriot not to wonder
how men can play the harlequin in their streets that are
trodden by the soldiers of foreign rulers. He and the
banker pass by an unmasked woman, the Princess
Rahoga, leaning on her husband's arm. She is a Pole,
married to a man unworthy of her. Captivated by her
misfortunes and her beauty, dimly conscious that he
has seen her before—in his dream—Henryk falls
desperately in love. This is a chapter of Krasinski's

autobiography. The woman is Delphina Potocka, the victim of a miserable marriage, and Venice was the scene of Krasinski's first love where as a youth he spent hours with Mme Bobrowa. Aligier warns Henryk against this infatuation. His soul, says the mentor, will grow old before its time under its influence. He will squander life, when the treasure of the Pole is "in pain, sacrifice, service, memories, hopes, immortal desires," and his place in the "great and dark forest." The youth answers that the woman's pain draws him to her: "Pain, whether here or whether there, whether in a brother, or in one of these my sisters, always sadness and pain call me, lure me." Here we know from similar expressions in Krasinski's letters that he is speaking of himself. Aligier reproaches Henryk for having already forgotten that the guide has promised to lead him "to the gathering of secret yearners where the spirit of the future is labouring to come forth." There Henryk, beholding all earthly history, will no longer find it worthy to dream of one fellow-countrywoman. How far Krasinski meant to work out Henryk's love-story and to link it to that of the indifferent husband in *The Undivine Comedy* we shall, as Count Tarnowski observes[1], never know. It ends here: and now he is conducted, still by Aligier, into the vaults of a Venetian palace where scene after scene is displayed to him representing the development of the Divine Thought through all the ages of history.

They are greeted by a choir:

Ye who would create the present and discover the future take first into the depths of your souls all the dead days of the past. For albeit history changeth there is one eternal thought

---

[1] St. Tarnowski, *Zygmunt Krasinski*.

and one only truth. Each thought, conceived in God, sent from eternity into space and time, as part of the truth, must suffer as the Son of God suffered in His flesh. It shall be manifested among men, and suffer and bear its cross, and have its grave. But each one has risen again in the one which followed it. Each has risen from the grave in another higher body.

The first to give their witness from the past are the Chaldeans. "Ormuzd and Ahriman war eternally. We craved to be delivered, to be purified, to flow on flame to thee, oh, unmoved light."

Their power died to give place to others. The Egyptian priests next rise before Henryk.

The mystery of mysteries was preserved among us. We first knew Thee Whose name is : " He was and is and ever shall be." Wherefore, oh, Thou Infinite, dost Thou elude us ? We were fain to teach a corrupted race the eternal truth. From the mighty pyramids, from the labyrinths, Thou didst depart from us to the setting of the sun.

Strains of aerial voices singing of roses and myrtles and the sea foam whence rose Aphrodite fall upon Henryk's ears, and the priests of Eleusis appear together with Plato. The Hellenic part in the world's advance is typified by the summons of this choir to love " the ideal beyond measure."

"Love," adds Plato, "with unequalled love, and flame in that love. Know thyself, and, knowing, raise thy butterfly-like wings. They shall carry thee to thy home, and thy home, thy native home, is the bosom of God."

They pass away with their eternal yearning for the "Desired of ages": and hence it is an easy transition first to the solitaries of Mount Carmel, expecting the advent of Christ, then to the Jewish sect of the Essenes living lives of austerity that preached the victory of the soul over the body, as they too awaited the Messiah.

They kneel, and the youth sinks on his knees also with Aligier : for they see the form of Christ in the skies, risen from the dead. An invisible choir sings that Sion, Greece, and Rome shall no more hold back the human race. The Son of God has died and risen. "Henceforth no people that has become a nation dieth on the earth. Henceforth no man who has become a spirit shall die in the grave."

The panorama of the "second part of history," with its "other trials of humanity," now unrolls itself. The various trends of human thought with their evil and their strain of good are depicted: the Albigenses, prophesying the arrival of a Paraclete; the Templars, in the dying words of their Grand Master, looking for the world to become one fold; the wanderings of magic and alchemy always seeking a perpetual elixir they cannot find; Freemasons in whom Krasinski saw the inheritors of the Templars, overthrowing kings and governments. In all these deviations of the human mind Krasinski beholds a spark of the Divine idea, which results in nothing because they did not embrace the entire truth, but only dimly saw one portion of it[1]. Revolution and war and bloodshed are everywhere, and: "as God was slain in man so is humanity slain in a nation." The youth now gazes on funeral obsequies, where three stand by a catafalque, holding sceptres surmounted not by a cross but a bayonet, and in whose crowns are shining the jewels of human blood and tears. In the coffin she sleeps, at the very thought of whose name the youth cries that he must kiss if but the earth. "She is my father and my mother, she is my all." She breathes still; but her executioners proclaim

[1] J. Kleiner, *History of the Thought of Zygmunt Krasinski.*

that there will be no peace till she is dead for ever. While young Henryk is rapt into patriotic passion, the choir chants: "From the day of the death of the just the European world shall not rest till itself becomes just. The nations live, and yet live not, because they cannot live according to the Thought of God[1]."

Since that sin against humanity the world is ruled by hatred. Choirs swear around Henryk to spread universal ruin. The guillotine is erected. The French Revolution shakes the world. Then there rises over its tempests the figure of Napoleon, beloved by the Polish mystics.

And now the Lord will say to his soul: "Go forward!" and nothing and no one shall stay it, and it shall pass on and find the further way in the darkness.

The choir takes up the panegyric:

Who is equal to him of those who have gone by till now? All human fates shall flow into that one man—all toils and triumphs, powers and defeats, joys and woes. As the world was created straight from God's hand out of nought, so he shall appear from nought among men and be raised from nought. He shall be heroic like unto the Greek Alexander, an emperor like the Caesar of Rome, a martyr as the saint of the first spring of Christ. And he shall die like unto Moses, alone in the sight of God, foretelling the will of God for the future days of the race of man.

But the light of him from whose uprising it at first seemed that "neither kings nor people were to wield power, but nations and the human race, and in the name of God," goes out. The three executioners of

---

[1] Here we may point out the striking analogy between what Krasinski said more than sixty years ago and the language of leading politicians and thinkers of our day, who have ascribed the great European war to the original crime of the partition of Poland, at the same time basing their hopes for the future of Europe on the restoration of Poland.

Poland, defeated by Napoleon, return after his fall. The so-called Holy Alliance is formed. "Diplomacy, police, gendarmerie," mutter subterranean voices, in answer to voices crying against them on high.

"Oh, Aligier, is this the solution of so many ages?" cries Henryk in despair. Have their visions only ended in this? Aligier would have him wait and hope. "This is only the ending of the past. Beyond this threshold begins the present." Voices hail them in ecstatic accents, calling them to come and gaze upon the promised hour. "All that is past and that pained, passing away shall return, shall live again, be higher raised, but shall pain no more." The doors are flung wide, and the last stage in the pilgrimage is reached.

The action is still in the vaults, and takes the shape of the initiation of a neophyte into secret rites. The president in a white toga is on the throne, and against the walls are ranged choirs of the different nations, each garbed in national colours, Italian, Irish, German, French, Slavonic, and Polish. At the head of the latter stands Pankracy. Henryk is to be received into this brotherhood whose purpose is to work for the hastening of Christ's kingdom on earth. Kneeling at the feet of the president he is commanded by the latter to give an account of what he has seen, and to utter a protestation of faith in the Trinity of which the history of man, says the president, is the reflection. Let the neophyte declare which of the past eighteen centuries since Christ has honoured Christ. He answers, None.

"That one," takes up the president, "will only honour Him who will make visible and tangible in all actuality His precept. Its accomplishment shall be the descent of the spirit, the deed the very Paraclete. Where is that deed? Dost thou behold it? Look in thyself. It is there. In thine as in every other heart. Neither in the individual nor in nations nor in humanity shall the eternal grace effect aught till their hands shall be raised towards it: for the will of the created is the half of the creation. Even if what is appointed to pass has passed, even if the times are fulfilled, even if the promised Spirit already bloweth over the vale of earth, if we ourselves do not gain Him by our service, by our yearning, by our deeds, if we do not make of ourselves an altar unto Him, He will not shine upon us, and we shall remain uncomforted. Are God's altars only under the arches of cathedrals? They are everywhere: in the parliament chambers, and in the tribunals, and in the metropolis and the market places, and in the factory and in the stock exchange, and in every art and in every science the Lord must be seen, known, honoured and His law fulfilled —it must be and it shall be. Each toil shall be changed into a vocation, each office into priesthood. Dost thou feel in the depths of thy being that thou expectest such a future, that thou believest in it and dost love it?"

Henryk. Since I have drawn breath I have desired with each beat of my heart beauty, liberty, happiness—and I live amidst hideous sorrows. I have never felt young, and thou dost promise me the renewed youth of the world.

The president then further enunciates the precepts which are already familiar to the reader of Krasinski that "only he has reached liberty who has made of his spirit such a masterpiece that it no longer wars with itself or with others": that love alone can create.

A dissentient voice is heard from Pankracy. This reign of justice may be in the future, but it must be reached by seas of blood. Pankracy, says Dr Kleiner, is not here the leader of men as in *The Undivine Comedy*, whose will sways the universe. With his entrance into the *Unfinished* Krasinski's idea of any connection with *The Undivine Comedy* wavered. He is merely an agitator placed there by the poet of the *Psalm of Grief* as a protest against the spirit of anarchic revolution[1]. A long dispute ensues between

[1] J. Kleiner, *op. cit.*

Aligier, the apostle of love and the antagonist of such a revolution, and Pankracy, who is assisted by Blauman, the man who rebels through ignorance and stupidity, and by a Julinicz in whom Krasinski caricatures Juliusz Słowacki, parodying the words his brother-poet had written in his attack upon the *Psalm of Love.* Considering the nature of the case Krasinski's treatment of his antagonist is not of a particularly scathing order. The contest between Pankracy and Aligier is on the lines of the *Psalms,* without their power or beauty. It ends in the president cursing Pankracy in the name of the Holy Spirit and of humanity: "for whoso is against the eternal love he, although he may conquer, shall perish." With Pankracy's expulsion from the brother-hood, in which he is unworthy to represent his nation, ends all that remains of the *Unfinished Poem.*

CHAPTER XIV

RESURRECTURIS: THE LAST WORDS OF THE ANONYMOUS POET
(1851–1859)

With the short poem *Resurrecturis* the Anonymous Poet
brought his work for his nation to its completed end.
He had struggled against the demons of despair. His
life had been beset by the most cruel of exterior circumstances. His years were cut short by the anguish that
he had endured for his country. And yet the last word
that put its seal to his life and labour was one of which
the title speaks for itself : *to those who are to rise again.*
Nothing may be found in *Resurrecturis* from which a
mind, unattuned to Polish mysticism, might turn away as
from things unsympathetic or uncomprehended. What
soul, tormented by perplexity and grief, has not asked
herself the everlasting question of the first lines of *Resurrecturis* ? To each the Polish poet gives his answer.

This world is a cemetery of tears, of blood, of mire. This
world to each is his eternal Golgotha. Vainly the spirit writhes
against its pain. There is no halting place in the storm of life.
Fate mocks us every moment. They who are holy die, the
worthy die: the hated live. All is confusion never to be solved.
Death is nigh ; and only far away, somewhere on the later
wave of ages—resurrection.

Then must we torpid grow and petrified, be without heart,
become murderers among murderers, felons among felons? Lie,
hate, slay, and mock: so will we give the world back what it
gives to us. Let us eat and drink. Let us stand for the comfort

of the body, the worthlessness of mind. So shall we be counted among the stupid and the happy.

Oh, let it not be so! My soul, draw back, oh, stay! Not with that weapon at the head of all humanity shall the vanquishers of evil pursue evil without mercy. One only power in the world, the quiet might of sacrifice, shall crush the crushing fate. This is the lion of the history of the world. Pride or abasement are but chaff which each breath of history casts into the pit.

Oh, know thyself for what thou art. Crave not for the mastery which is His Who is in heaven, nor choose to be as the brute beast fattening on the fields of pasture. On this side the grave, before the resurrection dawns, be thou in man the suffering which is of heaven, be thou the masterpiece of unbent will, be patience, mistress of misfortune that slowly buildeth up her edifice from nought. Be thou defeat, of distant aim, but which at last shall conquer for all ages. Be peace amidst the raving of the storm, order in chaos, harmony in discord. Be thou eternal beauty in the eternal war of life. Only for vile men and for Pharisees be menace, wrath, or silence sanctified; and with dissimulation have no league. But for all others be an angel's breath. Be thou the sustenance that giveth life to hearts. Be as a sister's tears to those that mourn, the voice of manhood when their courage faints. Be home to those who are driven forth from home, hope to those who have lost their hope, and to those sleeping in a death-like sleep be thou the awakening thunderblast. In the struggle with this hell of earth be ever, everywhere the strength that against death prevails by the stronger strength of love. Be thou the hell of love[1].

In the unceasing form of word and pattern give thine own self forth freely to thy brothers. Multiply thy one self by living deeds, and thousands from thy one self shall rise. Be even in chains unwearied toil. Let every pain, albeit it be pain, not pain thee. Be thou thy whole nation in thy one heart. Be thou the miracle uniting heaven to earth—be sanctity in bondage.

Hasten not to death till, seed in the soil, thy thought is sown in hearts, and brings forth fruit. So long as thy own martyrdom assures not victory, thy martyrdom will be to thy good only, not to humanity's. Shun martyrdom! The

---

[1] Meaning the colossal power of love. Against the objection of the critics to the term Krasinski stated that it was not his but St Theresa's. See *Letters to St. Koźmian.*

garlands of vain glory are grasped by madmen, into the gulf
of danger heroes leap, but the soul's higher strength heedeth
not these illusions.

Only then, when the bell of events, wailing, summoneth
thee to sacrifice thyself for their redemption, and thou, hearing
the earth's call, fallest with thy soul in humble penitence at the
dividing threshold of two worlds, and in thy soul sent thither
by God flows in the silence God's inspiring voice, then rise:
and as the champion who has reached the lists shake from thy
feet the dust from off this earth. Rise, and from the love which,
when it loveth dies, lift to the heavens thy upsoaring hands.
Rise, and to the executioners, hastening on thee, hasten thou
first; and calmly, sweetly, peacefully welcome those guests,
unmourning, with the pitying gaze of thy immortal soul. Then
end with thy rich witness in the future. Be by thy death the
highest bloom of life. What the world called dream and
mirage make thou awake and living, make of it faith, make
of it law, make of it what is certain, tangible, a holy thing
that as a poniard penetrates to hearts to pierce there without end, moving them albeit only by the breath of sighs: until
the world, thy murderer, shall kneel, confessing that God and
country are the conscience of the nations.

When thy thought takes the crimson of thy body's flowing
blood, thy thought shall be the stream of life flashing on high,
God's judgment on the godless multitudes below. Nor man
nor cannon shall keep it back, nor falsehood nor deception,
genius or glory, kings or peoples. And in the third span, on
thy suffering's grave, out of the deluge of events, over the
abyss of sorrows the unborn shall be born—and justice rise[1].

Resurrecturis was Krasinski's favourite among his
poems. From the time it appeared, overpowered by
physical sufferings, he could speak no more to his
nation. Yet during these last years he occasionally
wrote lyrics, intimate and sacred, but not for the public
gaze. They are his poems to his wife. It has been
pointed out that the character of Krasinski's love
poems is their passion and virility, which never degene-

---

[1] This last stanza has another reading in Krasinski's original MS. of
1846: "When thy thought shall take flesh from thy body's flowing blood,
thy thought shall be a sacrament, and in the third span they shall not find
thee in thy grave. God now is with thee, God now is in thee."

rate into sentimentality[1]. We have already drawn attention to another peculiarity that distinguishes them; they are the love poems of a patriot. The poet had uttered into the ears of his Beatrice his grief for Poland, illumined by the hope that had risen upon him from her look. As he neared his end it was his wife who was the recipient of the deepest and noblest love of his manhood and of the same high ardour of patriotism, but one that had been tried and proved victorious in the furnace of life[2]. During the winter of 1851–52, which Krasinski and his family passed in Rome, the poet was not only in fast declining health, but the victim of profound melancholy. Yet the Eternal City that had inspired his *Iridion* still had even in the midst of his sadness its message for him and Poland : and in the spring he wrote that most beautiful of poems, known in the earlier editions as *Roma*, but which Krasinski himself simply calls in his manuscript: *To Elisa.*

Oh, my loved, lovely one, blessed be thou, because tempted by the infernal foes thou hast trodden their false allurements unceasingly beneath thy feet. Oh, my loved, lovely one, blessed be thou, because upon thy brow thou bearest not the crown of pride, but the thorn of Polish woes and thoughts of Christ. Oh, Polish wife of mine, blessed be thou because, while the world is perishing and our country dies, thou hast among the whirlwinds of our time believed in hope, even against hope itself. Oh, Polish wife of mine, blessed be thou, because when the veil of time is rent asunder that hitherto conceals God's thought in space, they shall not be defeated who are conquered now, they shall not sorrow who shed tears to-day.

See, what around thee in the Roman plains is left of pride. Amidst a desert the turbid Tiber flows through ruins. And here in gold and purple the unjust trod. To-day the marbles of their temples sleep in the mire above their dust. And here they said : " We shall blot out the nations. Only Rome shall

[1] St. Tarnowski, *Zygmunt Krasinski.*
[2] *Op. cit.*

live." See in their circuses flocks feed and ivy crawls. Read from the ruins of the Campagna which was Rome's that Poland shall not die. Power without love is like to smoke: not we, but it, shall pass. As from yon catacombs that lie beneath the earth the cross victorious rose, so we shall from the grave go with victorious steps, immortalized by pain. Oh! let my witness be the nation's Forum, changed to a desert vale; let my witness be these sundered heads of the Corinthian pillars, these statues of the gods shattered to fragments, these Thermae, arches, aqueducts, transformed to wild and shapeless rocks. Let my witness be tombs without end from hill to hill. Let my witness be all that is here both far and near, on height or plain, the light of heaven and the human ruins, that Poland shall not die—that there is an avenging spirit that at God's decree pierces the deep heart of the history of mankind, that falsehood, perfidy, and treachery die, but Poland does not die; that the oppressor's destiny is ruin, that Roman triumphs and Rome's glory die, but Poland does not die; that at the judgment hour the thunderbolt of victory shall hurl the executioners to earth, that sinning centuries and sinning worlds shall die—but Poland does not die.

Again on Elisa Krasinska's name-day in 1856, the poet tells her that "in the flowerless winter of the world":

Flowers in my soul do ever grow to thee amidst pain's winters, because thou art my spring, because thou art the last sun of my life. All has deceived me ere my days shall end. Thou only on this earth hast not deceived me. Thy form lies not to those who gaze on thee, when thine eyes' light, the radiance of thy brow, proclaim the angel in thy soul. All I have seen was but a dream, a breath, a vapour. Thou only art no mirage; yet in thee the beauty of the ideal is. Then let me fall upon my knees before thee, and let my painstricken lips sigh forth, seeking in all humility thy garment's hem: "Thou beauty art." *St Elizabeth's Day* (Nov. 19th, 1856).

And on the same occasion of her feast-day two years before his death, the last lines with one exception that Krasinski ever wrote were again to "My Elisa": a cry of repentance and reparation.

Once did I dream that I was on the heights of bliss. I thought I was in the heaven of an inspiration without end: and yet I squandered all my life to nought, only because I did not love thee.

Oh! woe unto those hearts to whom it seemeth that the fires of sin are but the flame of youth : because their skies and paradise shall turn to ashes for them, eternal bitterness shall be their life.

Oh! woe unto those hearts by passion riddled. Even should an angel to their life descend, their future poisoned is with their past guilt, and an angelic happiness itself shall only pain them.

Oh! woe unto my heart because it lived on bitter bread, watered with tears of rage. Tell me, thou who to-day art my soul's only strength, why in the past did I not love thee?

Purest of peace on thy white brow, high o'er the billows of the turmoils of the earth; sweetest of mournfulness within thine eyes. Why in the past did I not love thee?

Oh, be to me henceforth the guide of my existence! Oh, be to me henceforth the ideal of all beauty! The poison of this life I have drunk unto its dregs; only because I did not love thee.

The treasure of my powers has fallen into nought. My mind has been divorced from inspired flame. My light went out, I have withered from boundless grief, only because I did not love thee.

And I gaze often with despairing eyes upon my past, lying a dead windfall, where are no immortal deeds of mine; only because I did not love thee.

Oh! look on me! Thou art on high, and I below. Let death not be for ever my only part. Take from my forehead with thy hand the pains of life; because now for ever I have loved thee. *To My Elisa* (Baden-Baden, St Elizabeth's Day. Nov. 19th, 1857).

The outer events of Krasinski's declining years were the Crimean war with, first the hopes, then the bitter disillusion that it brought to Polish hearts; the death of Adam Mickiewicz in Turkey while arming a Polish legion to fight in the war on the side of France and England;—Krasinski admired him with enthusiasm as the great poet and leader of his nation, although he was not in entire agreement with certain of his views[1]; the grievous loss of his youngest child in her fourth year. In his letters to his friends, often not written with his own hand but dictated in a condition bordering on blindness, the poet's deep and increasing religious faith is very noticeable. In his Roman Easter of 1852 he writes to Cieszkowski:

I found your letter this morning on my return from receiving the most Blessed Sacrament. Believe me, there is something above nature in Confession and Communion...All pain (and whose life is not pain!) must in the end have recourse for relief to them. This earth is the pain of pains; if God did not frequently come down to it and give Himself to lips hungering for Him, it would be hell[2].

In a later letter, after expressing his trust in Divine Providence, he adds:

My dear, dear August, the further we go into the forest of life, the more are there of thorny trees, the fewer flowers and shrubs and kindlier verdure. But the teaching of life is that God guides all, that He is at the helm, and men only row, and that submission to that Most Holy Will is man's only strength[3].

Such is the tenor of Krasinski's confidences to his friends. And still, despite every loss and disappointment and suffering, his faith in the resurrection of his country that he knew he would not live to see never failed him as he sank into his grave. To quote in detail what he wrote upon this subject to his confidants in the end span of his life would involve too much repetition of what has been already said: but among his last letters to his tried and beloved friends, Koźmian and Sołtan, there

---

[1] "Adam has gone from among us. At that news my heart broke. He was one of the pillars upholding the edifice, composed not of stones but of so many living and bleeding hearts. The greatest poet, not only of the nation but of all the Slavonic races, is no more." *Letters to Sołtan.* Baden, Dec. 5, 1855. For further details on Krasinski's relations with Mickiewicz, see my *Adam Mickiewicz.*

[2] *Letters to Cieszkowski.* April 12, 1852, Easter Monday.

[3] *Ibid.* Heidelberg, Feb. 6, 1855.

are two passages that bear the dignity and the supreme final outlook of dying words, with which we close our studies in the Anonymous Poet's correspondence. To Koźmian he writes in April, 1856:

> The upright disappear, great figures are shattered and fall into the abyss of the past. Puppets or the unworthy remain: but in spite of all this our faith should remain one and the same. All these are only tests—the necessary tests of *Resurrecturis*. Without such there is no *resurrectio*[1].

For Sołtan he records the saying he loved and which well typifies the character of his life:

> Once more I beseech you do not think gloomily about our cause. *Speravit contra spem*: that is a great and holy word of the sacred Scriptures[2].

He still from time to time gathered his sinking strength to address eloquent pleas for his nation to influential personages; to the aunt of Napoleon III, Stephanie, Grand Duchess of Baden, of whom the poet was a personal friend; to Napoleon III himself. In 1857 and 1858 Krasinski pleaded personally with Napoleon on behalf of Poland in two private audiences, of which he left a full account among his papers, and which was published for the first time in the Jubilee edition. These written appeals have that stamp of spiritualized patriotism, the high sense of Poland's calling, and—in the letters to the Grand Duchess—the conviction of miracle triumphant over earthly obstacle and against human probability, that we find in all Krasinski's work, linked to the clear, calm political reasoning with which he viewed the European situation, and which, says Count Tarnowski, was so unerring that events proved him a true prophet[3].

---

[1] *Letters to Koźmian.* Baden, April 3, 1856.
[2] *Letters to Sołtan.* Baden, April 14, 1856.
[3] St. Tarnowski, *Zygmunt Krasinski.*

Among his manuscripts were also found a few other papers in prose that were written at this time, all on the Polish question, and some unfinished verses. These latter were probably, according to the editors of the Jubilee edition, intended to be worked out into a longer poem, and then given to Poland as a piece of spiritual guidance. They are ascribed by the same critics to 1858, the year preceding Krasinski's death. Although at the end of a life of bitter national grief, the Anonymous Poet here speaks in quiet sadness of his country as an outcast, abandoned by all except her faithful companions of " wrong and deception," whose children are tempted within and without her boundaries, he addresses her as ever : " My Polish nation arising from the dead." He repeats to her the language of his *Resurrecturis*, begging her to believe that : "in the end there is only victory where is virtue, only resurrection where is Golgotha. He only shall make his enemies his footstool who hath loved much and suffered much." He points to the calamities that have fallen on France as her penalty for abandoning Poland. "I saw, oh, Lord, how earthly causes are as perishing grain, mown down in the evening though in the morning it was green. Rulers and sovereigns end. Virtue alone knows no end." Once more he looks to Christ crucified and to the reign of the Holy Spirit. " The last tears are falling from men's eyes, and the last fetters from men's hands. Sleep still, oh, earth ! Thy Lord shall wake thee soon." *In thy Rebirth from Death to Life* (1858).

These were Krasinski's last lines. In the vain journey made from place to place to save his life, he halted with his wife and children in the winter of 1858 at Paris on the way to Algiers. In November Wincenty Krasinski

Resurrecturis

313

died in Poland, his dying son being unable to attend his deathbed. Shattered with grief at his father's loss, in the intervals of physical suffering Zygmunt spent the last weeks of his life struggling to write a memoir of Wincenty Krasinski: but this work, by which he intended to vindicate the General's memory, could never be carried through. He survived his father scarcely three months. On the 23rd of February, 1859, at the age of forty-seven, the Anonymous Poet of Poland laid down the burden of the life that had been given to his nation and fellow-men.

We need add little more. The summing up of Krasinski's life and work is to be found not merely in his own words; in his revelation of the sublimest of national idealisms and of the history of a soul that ennobled and conquered suffering both for himself and for his people, told in the language of a great poet; but also in the testimony borne by his fellow-Poles to what his teaching has done for themselves and for their country. So recently as the eve of the European war Polish political writers have urged upon their persecuted nation the moral of *Iridion*[1]. In Krasinski's writings, banned by the government of the Tsars in Poland, smuggled as penal contraband into the country for which they were intended, young Poles have learnt the defence and guidance of their souls amidst the unspeakable temptations by which their youth—the youth of the oppressed —has been beset. They can look back to the day when Krasinski's words, carried to them in secret over the frontier, first reached their hands as the day of their spiritual awakening[2]. Sons of Polish exiles, born and

[1] E. Starczewski, *L'Europe et la Pologne*. Paris, 1913.
[2] M. Zdziechowski, *The Vision of Krasinski*, Cracow, 1912, where the

brought up in a foreign land, living under foreign influences, who have never beheld their own country, tell us that to their studies of Krasinski they in great part owe the preservation of their own intense Polish nationality. In these things resides the immortality of the Anonymous Poet of Poland.

author, a distinguished Polish professor, describes as above the effect upon his character of Krasinski's works. They were brought to him in his boyhood by one of the ladies of his family, hidden in her petticoats to elude the Russian police.

BIBLIOGRAPHICAL NOTE

I. BIOGRAPHY AND CRITICISM

Józef Kallenbach, *Zygmunt Krasiński: Życie i Twórczość Lat Młodych* (1812–1838). 2 vols. Lwów, 1904.

Juliusz Kleiner, *Zygmunt Krasiński: Dzieje Myśli*. 2 vols. Lwów, 1912.

Count Stanisław Tarnowski, *Zygmunt Krasiński.* Cracow, 1892, and later edition of same, Cracow, 1912.

Maryan Zdziechowski, *Byron i jego Wiek.* 2 vols. Cracow, 1894–97.

Maryan Zdziechowski, *Mesyaniści i Słowianofile.* Cracow, 1888.

Maryan Zdziechowski, *Wizya Krasińskiego.* Cracow, 1912.

M. Mazanowski, *Zygmunt Krasiński.* Lwów.

Julian Klaczko, *La Poésie Polonaise au Dix-Neuvième Siècle et le Poète Anonyme.* Revue des Deux Mondes. 1862.

Adam Mickiewicz, *Les Slaves.* Paris, Musée Adam Mickiewicz, 1914.

T. Pini, *Zygmunta Krasińskiego tak zwany " Niedokończony Poemat," Próba Genezy.* Lwów, 1896.

Gabriel Sarrazin, *Les Grands Poètes Romantiques de la Pologne.* Paris, 1906.

Pamiętnik Literacki. Zeszyt Jubileuszowy Krasińskiemu poświęcony. Lwów, Feb. 19, 1912.

F. Hoesick, *Miłość w Życiu Zygmunta Krasińskiego.* Cracow, 1909.

II. CORRESPONDENCE OF KRASINSKI

Correspondance de Sigismond Krasinski et de Henry Reeve. Préface de J. Kallenbach. 2 vols. Paris, 1902.

Wyjątki z Listów Zygmunta Krasińskiego. Paris, 1860.

Listy Zygmunta Krasińskiego do Konstantego Gaszyńskiego. Lwów, 1882.

Listy Zygmunta Krasińskiego do Adama Sołtana. Lwów, 1883.
Listy Zygmunta Krasińskiego do J. Słowackiego, etc. Lwów, 1887.
Listy Zygmunta Krasińskiego do Stanisława Małachowskiego. Cracow, 1885.
Listy Zygmunta Krasińskiego do Augusta Cieszkowskiego. 2 vols. Cracow, 1912.
Zygmunt Krasiński. *Listy do St. Koźmiana.* Lwów, 1912.
Zygmunt Krasiński i Ary Scheffer. Listy z Nieznanych Rękopisów. Ed. L. Wielisch. 1910.
Listy Zygmunta Krasińskiego do Adama Potockiego. Ed. Adam Krasiński. *Biblioteka Warszawska.* 1905.
Nieznane Listy Z. Krasińskiego do Delfiny Potockiej. Ed. R. S. Kamiński. *Tygodnik Illustrowany.* 1898, 1899.

III.   WORKS OF KRASINSKI

Pisma Zygmunta Krasińskiego. Wydanie Jubileuszowe. 8 vols. Cracow, 1912.
Zygmunt Krasiński. *Pisma.* 4 vols. Lwów, 1902 (with an introduction by Count Tarnowski).

INDEX

32; 35; 38; son's struggle with
during Rising, 45–52, 54, 57, 59, 60,
67, 69, 76, 182; son's sacrifice for, 53,
55, 64, 65 n., 66, 82, 182 ; 58 n. ; 71 ;
74 ; 75 and n. ; 79; 80; 86; represented
in *Undivine Comedy*, 105–7, 110;
112; 138; 171; 179; 181 ; in *Summer
Night*, 182 ; in *Temptation*, 191; 195 ;
208; 222; 223; 225 ; death, 312, 313;
son's attempted biography of, 313
Krasinski, Zygmunt, general characteristics of life and work, 1, 2 ; work for
Poland, 1, 2, 65–7, 79, 80, 179, 183,
184, 189, 230, 238, 251–3, 255, 260,
268, 269, 277, 282, 285, 304; early
incapacity for verse, 1, 11, 26, 32 ; his
anonymity, 1, 55, 61, 64, 65 n., 66,
76, 77, 79, 80, 90, 91, 94, 107, 149,
167, 181, 185, 223, 246, 256, 270;
birth, 2, 3 ; relations with father, 2,
4–6, 10, 18, 20, 21, 45–9, 77, 81, 82,
110, 170, 175, 177, 182, 208, 249,
250; his mother, 2–5, 47, 49, 106,
111 ; childhood, 3–7, 105–7; cult of
Napoleon, 3, 30, 225, 226, 300;
character, 4, 8, 9, 12, 13, 15, 17, 20,
26–8, 30, 32, 40, 50, 69, 76, 88, 89,
106, 111, 112, 136, 138, 170, 171,
178, 183, 221, 222, 224, 234, 250,
254; his devotion to his country, 5–8,
15, 19–21, 24, 26, 28, 31, 32, 39–41,
45–9, 53–5, 57–65, 69 n., 72, 74, 78,
80, 82, 140, 161, 172, 176, 180, 181,
183, 187, 194, 200, 229, 238, 246,
253, 265–8, 272, 277, 282, 285, 304,
310 ; contrast with Mickiewicz, 5,
11, 33, 253, 282, 283; early Polish
writings, 7, 10, 11, 17, 25, 34 ; life
at school, 7, 8; influenced by Scott, 7,
9, 11, 17 ; friendship with Gaszynski,
8, 12, 16, 75, 77, 80, 91, 137 n., 248,
289; letters to Gaszynski, 8, 19, 27,
65 n., 75–80, 86, 89–91, 137, 149,
167–70, 174, 176, 194 n., 209, 219,
248, 266, 276 n., 289; his blindness,
8, 48, 54, 74–83, 87, 89, 92, 107,
111, 112 n., 171, 289, 310; life as
University student, 8–10, 12 ; love for
Amelia Załuska, 9, 10, 81, 135 ;
letters to Reeve, 10, 16 n., 18, 22,
23, 27–32, 35–44, 49, 51–63, 64 n.,
65 n., 67–74, 69 n., 75 n., 79–88,
89 n., 91, 96, 110, 135–7, 139, 140,
150, 169, 175, 179, 182; on *Konrad
Wallenrod*, 11 ; struggle with hatred,
11, 70–2, 84, 140, 167, 196; influenced by Byron, 11, 26, 28, 34,
43, 55, 180, 190, 274; letters to
father, 11, 12, 19–21, 26, 33, 45–8,
59, 60, 72, 73, 75, 135, 170, 176,

177, 181 ; episode in University, 15–
17, 70, 75, 88, 221 n., 292; friendship
with Danielewicz, 16, 88–91, 140, 170,
183, 208, 209, 219–22, 221 n., 289,
290, 292 ; removed from University,
17 ; last days in Poland, *ib.*; leaves
Poland, 17–19 ; life at Geneva, 19–32 ;
friendship with Reeve, 20, 22, 23
and n., 24, 26, 30–2, 35, 41–4, 50–3,
55, 56, 58, 59, 62, 69 n., 75, 79 and
n., 80, 91, 137 n., 170 ; love for
Henrietta Willan, 22–5, 27–9, 31–3,
35, 36, 39, 41, 53, 55, 69 n., 81, 135 ;
early French writings, 23–7, 29, 30,
33–5, 69, 70; love for Delphina
Potocka, 24, 192–7, 206, 208, 220–3,
229–32, 247, 250, 264, 271, 272, 289–
91, 294, 296, 297, 307 ; his poems to
Delphina Potocka, 24, 174, 194–6,
208, 250, 306, 307 ; letters to Sołtan,
27, 137–9, 171, 174, 176, 177, 180,
192, 193, 196 and n., 201, 206–9,
222, 223, 251, 252, 310 n., 310, 311 ;
his relations with the Rising, 29, 38–
64, 67, 76, 80, 94, 183 ; Odyniec on,
32 ; relations with Mickiewicz, 32–4,
36, 274, 309, 310 and n. ; as a poet of
nature, 33, 270, 271 ; visit to Chillon,
33, 34, 274 ; leaves Switzerland for
Florence, 35, 36; first impressions of
Rome, 36, 37 ; inspired by the Coliseum, 36, 37, 55, 165 ; in Florence,
42, 43 ; return to Geneva, 43 ;
struggle with father during Rising,
45–52, 54, 57, 59, 60, 67, 69, 76,
182 ; sacrifice for father, 53, 55, 64,
65 n., 66, 82, 182 ; letter to Stanisław
Krasinski, 53, 54 ; his *Adam le Fou*,
54, 55 ; his conception of the poet,
56, 87, 88 ; his spiritual wandering,
58, 59, 62, 86, 136, 137, 142, 169,
172–5, 179, 180, 183, 190, 194,
195, 198, 199, 205, 221 n., 224, 230,
231 ; his national mysticism, 60, 63,
67, 68, 73, 74, 77, 78, 84, 141, 149,
166, 173, 179, 183, 184, 187, 189,
190, 202–7, 211–3, 215–8, 224–
30, 233, 234, 236, 237, 241–6, 251–
3, 257–63, 265–7, 271–4, 277,
279–85, 286, 295–302, 307, 308,
311–3; in Geneva after end of
Rising, 67–79 ; on life, 68, 69, 85, 86,
88, 207 ; on the social revolution,
72–4, 85, 89, 90 ; summoned by
father to Poland, 74, 75 ; his fear of
Siberia, 74, 76, 77, 176, 275, 276 ;
journey to Poland after Rising, 79,
80; meeting with father, 80, 81 ;
winter in Petersburg, 81–7, 185, 186 ;
analogy between Mickiewicz and, 83 ;

For EU product safety concerns, contact us at Calle de José Abascal, 56–1°,
28003 Madrid, Spain or eugpsr@cambridge.org.

www.ingramcontent.com/pod-product-compliance
Ingram Content Group UK Ltd.
Pitfield, Milton Keynes, MK11 3LW, UK
UKHW010350140625
459647UK00010B/968